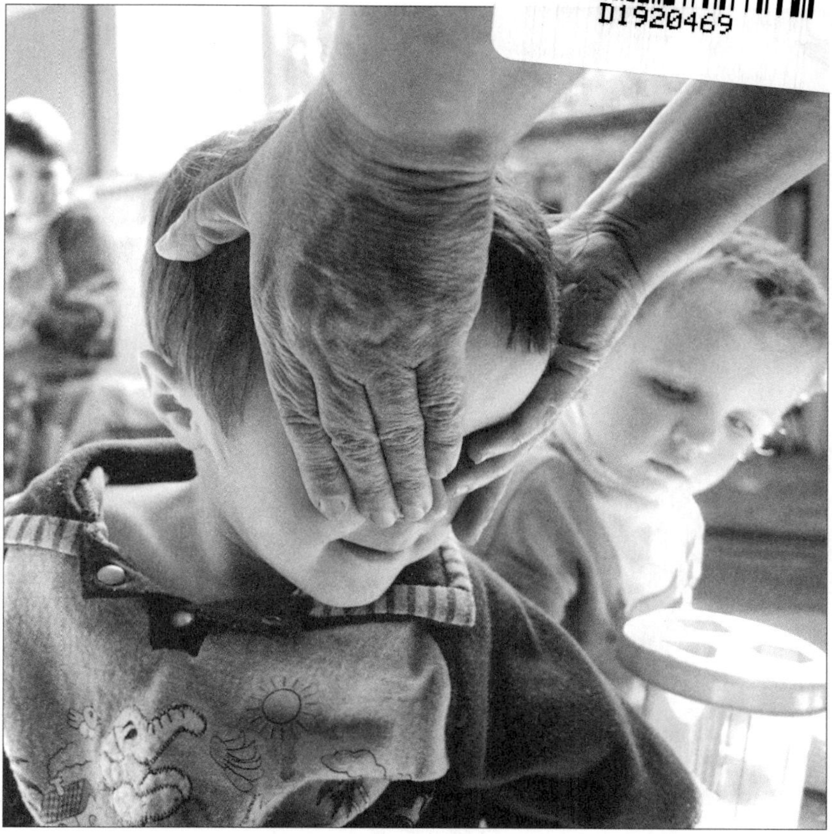

UNICEF/HQ97-0611/Roger Lemoyne

A woman health worker playfully covers the eyes of a disabled boy with her hands, at the UNICEF-assisted Kaspi Centre for Handicapped Children, in the village of Kaspi near Thilisi, the capital of Georgia.

Involving People Evolving Behaviour

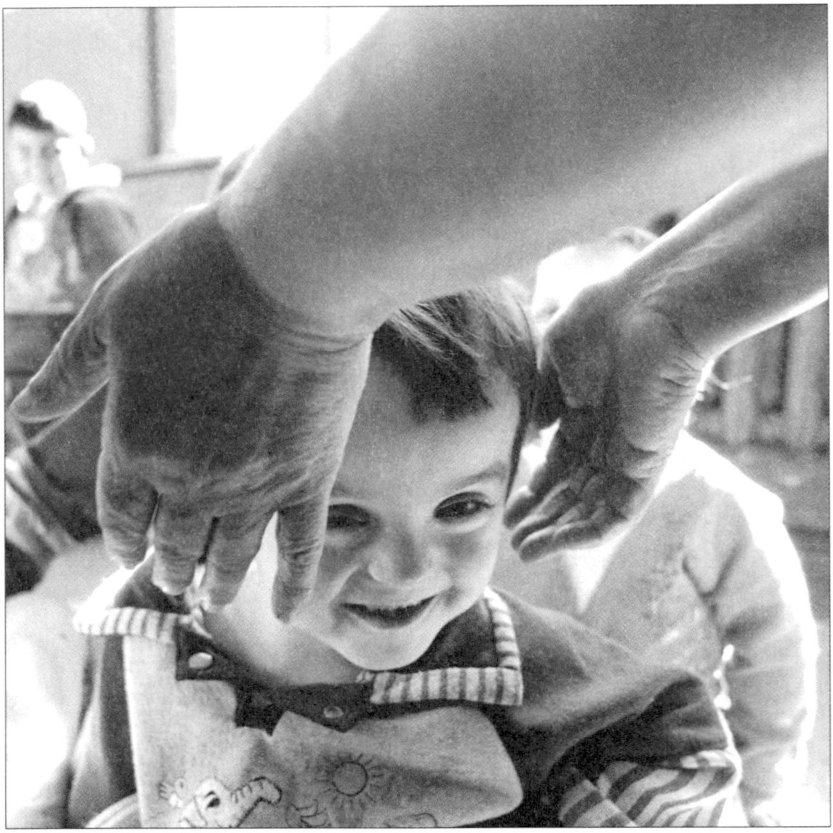
UNICEF/HQ97-0611/Roger Lemoyne

Involving People Evolving Behaviour

EDITORS

Neill McKee
Erma Manoncourt
Chin Saik Yoon
Rachel Carnegie

CONTRIBUTING AUTHORS

Mira B. Aghi
Rachel Carnegie
Bruce Dick
Erma Manoncourt
Neill McKee
Pamela Reitemeier
Douglas Webb
Rhona Birrell Weisen
Esther Wyss
Chin Saik Yoon

SOUTHBOUND
Penang

unicef
United Nations Children's Fund

The material in this book has been commissioned
by the United Nations Children's Fund (UNICEF).
The contents are the responsibility of the authors and
do not necessarily reflect the policies or the view of UNICEF.

The designations employed in this publication and the presentation
of the material do not imply on the part of UNICEF the expression of
any opinion whatsoever concerning the legal status of any country
or territory, or of its authorities or the
delimitations of its frontiers.

Published by
Southbound Sdn. Bhd.
Suite 20F, Northam House
55, Jalan Sultan Ahmad Shah
10050 Penang
Malaysia
Fax: 604-228 1758
E-mail: chin@south.pc.my
Web Address: http://www.southbound.com.my

Picture research by Nicole Toutounji, UNICEF, New York.
Cover photograph: UNICEF/Giacomo Pirozzi/1995.
Typeset by Chin Kooi Hong in Baskerville 9.5/12.5 points.
Front and back cover design, digitised photographs and graphics by
Adrian Cheah, C-Square Sdn. Bhd., Penang, Malaysia.
Pre-press services: Eefar Lithographic Sdn. Bhd., Penang, Malaysia.
Printed by Jutaprint, Penang, Malaysia

Perpustakaan Negara Malaysia Cataloguing-in-Publication Data

Involving people, evolving behaviour / editors Neill McKee;
Erma Manoncourt; Chin Saik Yoon; Rachel Carnegie;
contributing authors Mira B. Aghi . . . [et al.].
Includes bibliographical references
ISBN 983-9054-22-8
1. Human behaviour. 2. Behaviour modification. 3. Behavioural
assessment. 4. Information technology. I. McKee, Neill.
II. Manoncourt, Erma. III. Chin, Saik Yoon. IV. Aghi, Mira B.
302

Contents

UNICEF/Giacomo Pirozzi/1995

Editors' Foreword

Behaviour and Human Rights

As the 21st Century dawns, UN organizations and international bodies have become much more cognizant and preoccupied with human rights. Faced with a growing number of international and civil wars and ethnic conflicts, following the collapse of the Cold War, the various conventions which were ratified by most governments around the world, for example – the Universal Declaration of Human Rights, the Convention on the Rights of the Child and the Convention on the Elimination of All Forms of Discrimination Against Women – have become paramount instruments for developing and guiding programme interventions. One of the main motivations for this has been the behaviour of people towards "others", the outright atrocities committed by various groups against innocent civilians, including women and children, and the realization that there needs to be a "sea-change" in the hearts and minds, values, attitudes and practices of people and their governments if human kind is to survive the next 50 years, let alone the next millennium. The other motivation is the evident widening gap between the rich and the poor within the free market philosophy which has swept the globe, where an ever-growing number are slipping below the poverty line. If the fall of the Berlin Wall signalled a new era for civil and political rights, the same cannot be said for social and economic rights, which remain largely unrealized for over half the world's population.

Recently, it has been a preoccupation of many development organizations to articulate their programme concepts and procedures in a rights-based framework. This has led to a revision of language used in programme descriptions, especially the shift away from "stakeholders" and "target groups" to "duty bearers" and "rights holders". The State is the primary duty bearer when it comes to the realization of human rights. The State may also be responsible for gross violations of human rights. From one point of view, the signatory for the State on UN conventions is government and, therefore, the government is the primary "duty bearer", while there are various interests groups in civil society whose prime concern is to monitor the performance of the government and apply pressure and opposition or encouragement, as needed. However, the concept of "duty bearer" is being extended, in the context of international development work, to include a broad spectrum of partners, including lower levels of government, NGOs, special interest groups, community-level organizations, and even, in the case of children's rights, parents and the community at large.

The most important concept within a rights-based approach is the shift away from the fulfillment of needs, often motivated by charity, to the recognition that many people's rights are being violated and must be fulfilled. Whereas in the needs-based approach, an organization may be satisfied with 80 percent coverage of latrines and safe water supply, in a rights-based approach, the rights of 20 percent of the people remain abused or unrealized.

Furthermore, human rights are universal and indivisible. We cannot decide that certain rights are owed to this particular group of people and not to others. However, the actions taken to realize the rights of people can be prioritized according to the resources available to a particular country, government or organization at a particular time. This is not to detract from the duty bearers' need for a longer-term plan to fulfill all rights – the realization of social justice.

What does all this have to do with the subject of this book, behaviour? Within rights-based approaches, there is analysis concerning the capabilities and roles of the duty bearers in the fulfillment of their obligations. There is also a need to study the networks or patterns at work in society in order to understand how the duty bearers can best fulfill their obligations in a coordinated way. The analysis put forward in this book actually addresses these very questions. It would be a mistake to throw aside our learning on human behaviour over the past 50 years as non-rights-based and therefore not applicable in a rights-based approach. This is because, whether we use rights-based programming concepts and language or not, it is the individual and social behaviour of people which will principally determine whether the rights of rights holders are realized or not.

In the case of civil and political rights, direct or confrontational approaches have proven very useful, at times, to embarrass the duty bearers, pressuring them to release political prisoners or withdraw authoritarian legislation. The danger inherent in rights-based programming, especially as applied to social and economic rights, is that we use such forceful methods at all levels, including the community and family, without understanding, or even taking advantage of, the social context and traditions of the communities in which we are working. In some instances, organizations have simply applied their advocacy messages, suitable for the national political level, to the community level. Very often such approaches meet with resistance because they do not take into consideration the values, attitudes, perceptions or even the language of the community, nor the need for a gradual or progressive approach. As a result, rights-based approaches and concepts are often categorized as "western" or "alien" by the recipients of messages.

If there is anything that this book is about, it is the fact that human development depends on the involvement of people in a critical reflection of their own behavioural patterns and the roles of various actors in their society. Such involvement can be called a realization of the "participation rights" of people. Set in this context, the chapters which follow concern the information, motivation, skills and enabling environment that duty bearers and rights holders both need in order to make real progress on human development and the realization of human rights in the new millennium.

ACKNOWLEDGEMENTS

The editors and contributing authors would like to thank all their friends and colleagues who helped in the research, review, and preparation of this book for publication. They would like to acknowledge in particular:

• The participants and faclitators of all the development projects cited in this book for sharing their invaluable field experiences;

• Our colleagues below who reviewed and commented on the draft manuscripts for the book. While their suggestions and feedback provided us with much appreciated guidance in finalising the book for publication, we are solely responsible for the views and content published between these covers:

Prof. Peter Aggleton, Thomas Coram Research Unit, Institute of Education, University of London
Dr. Gary Coldevin, Communication and Education Consultant, Montreal
Dr. Eugenia Eng, Associate Professor, Department of Health Behaviour and Health Education, School of Public Health, University of North Carolina-Chapel Hill
Dr. John Mayo, Dean, College of Communication, Florida State University, Tallahassee
Dr. Claire Viadro, Research Associate, Lineberger Comprehensive Cancer Center, University of North Carolina-Chapel Hill

• Nicole Toutounji and Ellen Tolmie of the Photograph Library, UNICEF, New York who carried out the painstaking research for the photographs which appear in the book.

UNICEF/Giacomo Pirozzi/1996

Enabling Environment
Ability to Act
Motivation
Information
Values
Family
Self
Community
Peers
Timely accessible & relevant
Effective Communication
Life Skills
Policy/Legislation, Services, Education, Religion, Politics, Economics, Physical & Organizational Environment

INTRODUCTION

This book is aimed at people who are involved in designing, implementing and monitoring social sector programmes and projects for developing and disadvantaged communities, anywhere in the world. The intended reader may wear many different hats: programmer, programme planner, communicator, communication programmer, evaluator, researcher, economist, etc. The reader may be working in the fields of education, health, water and sanitation, agriculture extension or in intersectoral programmes such as HIV/AIDS prevention and care, community development, emergency relief, child protection, etc. He or she could be from a government ministry or department, a national or international non-governmental organization, a United Nations or bilateral agency, or the private sector.

Very often such "development professionals" work in a compartmentalized way. Each applies his or her own skills and knowledge to a particular problem area. This book is an attempt to bring together the best practices from a number of different disciplines into programming for behaviour development and behaviour change, an area of growing interest around the world today.

Why is there such a growing interest?

Development professionals are experiencing increasing pressure to bring about sustainable change within the communities and areas in which they work. This push is coming from the sponsors of development projects and from the management of development agencies who are concerned with an apparent stagnation in the progress of their programmes, after almost four decades of activity in the developing world. Recent deep cuts in the budgets of almost all international development agencies has driven the issue to crisis levels.

A large part of the current discontent stems from apparently insurmountable obstacles to developing long term changes in the practices of people who are the intended "clients" of projects. Evaluation of completed interventions, carried out immediately upon the termination of projects, may reveal "satisfactory" levels of practising the desired behaviour. However, follow-up studies often show sharp drops in these levels.

The shift in evaluation emphasis, from quantifying physical outputs to less tangible appraisals of the changes in people's behaviour, is part of a broader thrust aimed at promoting sustainable development. Many programmes seek to influence the development of behaviour, especially of children and young people, or to change unhealthy behaviour, especially of adults. This new emphasis on behaviour development and change, seeks to engage people in adopting new ideas about the physical or social environment, internalising them, and then expressing them in new practices.

Behaviour development and change

Adopting new kinds of behaviour has been the chief aim of the health sector for a number of decades. It was the primary focus of numerous health education campaigns before such initiatives were taken up by organizations working on environmental concerns. The escalating numbers of people testing HIV-positive has spurred this thrust within the health sector and because HIV/AIDS prevention and care have become national priority areas in many countries, behavioural approaches in programming have attracted much attention and interest from other sectors of the development community.

However, development professionals, in general, are discovering very quickly what those working in the health sector have known for a long time – that developing healthy behaviour, or changing unhealthy behaviour, for individuals and communities, is very difficult. At the same time, they have discovered that when this is successful, the impact is long-term and extremely rewarding.

Effective solutions to challenges posed within programmes dedicated to behaviour development and change have been available for some time. They remain elusive to programmers because the solutions are dispersed across many sectors and amongst many professions. Although much of past development programming may not have been designed primarily to influence people's behaviour, it has addressed behaviour issues indirectly. As a result, we have a pool of highly relevant programme design and management experiences, which, when brought together, offer programmers solid ground on which to design and mount behavioural interventions.

This book is a multisectoral and interdisciplinary synthesis of field experiences and lessons learned, which offers fresh insight and debate in the context of behaviour development and change. Its aim is to challenge traditional approaches to programme design, using a range of different perspectives from the personal to the political, with a view to increasing the impact and sustainability of international development programmes.

Chapter One: "What Makes People Change Their Behaviour? Theories and Frameworks" is intended as an introduction to the area for those interested in the theoretical side of their work. It offers a clear and wide-ranging overview of behaviour theory from the interrelated perspectives offered by sociology, psychology and anthropology. The chapter explains and describes the key elements of salient theories and frameworks, identifying key behavioural determinants and translating these into lessons to be learned for sustainable programme design. However, the author emphasizes that many theories of behaviour are grounded in Western individualistic culture and demonstrates how they must be adapted when applied to developing country contexts. The author concludes that programmes are most effective when supported by behavioural theories or conceptual frameworks which take into account local realities.

Chapter Two: "The Age of Information" situates behaviour in the context of contemporary society, which is evolving at an unprecedented rate, driven to a great extent by new information-communication technologies. It contains case studies which illustrate how information has been a catalyst for change but, from a development perspective, it reminds us of the risks inherent in an information-centred approach. It reviews the different roles assigned to information by various development paradigms, and concludes with the argument that information is a necessary but insufficient ingredient for change.

Chapter Three: "Motivation To Act: Effective Communication" describes the process of effective programme planning from a communication perspective and offers concise definitions of concepts used in communication for development. It highlights some key components of successful programme design and reviews some effective methods of communication used to motivate people, such as interpersonal communication and social mobilization. It draws upon concrete experiences from different continents and cultures, covering a variety of programmes.

Chapter Four: "Ability to Act: Strengthening People's Life Skills" distils a rich body of experiences from the field of participatory learning. Life skills programmes set out to equip people with the necessary skills to interact effectively within their community and to play a meaningful part in bringing about the behaviour change which they desire. In principal, this approach aims to empower everyone – especially the minority and disadvantaged members of the community – not only with knowledge and skills, but also with the confidence and ability to initiate and sustain changes in their lives.

Chapter Five: "Making Change Possible: Creating an Enabling Environment" addresses the role of the wider environment in either facilitating or constraining change. The environment here includes not only the natural and physical environment, but also factors which can affect how we behave, such as: policies and legislation, economic status, provision of health and education services, cultural norms and religious beliefs. The authors argue that people need more than information, motivation and skills to initiate and sustain behaviour change – they also need an enabling environment, which facilitates rather than blocks the changes they wish to make.

Chapter 6: "Behaviour and Beyond: An Evaluation Perspective" describes the different methods which development professionals can adopt to evaluate the progress and results of their activities in evolving desired behaviour, amongst the communities they serve. Evaluation is recommended here, not simply to satisfy project administration requirements, but to give programmers criteria which will allow them to choose between different strategies and approaches, with the participation of programme clients. Such systematic reflection helps them to acquire and accumulate invaluable data, enhancing and expanding the skills of those involved.

Overall, the chapters of this book elaborate a new model (see page xvi) which, it is proposed, encompasses all of the necessary ingredients for behaviour development and behaviour change programmes and, ultimately, the empowerment of people. Providing timely and relevant information, employing appropriate and effective communication for motivation, supporting people's ability to act through the acquisition of life skills, and fostering an enabling environment – these are proposed as the essential elements required for sustaining behavioural change and developing healthy behaviour. When combined with extensive research on the perceptions, attitudes and beliefs which are the expressions of people's value systems, these elements provide a model which offers clarity in a difficult area, as well as a promise of greater success in our programmes.

Behaviour development and change model

At the centre of the model is the "self". However, the pages which follow will reveal that in most cultures in the developing world, it is difficult to separate the self from family, peers and community. It has been proposed that individuals in developing societies are more governed by these social forces than they are in Europe and North America. Therefore, behavioural theories must be critically examined adapted and modified when they are applied in developing country contexts. However, behaviour theories provide a conceptual framework and are very helpful in analysing situations and developing objectives and strategies.

Information must be provided in a timely, relevant and appropriate manner to the different groups who are being addressed by a programme. The same information should not be offered in the same form to all. And without carefully shaping the information into communication formats which provide motivation to act, people will simply ignore the messages. In other words, information can be formulated in interesting ways and communicated through various media in a manner that keeps people's attention and involves them. Effective communication strategies often allow people to use and shape the information themselves, through participatory processes. This is when information becomes knowledge.

However, if people do not have the skills or abilities to use the knowledge they have acquired, the preceding efforts may be fruitless. People need essential life skills. Traditionally, educational systems have concentrated on cognitive skills, such as reading and writing, and vocational and physical skills. However, today it has been recognized that psychosocial life skills are vital. These skills consist of decision making, problem solving, critical thinking and creative thinking, communication skills, interpersonal relationship skills, empathy, self awareness, and coping with stress and emotions. Home and school environments often constrain the development of such skills. Children are taught to learn facts and not to question authority. Creative problem solving is not encouraged.

However, even if people acquire information, motivation and relevant skills, they still may be unable to act if they do not live in an enabling environment. Besides the social environment, mentioned above, appropriate and accessible health and social services and supplies must be present. There should be appropriate policy and legislation to ensure that the programme remains a national priority and will not be withdrawn. In addition, educational systems and cultural, religious, sociopolitical, socioeconomic and physical environmental factors will assist or hinder the adoption of new behaviour. These elements of the environment must be carefully considered when designing programmes. Also, organizations may be very facilitating or very disempowering. It is difficult to promote empowerment in a disempowering organization. Facilitating organizations allow their employees the scope to foster positive behaviour change and, sometimes, the empowerment of people.

Finally, the values held by people in different cultural contexts are of paramount importance when designing programmes. The issue of values cuts across all of the above factors. Values are expressed by perceptions, attitudes and beliefs and these must be carefully researched and understood for programmes to be effective. If we do not take people's value systems into account, the programme will hit a brick wall.

The chapters which follow will explore the above ideas in greater detail. But to summarise:

- Accurate and timely information is a necessary, but not sufficient, prerequisite to behaviour development and change. Information alone seldom leads to behaviour change;

- Communicating information through appropriate channels in motivating formats is one essential component of successful programmes; however,

- People need essential life skills to act on the information received, no matter how motivated they are; and

- Their wider environment must support and facilitate change for programme effects to be sustained.

In addition, it is hoped that the reader will learn two key lessons through the following analysis:

- Specialists working in different development sectors should coordinate and integrate their efforts; and

- Programmes must be participatory in nature, or "people-centred".

There is no "quick fix" or "magic bullet". We must take the longer road of involving people in evolving new and positive behaviour.

UNICEF/HQ94-0892/Roger Lemoyne

A boy aims a toy gun at a girl as they play on sand bags protecting a bunker in Dobrinja, a heavily damaged "front line" suburb during the siege of the capital city of Sarajevo, Bosnia and Herzegovina in 1994.

1

Why do people behave as they do?

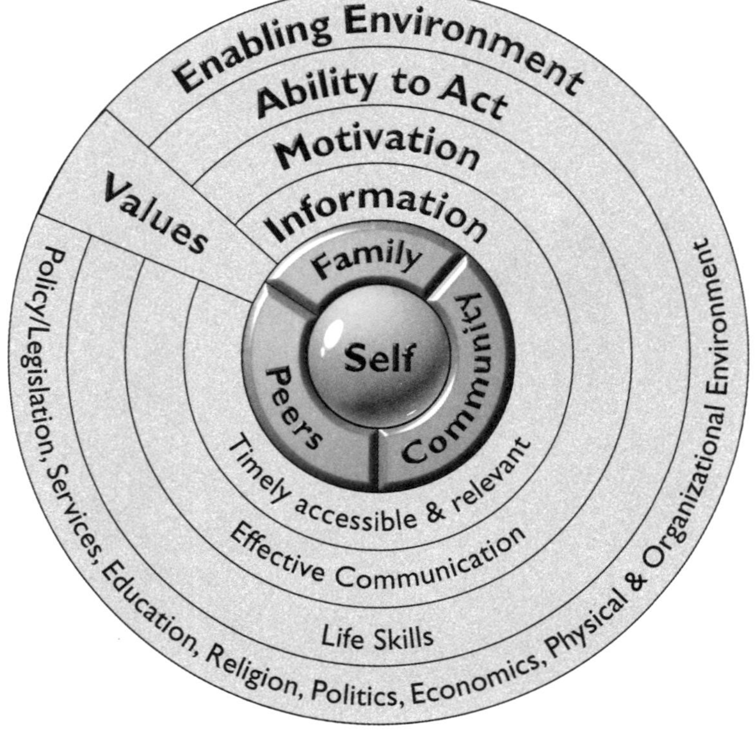
Enabling Environment
Ability to Act
Motivation
Information
Values
Family
Self
Community
Peers
Timely accessible & relevant
Effective Communication
Life Skills
Policy/Legislation, Services, Education, Religion, Politics, Economics, Physical & Organizational Environment

ONE

Why do people behave as they do? Theories and frameworks

Erma Manoncourt

Introduction

Understanding people and their behaviour is one of the keys to successful development programmes. The actions and practices of an intended beneficiary or a stakeholder can directly affect the evolution of many social and health-related problems. The political and social sciences, especially the disciplines of sociology, psychology and anthropology, have contributed much to our understanding of why people behave the way they do and the respective roles of their motivations, fears, social pressure, environmental factors, etc. on individual and collective behaviour. In order to increase programme impact, and develop interventions that are strategically applied, it is important that development professionals determine, and understand, the various factors that influence an individual's, or community's, decision to perform or not perform specific behaviours (see Box 1).

1 *Some important behaviours in health and social programmes*

- Adoption of health-promoting behaviours e.g. giving Oral Rehydration Therapy (ORT) to children with diarrhoea; using iodised salt; exclusive breast-feeding of infants for their first six months; using impregnated mosquito nets; child-spacing; drinking potable water;
- Individual and collective action e.g. Promoting and maintaining clean, safe environments; building sanitary latrines;
- Reduction of negative health-related behaviours e.g. having unprotected sex; smoking; excessive drinking;
- Adoption of behaviours that promote, for example, child rights e.g. preventing employment of child labourers; advocating for children's participation; developing policies that empower women.

The current social ecological perspective identifies these factors as multiple levels of influence – individual, interpersonal, institutional or organisational, community and public policy – and highlights the importance of the interaction and interdependence between individuals and their environment. More specifically, this perspective reinforces the idea that behaviour must be addressed and framed within its social environment since it both influences and is influenced by its social context. In terms of practice, this suggests that programme communication is more likely to be successful when problems are analysed and programmes planned in the light of multiple levels of influence and include multi-level interventions.

Applying a behavioural perspective to the programme planning process enables one to identify the populations most ready for change; to examine the behaviours most easily influenced, along with their most important determinants; and to design interventions that are most likely to have the desired influence on these determinants. Behavioural frameworks are not only useful for identifying determinants of both desired and undesired behaviour, but also assist programmers in identifying potential points of intervention. As numerous practitioners and researchers alike have noted, successful programme strategies need to be based on theories of behaviour and change.

The relationship between programming and behaviour is critical in developing programmes that address key social and development problems. During the situational analysis phase of a programme, theories influence need assessments by pointing to the types of information that would be most helpful in guiding programme decisions and by identifying behavioural factors that are more important among target populations. In the planning phase, theories direct attention to important explanatory factors (how different factors relate to behaviour), thus identifying intervention targets. During programme implementation, theories identify change processes that can be targeted. As part of the evaluation phase, such frameworks are used to identify important explanatory factors for observed behaviours. They also signal factors that need to be measured, in order to understand whether or not the hypothesised change or developmental process occurred as planned.

What is meant by "behaviour"?

General discussions about behaviour development and change can become confusing due to the diverse terminology that is often used by different practitioners, representing various professional orientations and previous experiences.

This chapter begins with a set of key definitions (see Box 2), that can be used as a common frame of reference. It continues with a description of common behavioural perspectives, frameworks or theories that have been tested in, and applied to, different types of programmes. Although they can be used to explain or predict human behaviour in general, particular emphasis is placed on those relevant to child survival, protection and rights.

A variety of behavioural frameworks (models, theories) will be discussed in this chapter but for illustration purposes, emphasis will be placed on health programmes and consequently the use of health behaviour examples. Nonetheless, the reader is reminded that the discussion that follows has a wider application to other social and development programmes, such as sanitation and girls' education.

Although one often hears the term "health behaviour", it has different meanings depending on one's professional training. For programming purposes, distinguishing between health-directed and health-related behaviour is useful. The former refers to observable acts that are undertaken with a specific health outcome in mind. In direct contrast, health-related behaviours are those actions that a person does that may have health implications, but are not undertaken with a specific health objective in mind. Example: A mother is observed breast-feeding her five-month old infant. Using a health-directed frame of reference, one might easily assume that she does this because she is concerned for her child's health and believes that breast milk is the best food at that age. However, supposing further investigation showed that the mother has chosen to breast-feed because she likes the bonding with her child and all her friends also breast-feed. In this case, one could classify her behaviour as health-related – it has an impact on health, but was not undertaken in a conscious effort to promote health, or prevent a health problem from occurring.

With respect to health programmes, research has identified three types of health-related behaviour which reflect different motivations to act. They are:

(1) Preventive health behaviour – action taken when a person wants to avoid being ill or having a problem. Example: a mother who takes her child to be immunised to avoid having measles or goes to a traditional healer to ensure that her child is protected from 'bad spirits'.

(2) Illness behaviour – action taken when a person recognises signs or symptoms that suggest a pending illness. Example: a mother gives her child cough medicine after hearing her wheeze.

(3) Sick-role behaviour – action taken once an individual has been diagnosed (either self or medical diagnosis). Example: a mother decides that her child has malaria and takes him to a traditional healer for local medicine.

In each of the above situations, the mother has reacted, and responded, but the sense of urgency that motivates her to act, or to perform certain actions, is tempered by her perception of the behaviour needed.

Whose behaviour is the focus of an intervention target?

When formulating interventions, it is important to clarify who is the subject of the action – by age or cultural group, gender, religion, ethnicity or some other characteristic. Example: Is the programme interested in the actions of adults, or adolescents, or young school children? Should an HIV/AIDS programme focus on female prostitutes or male truck drivers who frequent their services? Different target groups require different considerations when

2 ***Key definitions***

Behaviour is defined as: "an observable act, such as stepping on a weighing scale". Technically speaking, a behaviour category is used to refer to a composite of discrete actions. For example: "weighing a baby" is composed of several actions: "putting the child in a harness," "calibrating the scale measurement," calculating the kilogrammes on a scale", etc.

Behavioural determinants are factors that either influence or cause an action to occur, or not occur. Also referred to as **mediating factors**, they may be internal (anxieties, beliefs, etc.) or external (peer pressure, supportive setting, etc.) In the example of "losing weight," the determinants could be internal (e.g. an individual's personal attitude towards being overweight) and/or external (e.g. having close friends who are on diets). Research has shown that these factors will vary in importance for different behaviours and across different settings; therefore a clear understanding of when, where and under what conditions the desired behaviour should occur (or undesired practices should cease) needs to be determined.

A discussion of behavioural terminology is incomplete without mention of two key internal behavioural determinants, knowledge and attitudes, that affect how human beings act.

Attitudes are feelings, opinions or values that an individual holds about a particular issue, problem or concern.

Knowledge is internalised learnjng based on scientific fact, experience and/or traditional beliefs. Experience shows that knowledge is necessary but not sufficient to produce behaviour change, which occurs when perceptions, motivation, skills and the social environment also interact. In Chapter 2, the role of information on knowledge acquisition will be explored further.

planning interventions, since their needs and perceptions vary. For example, when communicating to young people, behaviour initiation and development are paramount concerns. In comparison, changing or maintaining current behaviours is most often the focus of behavioural interventions that target adults.

Decisions about which groups to target help us make choices amongst the variety of theoretical models and conceptual frameworks that are based on empirical programme experience. Realising that change in society occurs at many societal levels, programme staff are often faced with choices as to whom they should direct their efforts – individuals, families or households, communities or the wider society as a whole. In practice, these choices are influenced by time and resource considerations and should be informed by an understanding of behaviour as a developmental and change process. Knowledge of the available theories or models can also guide programme planning and clarify the relationships between different factors that influence individual, interpersonal and group behaviour.

Explaining behaviour and behaviour change

When professionals first become interested in changing health-related behaviour, the emphasis is on providing information to patients or the public. The assumption is that a well-informed population would take the necessary action to protect itself from, and prevent, illness. Early analysis revealed that information alone is not sufficient to produce the desired behaviour.

The lack of success in early attempts to promote changes in health behaviour eventually led to the development of a variety of theoretical models, as illustrated in Box 3, that were developed in various professional disciplines. These theories and models can be distinguished and categorised according to their explanation of the different pathways leading to behaviour development and/or change. First, they provide an explanation for the process through which individuals can change. Secondly, they identify the unit of practice by clarifying the societal unit to whom the change process will be directed – referred to level of change. Finally, they differentiate the specific targets of change, as well as, the type of strategies and/or skills relevant to addressing the change process. All are designed to explain or predict why people behave as they do and to provide insight into interventions that might be more effective. Each theory provides a perspective of the overall behaviour change process that can be relevant to development programmes that aim to influence behaviour at the individual, community or societal levels. In summary, theories can guide programme strategies by providing answers to four key questions:

- What? Potential behaviour – actions, practices – as targets;
- Why? Reasons or influential factors that explain why a particular behaviour occurs;
- When? Insights about the timing and sequencing of interventions;
- How? Important behavioural influences to be changed, or modified, and methods that could be used to achieve the change.

Although there are numerous models available, space limitations do not allow for an exhaustive discussion; nor is the purpose of this book to provide in-depth instruction on behaviour change theory and its use. This chapter summarises a selected number of theories that:

(1) have been empirically tested;
(2) are most commonly used in intervention programmes; and
(3) show promise for cross-cultural application to development work.

It highlights theoretical models that attempt to explain behaviour at different levels – individual, interpersonal and group actions. However, we should note that none of the theories below can explain all behaviour by themselves and that different theories will address different dimensions of the behaviour reality (Earp and Ennett, 1991).

Furthermore, Aggleton (1996) reminds us that most of these frameworks were developed in the West and have encountered difficulty when applied to other cultural contexts. He noted specifically, in the context of HIV/AIDS intervention research that "some of these models were originally developed in North America and Europe, where they have not gone without criticism. Generally it has focused on their neglect of the social context within which particular actions become meaningful and for the assumptions they make about rationality." His analysis also indicates that efforts to transplant such frameworks to developing countries have encountered difficulties; because social norms, duties and obligations may be different in strength and kind to those encountered in the West. Furthermore, he also found that their emphasis on individual behaviour may be inadequate for understanding actions taken in social contexts where personal behaviour may be as much a community-based process, as it is one governed by individual decision-making.

This observation makes clear that the theories or models discussed in this chapter should not automatically be assumed to be relevant to developing countries without testing their relevance and applicability to different cultural milieu. Clearly, theory-based interventions need to be adapted to and modified

3 Theoretical Frameworks/Conceptual Models for Human Behaviour

Levels of change	Change process	Theories or models	Targets of change	Strategies and skills
Individual	Psychological	Value expectancy Attitude change Control theories Personality theories Attribution theories	Personal behaviour Developmental processes Knowledge Attitudes Values Skills Self-concept, efficacy & esteem	Testing & measurement Programme planning Educational approaches Mass media Social marketing Skills development Life skills Resistance to peer pressure
Interpersonal	Psycho-social	Network Theory Social Learning Theory Social Support Theories Role Theory Social/Influence/Experience Models Social Comparison Theory	Interpersonal behaviour Social networks Social support Families Peers Neighbours Work groups	Social network enhancement Family counselling or support Social support groups Increasing access to normative groups Peer influence/education/counselling
Community	Cultural & Social	Cultural change theories Social change theories Community development Diffusion of innovations Community power Community decision making	Group behaviour Area economics Community resources Neighbourhood organisations Community competencies Social & health services Organisational relationships Folk practices Government structures Formal leadership Informal leadership	Change agents Community development Community coalitions Empowerment Participatory methodology Conflict resolution strategies Mass media

Adapted from McElroy (1994)

by local realities, ideally with the active involvement of target groups. However, successful intervention strategies also point to the need for development workers to make explicit their assumptions about perceived relationships among various behavioural factors (Glantz *et al.*, 1990). This suggests that there is a role for theory – whether deductive and/or empirical – in development programmes that promote social change and focus on behaviour. As respondents in Aghi's ethnographic study (see pages 35-39 at the end of this chapter) eloquently stated:

> Yes one can change one's behaviour. I have to have a reason for changing my behaviour . . . The circumstances have to be different, they have to change before I can change my behaviour . . . There has to be motivation, something new, something different, things have to change, they have to improve . . . or else things have to somehow appear different, they have to be presented in a special way. This can only occur if the individual is called upon to get involved in the new way of doing things from the point of why, how, where, etc. There has to be a seen advantage to change behaviour, some kind of profit, financial or otherwise . . . I have to be convinced that new behaviour will be profitable . . . It has to improve my situation in order to be attractive . . . It has to be in keeping with my life . . . .

This is the task of development workers and practitioners – influencing human behaviour as a means of achieving social, health and economic goals.

Some theoretical frameworks which explain individual behaviour

Health Belief Model (HBM)

The Health Belief Model is the most common and well-known theory in the field of public health and has been used more widely than any other to guide behaviour interventions in development programmes. Developed in the early 1950s by Godfrey Hochbaum and other social psychologists at the US Public Health Service, it was used to explain patients' responses to tuberculosis preventive actions. The HBM model is based on the premise that one's personal thoughts and feelings control one's actions. It proposes that health behaviour is therefore determined by internal cues (perceptions or beliefs), or external cues (e.g. reactions of friends, mass media campaigns, etc.) that trigger the need to act. It specifically hypothesises that individual behaviour is determined by several internal factors:

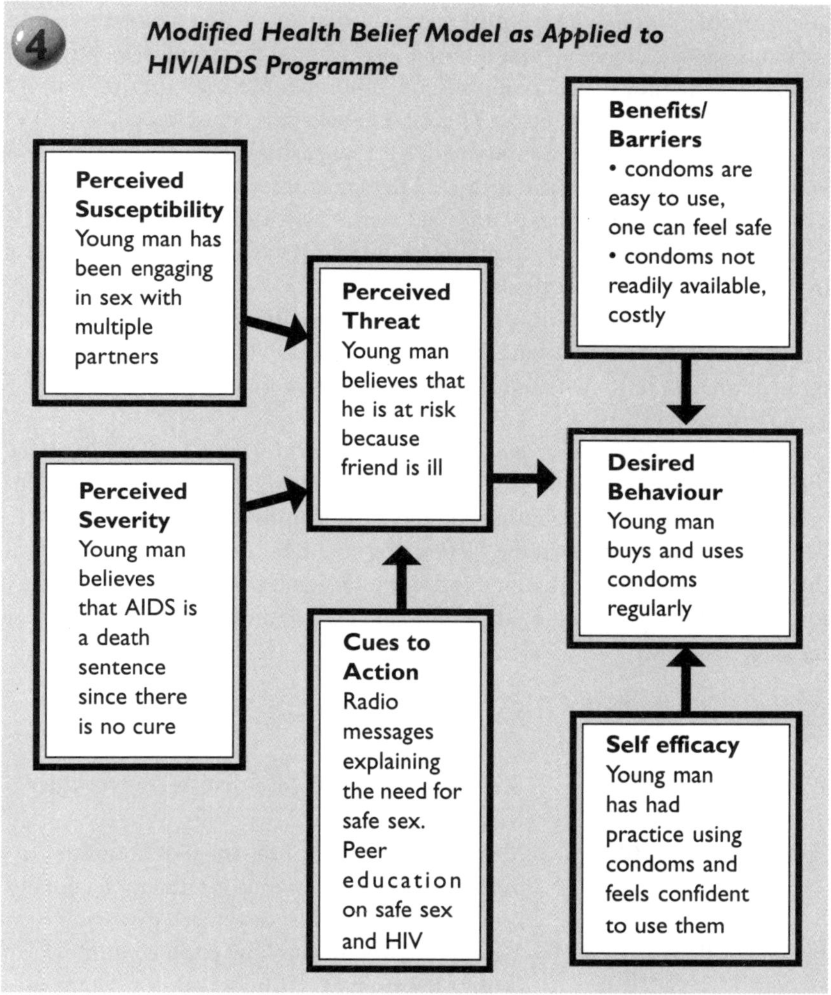

- Belief about one's chances or risk of getting an illness or being directly affected by a particular problem or illness (perceived susceptibility);
- Belief or one's opinions about the seriousness of a given problem or illness (perceived severity);
- Belief about the efficacy of an action to reduce risk or severity (perceived benefits) compared to one's opinion about the tangible or psychological risks or costs for proposed action (perceived barriers).

According to the HBM, the first two beliefs jointly form one's conviction and influence the degree to which an individual may be motivated to act on a given problem. The theory also suggests that the above reflections and thoughts are triggered by both internal (e.g. sweating, nervousness, etc.) and external influences (e.g. reactions by other people and/or opinions of significant others, media, etc.). These are labelled as "cues to action".

Once an individual is motivated to act, the actual behaviour undertaken will be determined by a third factor – a personal perception of "cost-benefit". This framework further explains that before deciding to act, individuals consider whether or not the benefits (positive aspects) outweigh the barriers (negative aspects) of a particular behaviour.

In a more recent formulation of this theory, the concept of self-efficacy has been added. This addition takes into account individual beliefs or personal perceptions of one's own ability to undertake a particular action.

Practice applications/implications: This model has several practice implications in that it can be useful in trying to explain health-related behaviour and in developing messages that could persuade individuals to make positive decisions. Keeping in mind the factors presented in Box 4, let us assume that this theoretical framework alone is used to design a communication strategy for HIV/AIDS prevention. It would suggest communication activities or messages such as:

Concept	Practice Application
Perceived Severity	Messages that emphasise that AIDS is a killer with no cure;
Perceived Susceptibility	Messages that try to show the extent of the problem and that everyone is vulnerable, not just prostitutes or long-distance truck drivers;
Perceived Benefit/Costs	Messages that indicate how people could protect themselves – using condoms, which is simple to do (benefit) and inexpensive (cost). The latter assumes that condoms are available and at low cost;
Cues to Action	Messages on how to use condoms and reminders when to use them;
Self-efficacy	Messages highlight that condoms are readily available and easy to use.

Theory of Reasoned Action (TRA) and Personal Behaviour (TPB)

Similar to the HBM model, the Theory of Reasoned Personal Behaviour also supports the notion that one's thoughts and perceptions are important determinants of behaviour. Developed by Fishbein and Azjen (1980), this theory added a new dimension to our understanding of behaviour by introducing the concept of behavioural intent. According to their behaviour research, the most critical factor in determining whether individuals will actually perform a desired behaviour is their behavioural intent. Behavioural intent reflects the level of commitment that an individual has to undertake a desired behaviour and likelihood that an individual will perform the desired behaviour: It is influenced by:

Personal attitudes – a person's judgement of a behaviour as good or bad *combined* with some views on its worth for carrying it out or not. This judgement is based on beliefs about either good outcomes (favourable attitudes) or negative ones (unfavourable attitudes).

Perceived social pressure/norm – beliefs which individuals have about what opinions their "significant others" or reference groups (i.e. family, friends, peers) hold, related to a desired behaviour, *combined* with the extent to which they feel that they are motivated by or should go along with the opinions of others.

In later formulations of TRA, the concept of perceived behavioural control was added to the framework. This was an attempt to reflect that factors outside an individual's control could also affect actual performances of a particular behaviour. As such, it can be defined as follows:

Perceived behavioural control – beliefs which individuals have about the availability of resources and obstacles to performing a behaviour, combined with perceptions of the impact of these, or power of each to resource or obstacle to either facilitate or inhibit desired behaviour.

Clearly, this theory acknowledges the joint influence of attitudes, norms and perceived control in affecting behavioural intention as a motivating force in the behaviour process. It also clarifies that perceptions of control, similar to behavioural intention, have a direct influence on one's taking action. However, the relevant importance of each of these dimensions is dependent on the behaviour goal, itself. TPB posits that individuals who have positive attitudes towards performing a particular behaviour, and who believe that "significant others" are in favour of or support the desired action, will more likely attempt a particular behaviour. For some people, their own personal attitudes will have a greater influence on their behaviour than perceived social pressure, and vice versa for others.

For example, in a small ethnographic study conducted for the purpose of understanding the dynamics of human behaviour, Aghi (see pages 35-40 at the end of this chapter) interviewed 30 individuals (selected randomly with no special specifications in mind) to determine how they viewed their own behaviour. Their responses to the question – "Why do you think people behave differently than usual in front of those they respect, love or are in awe of?" –

capture Fishbein's concepts of perceived social pressure and personal attitude as well as the pivotal role they play in fostering one's intent to do something:

> *Perceived social pressure*: "People inspire other people to behave in a particular manner. We behave differently in front of people we love or respect because we want to be liked by them . . . I do this because I want to have an approval . . . I want him/her to think highly of me, etc."
> *Personal attitude*: "My reason for doing this is because I want to feel elated . . . I want to feel good . . . (so) . . . I behave deliberately."

Practice applications/implications: Using the example of HIV/AIDS prevention and condom use, this theory would identify the potential intervention entry points to persuade individuals to make positive decisions and would suggest messages and/or activities such as:

Concept	Practice Application
1. Personal Attitude	Messages that emphasise that condoms are effective protection against AIDS and are something that even young people can use;
2. Subjective Norm	Messages and media images that show adolescent peers who think that using condoms is an okay thing to do and encourage their friends to practice safe sex;
3. Behavioural Intention	In peer group discussions or sessions, sexually active adolescents are encouraged to make verbal commitments to use condoms;
4. Perceived Behavioural Control	In PSA spots, adolescents are shown purchasing condoms from vending machines.

Stages of Change Theory

The Stages of Change Theory is based on the premise that behaviour change is a process and explains the psychological processes that people undergo are

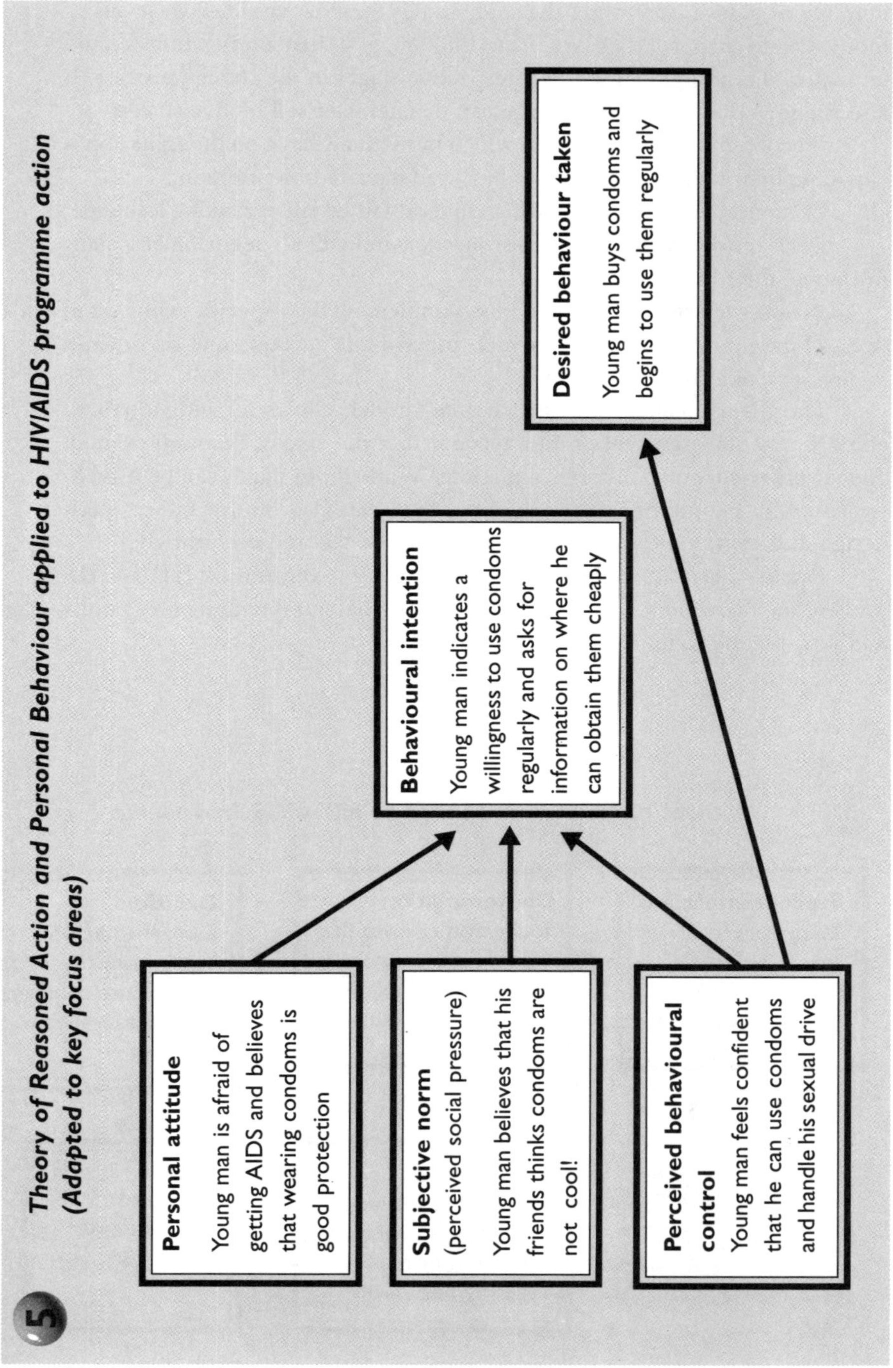
5
Theory of Reasoned Action and Personal Behaviour applied to HIV/AIDS programme action
(Adapted to key focus areas)
Personal attitude
Young man is afraid of getting AIDS and believes that wearing condoms is good protection
Subjective norm
(perceived social pressure)
Young man believes that his friends thinks condoms are not cool!
Perceived behavioural control
Young man feels confident that he can use condoms and handle his sexual drive
Behavioural intention
Young man indicates a willingness to use condoms regularly and asks for information on where he can obtain them cheaply
Desired behaviour taken
Young man buys condoms and begins to use them regularly

iterative in nature. Assuming that individuals experience different levels of motivation to change, Prochaska, *et al.* (1992) suggests that interventions should be matched to individuals at their respective stages in the change process. It also suggests that behaviour change can be characterised by five stages:

Precontemplation – phase in which individuals have no thoughts about changing their behaviour because they are unaware of a problem;

Contemplation – phase in which individuals consider making a change;

Decision/determination – phase in which individuals begin making plans to change their behaviour;

Action – phase in which individuals implement their specific action plan;

Maintenance – phase in which individuals sustain new or desired behaviours, over time.

The theory, conceived as a circular model, allows for individuals to enter at any stage and takes into account that the stages, themselves, may appear different, given different situations. While these stages can be used to explain why people behave as they do, they can also inform intervention design and communication messages that can be tailored accordingly.

Practice applications/implications: Using the example of HIV/AIDS prevention, this theory would identify the potential intervention entry points and possible messages and/or activities such as:

6 Stages of Change as applied to HIV/AIDS Programme

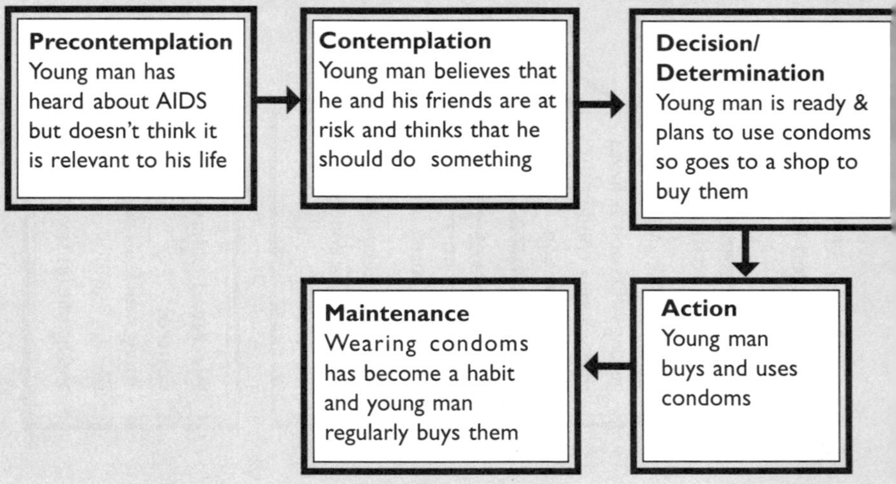

Concept	Practice Application
Precontemplation	Messages that show the extent of the AIDS problem and that everyone is vulnerable, not just prostitutes or long-distance truck drivers;
Contemplation	Peer education sessions held where teenagers encourage friends and class-mates to practice safe sex;
Decision/determination	Messages that provide information about how to practice safe sex and where to buy condoms;
Action	Peer educators available to help other teenagers develop life skills to handle sexual situations;
Maintenance	Students who practice safe sex recruited as peer educators to help others like themselves.

Some theoretical frameworks which explain interpersonal behaviour

Social Cognitive Theory (SCT)

Developed by Albert Bandura (1986), Social Cognitive Theory assumes that individuals interact constantly with their social environment and that they influence, and are influenced by their social milieu – friends, family, co-workers etc. Central to this theory is the premise that behaviour is a result of a three-way, reciprocal interaction between personal factors (i.e. one's own feelings and reactions) and environmental influences (i.e. thoughts, advice and feelings of "significant others"). In contrast to the previously-discussed conceptual models, this theory emphasises the role of one's own experiences and observations of others and the results of their actions on personal behaviour. SCT explains human behaviour as a multi-dimensional and reciprocal process. It uses four concepts that can be used to guide programme development and behavioural interventions at an interpersonal level:

- Reciprocal determinism – behaviour changes result from a bi-directional interaction between person and environment;
- Behavioural capability – knowledge and skills to influence behaviour;
- Outcome expectations – personal beliefs that if one behaves in a particular way, then a desired outcome will result;
- Self-efficacy – self-confidence in one's own ability to successfully perform a given behaviour at the needed level of competence. More specifically, SCT proposes that if individuals believe they have skills or ability to perform a task, or take a specific action, they will be more likely to try it and maintain it.

SCT is centred on the premise that people learn their behaviours from their own experiences (trial and error) and the results of their actions and by observing others.

Observation, and consequently effective role models, are important in learning new behaviours. Empirical study shows that the more similar a role model is to a particular target group, the more the group will identify with the model and try to emulate his or her behaviour.

Practice, trial and error, is the most powerful source of learning. It takes into account that the individual's mastery of tasks is important and that the more they practice and are able to accomplish a particular task, the more motivated they will be to attempt a desired action.

According to Bandura, one's sense of self-efficacy is also learned through emotional reactions or feelings about a situation or from persuasive arguments and encouragement by credible people within an appropriate social context.

Practice applications/implications: Using the example of breast-feeding promotion, this theory would identify the potential entry points to persuade individuals to make positive decisions and would suggest messages and/or activities such as:

Concept	Practice Application
Reciprocal determinism	Mother support groups are formed to assist and guide new mothers in infant care and how to breast-feed effectively;
Behavioural capability	Messages and media images that use young mothers to provide information about how to breast-feed correctly;

Outcome expectations	Messages and media images that explain the importance of breast-feeding as a natural means of protection for young babies and the basis for good health;
Self-efficacy	Practice sessions with a nurse wherein mothers learn how to express milk for their babies when they have to work.

Social Experience Model

Using a human development perspective, Bloomberg *et al.* (1994, p. 455) developed a framework for understanding the critical interaction between elements of the social environment and health. They concentrated on the concept of social experience, and the ways in which social the immediate and wider environment of an individual can affect his/her behaviour. This theoretical model emphasises that human behaviour is the result of interactions with "significant others" and the ways that one is treated due to his/her status or membership in a particular group. It also explains that social context and relationships in which one is involved influences his/her self-perceptions of personal competencies and expectations and can ultimately affect various social or health outcomes.

According to Bloomberg and his colleagues, an individual's socio-demographic background plus his/her own personal traits determine the social context of interactions with others. They noted that factors such as environment resources, parental education, family income, occupational status are key socio-demographic characteristics that play a role. More importantly, this theory suggests that the opinions and behaviours of one's friends, family, or social network influences one's own personal perceptions and actions. This social experience has a direct impact on one's actions and ultimately, social, health and other development outcomes. A more detailed discussion on the role of social context is taken up further in Chapter 5: "Creating an Enabling Environment".

Practice applications/implications: What does this model mean to programme staff? Bloomberg *et al.* suggests that developing effective programmes entails setting aside sufficient time and resources to prepare learning situations that are conducive to behaviour change. Using the example of breast-feeding promotion, this theory would suggest potential interventions that include messages and/or activities such as:

Concept	Practice Application
Social Experience	Mothers support group established wherein young mothers are encouraged to breast-feed. Members include friends and other women of similar background and status who have successfully breast-fed and are able to provide advice and feedback.
Perceptions	Young mothers who breast-feed express a sense of accomplishment and increase their confidence and capabilities related to breast-feeding.

Social Network and Social Support Theory

The theory explains the mechanisms by which social interactions can promote or inhibit individual and collective behaviour. As defined by Israel *et al.* (1985, 1990) and other researchers, a social network is person-centred and refers to the set of linkages and social relationships between people. An understanding of network theory enables programmers to better analyse how friends, families and other significant people might impact on the same individuals and groups that they are trying to influence. In developing appropriate interventions, the following network characteristics should be considered:

- Structure, i.e. size and number of members in the network;
- Interaction, i.e. the frequency of contact, strength of the bond and reciprocal nature of different contacts;
- Density, i.e. extent to which everyone knows each other;
- Reciprocity, i.e. extent to which resources and support are both given and received in a network relationship.

Social support, on the other hand, refers to the content of these relationships – i.e. what is actually being shared or transmitted during different interactions. As such, assistance provided or exchanged through interpersonal and other social relationships can be characterised into four types of supportive action:

- emotional support (caring, esteem, love);
- instrumental support (money, tangible aid or services);
- informational support (advice, suggestions or information useful in

solving problems);
- appraisal support (information that is useful for self-evaluation, feedback).

Practice applications/implications: Using the example of breast-feeding promotion, this theory would identify the potential intervention entry points and persuade individuals to make positive decisions with messages and/or activities such as:

Example: A young mother wants to breast-feed her first child. She has older sisters around her, who also have children whom they breast-feed. She lives in an extended family household with her mother-in-law and husband's family <dense network>. The older women around her are always ready to give her encouragement and advice <informational support> on how to handle feeding and cope with difficulties. From a behavioural viewpoint, further support and suggestions on breast-feeding should take into account the advice that the young mother already receives. Rather than singling her out, it is more effective to also talk with, and convince, the women to whom she goes to seek advice on a regular basis. Therefore, communication messages might be designed to target the family as a whole and emphasise the important supportive role which family and in-laws have in helping introduce their younger family members to the value of breast-feeding.

From a programme planning perspective, it is the social support functions of social networks that are of most interest. Although interrelated, they are two distinct concepts since evidence shows that there are negative aspects of relationships (i.e. mistrust, conflict, etc.) which can adversely affect health and cause other social problems. This suggests that social networks may or may not provide social support.

Some theoretical frameworks which explain community or societal behaviour

Diffusion of Innovations (DOI)

Based on his study of collective human behaviour and responsiveness to novelty and the introduction of change, Everett Rogers (1983, 1986, 1995) developed a theoretical model entitled Diffusion of Innovations Theory. Based on agricultural extension work in USA and East Africa, this theory explains the progression over time by which members of a community or society adopt new, or different, ideas and practices. It is based on the premise that social change or changes in human behaviour can be understood by the way that individuals and groups respond to new or different ideas and behaviours that are introduced. The theory also provides insight into the impact of social influence on individual and household behaviour.

Commonly referred to as "innovations", these new ideas can in fact be technologies, attitudes, behaviours, policies, practices or even programmes. In development work, some examples of present-day innovations are:

- making ORT to combat dehydration;
- buying iodised salt;
- vaccinating children against immunisable diseases;
- advocating against the practice of female genital mutilation.

Experience has taught us that these innovations are not always recognised initially as being necessary, useful, or important, by the target population. Their acceptance, and adoption, on a wide-scale basis begins slowly, as a few people or groups try the idea out first before it gradually spreads to others, as a social momentum may be created or the social climate becomes more accommodating. The theory also posits that the adoption is a process. All eventual adopters pass through five stages: (a) awareness of the innovation; (b) interest in it; (c) trying it out; (d) making a decision to accept or reject; and (e) adopting or adapting the innovation into one's daily life.

Role of communication channels: Based on a premise that communication is a two-way process, rather than just persuading individuals or a group to take action, DOI theory posits that communication channels play a critical role in the decision-making process described above. While recognising the importance and widespread effect of mass media in promoting innovations, the theory also emphasises the value of social networks or interpersonal communication in individual adoption decisions concerning a new or different idea or action being promoted. Describing diffusion as a two-step flow of communication, opinion leaders are seen as having an important mediating influence on the impact that mass media will have on specific reference groups or a population. In practice, this suggests that radio broadcasts might be most effective in raising the awareness on a large scale about a particular practice, such as using ORT to prevent dehydration. But in a complementary manner, if a respected community health worker reiterates this information and then shows the mother how to use ORT, the mother is more likely to use it at home when her child is sick.

Link between innovation characteristics and acceptance: The DOI theory also provides insight into factors that influence the speediness and extent of adoption of a desired idea, or practice, by a specific population. First, it acknowledges that the characteristics of the desired change have an influence. Interventions in the field have shown that perceptions held by individuals about the new idea or desired behaviour are related to its characteristics and can affect their receptivity to and likelihood of undertaking a new or different action or proposed change. Thus, five types of considerations are crucial to decisions made by individuals and groups concerning new, or different, behaviours being promoted (see Box 7).

7 ***Innovation characteristics***

Relative advantage – How much better is the new idea or desired behaviour seen to be compared to the existing ones that it aims to replace?

Complexity – How simple or difficult is the new idea or behaviour to understand, act on and adopt? How many sub-steps or actions are necessary to complete the behaviour?

Compatibility – How compatible is the desired behaviour with existing practices, values and cultural norms of the intended audience?

Trialability – How much can the desired behaviour be tried out before making a commitment to act on or to adopt?

Observability – How visible are the results and outcomes of the desired behaviour to the intended audience?

Practice applications/implications: Using the example of promoting ORT during episodes of diarrhoea in young children, this theory would identify the potential intervention entry points to persuade individuals to make positive decision, taking into account the following points:

CONCEPT	PRACTICE APPLICATION
Relative advantage	Messages that emphasise where Oral Rehydration Salts (ORS) sachets are available, at an inexpensive price. This would facilitate mothers giving their children needed fluids while saving time by not having to measure and mix a sugar salt solution;

Compatibility	In some cultures, fluids are automatically withheld from children with diarrhoea in the belief that they will make the situation worse. Messages using counter-arguments to promote ORT, coupled with visual aids that show the revitalising effect of water on a drooping plant, are often used to explain a similar effect on a child's body;
Trialability	In educational sessions, workers provide young mothers with opportunities to actually mix, prepare and taste ORS and then practice giving it to their sick children.
Observability	In severely dehydrated children, mothers can observe the change in their appearance once they have received sufficient fluid, within a relatively short period of time.
Complexity	As noted in Box 8, different hygiene-related behaviours require and are the result of several steps or smaller actions being completed. Each choice of action has a range of activities, and necessary preparations, that differ and will have a different need for a mother's time or skills. For example, a mother's decision as to which behaviour to undertake – i.e. maintaining personal hygiene or a clean household environment – and will be influenced by the amount of effort needed. This is an example of a complexity consideration.

From a practice viewpoint, the general rule of thumb is that the more complex the behaviour, the longer it will take to be accepted and the more inconsistent to current practices, the longer it will take for acceptance. We also know that the more individuals can practice and learn a new behaviour and see the visible effect of their action, the more likely they are to adopt it. Finally, it is also clear that adoption of a new or different behaviour is more likely to happen if we can emphasise the benefits over the negative outcomes of a desired change.

8

Overview of hygiene-related behaviours by major behavioural domains

Domestic and environmental hygiene
wiping surfaces
sweeping & cleaning compounds/floors
removing shoes before entering house
controlling insects
cleaning streets and community
disposing waste water
using & washing clean food utensils
feeding small children & babies

Disposal of human faeces
choosing place to defecate
disposing faeces
anal cleaning
hand-washing

Water and personal hygiene
water handling
storing & treating storage
reusing water
disposing of waste water
washing hands/cleaning nails
washing face
bathing
practising good hygiene after defecation
washing clothes, towels etc.
personal hygiene during natural events such as childbirth

Food hygiene
cleaning kitchen/floor preparation areas
hand-washing
using clean utensils & work surface
disposing of garbage & waste water
washing raw food & fruits
length of cooking
temperature/length of storage
storing leftover foods

Boot and Cairncross (1993)

Conceptual Model of Community Empowerment

Many theorists are not satisfied with individual behaviour change alone. They maintain that we should be more concerned with empowerment of people for long-term change (Freire, 1970; Wallerstein, 1992; Steckler *et al*, 1993). A review of literature (mainly health education articles) reveals that there are a variety of definitions for the concept of "empowerment". For some it is:

- largely a personal process in which individuals develop and employ necessary knowledge, competence and confidence for making their own decisions/voices heard, or,
- participatory competence: the ability to be heard by those in power, or,
- a social process of recognising, promoting and enhancing people's abilities to meet their own needs, solve their own problems and mobilise the necessary resources in order to feel in control.

Central to an understanding of the community empowerment process is the recognition that communities are composed of individuals and organisations that interact in a variety of social networks. This interdependence supports the notion that changes in one part of the social system has rippling effects in other parts. As a result, development programmes that aim to facilitate community ownership, competence and commitment to change must explore the concept of empowerment at three levels of practice:

- Individual empowerment has a focus on personal efficacy and competence. It also takes into account one's sense of mastery and/or control over a situation.
- Organisational empowerment emphasises processes that enable individuals to increase control within a formalised structure, and the organisation itself to influence policies and decisions in the larger community. In practice, it also provides opportunities for individual growth and access to decision-making processes.
- Community empowerment centres on collective action and control that is based on participation of both individuals and organisations within a specific social context. Some of its benefits, on a group level, are greater economic independence and social recognition.

Gershick *et al* further point out that "an empowered community is one within which individuals and organisations apply their skills and resources in collective efforts that lead to community competence. Through such participation and control, the community is able to meet the needs of its individuals and organisations." (Gerschick *et al,* 1990: 7)

As indicated in Box 9, the work of Zimmerman and Rappaport (1988) highlights the synergy and interdependence that exists between these levels by conceptualising community empowerment in terms of perceived control. As such, the concept of community empowerment is grounded in the recognition that communities, themselves, are composed of individuals and organisations who interact. For instance, individuals who experience personal change through work, can be motivated to create change within the community or influence public policies. Organisations affect both individuals working within them and the distribution of resources within the larger community. Communities in turn affect both individuals and organisations by sharing access to social, political and economic resources.

9 ***Conceptual Model of Community Empowerment (Perceived Control)***

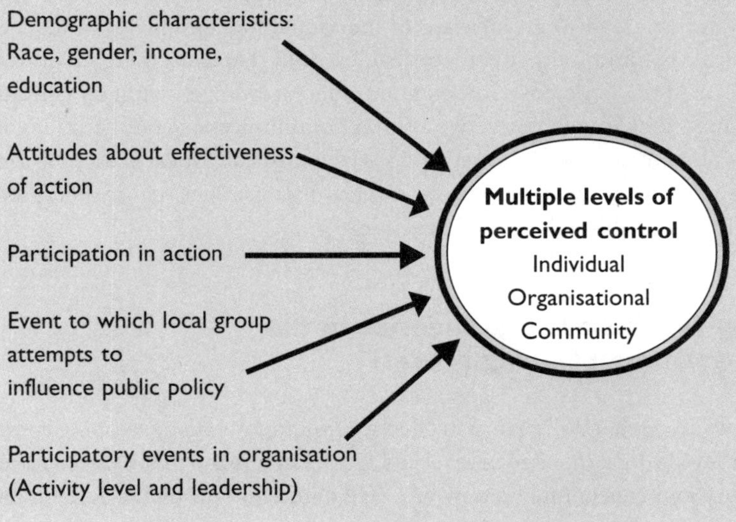

Practice applications/implications: Using the example of ORT promotion, this theory would support interventions as follows:

Example: A National Boy Scouts organisation agrees to participate in a campaign against child deaths caused by diarrhoea and dehydration. Young Scouts, working closely with health programme staff and local community groups, are involved in distributing information door-to-door and meeting with parents to discuss the importance of giving ORT to sick children who are suffering from diarrhoea. Through their interaction, young people develop confidence. Simultaneously, mothers and fathers through meetings and discussions discover ways in which they can combat health problems over which they may have felt no control and by working with others like themselves, develop strategies to make a real difference in the lives of their children. In a best-case scenario, the young people are strengthened; parents through their participation in local groups or organisations, gain new skills and knowledge; and finally, the organised community groups refine their problem-solving skills and approaches and begin to tackle other problems that may face their community.

Based upon the above discussion, it is clear that empowerment is not just a single, but a multi-dimensional concept, around which effective programming can be oriented. In other words, by targeting behaviour interventions at the community level, programmers inherently have an impact on individual changes as well. This suggests that programme strategies, which facilitate real participation in community and organisational decision-making, may in turn lead to an increase in individual perceptions of influence and control, as community members develop skills that assist them in influencing others. At the same time, interventions that encourage voluntary community organisations to take an active role in community and public policy issues may also increase personal perceptions of control (an aspect of empowerment), when individuals who participate in these organisations realise their potential for influence through collective action.

Applying behavioural theories to the programme planning process

While discussing the barriers to effective programmes in developing countries, Hubley (1986: 235) cited several key factors that relate to the use or misuse of theory and conceptual frameworks. He found that problems in the planning process can be attributed to:

- an over-emphasis on behaviour change – without accompanying economic and social development to address poverty and social inequities;
- a failure to ensure that all the required enabling factors are available (i.e. money, resources, time, accessible services);
- too much focus on traditional beliefs as the cause of a problem without looking for other possible explanations;
- targeting programme interventions at the individual level without taking into account the influence of "significant others", at community and national levels.

Clearly, there are numerous theories and conceptual frameworks that are used to explain health behaviour and identify critical factors in developing and changing knowledge, attitudes and practices. It is important to keep in mind that by specifying how these factors relate to behaviour, a model or framework can identify leverage points for behaviour change or development. At the same time, we recall how no single theory or conceptual framework can explain all behaviour and different theories tend to address different dimensions of reality.

Although they are not a substitute for professional judgement, theories of behaviour and social change can be useful in making decisions about and planning interventions that are designed to affect behaviour. In fact, they provide a basis for strengthening programme justification, promoting effective and efficient use of available resources, improving accountability and reinforcing professional credibility. Lawrence Green and his collaborators (1986, 1991), through their Precede/Proceed Model, have contributed much to programme planning in behaviour change communication. Based on the premise that sustainable behaviour change is voluntary by nature, this model reflects a systematic planning process that seeks to empower individuals with knowledge, motivation, skills and active community participation.

The Precede/Proceed Model encompasses nine phases, of which the first five are diagnostic and the latter focus on programme implementation and evaluation (see Box 10). These diagnoses require an understanding of the target community and intervening organisation as a means of identifying goals, setting priorities and developing a plan of action with strategies that are informed by findings and assumptions learnt in the diagnostic process. Theory is most useful in signalling which factors should be examined in each diagnostic category.

Given this chapter's focus on behaviour development and change, particular attention is paid to the educational diagnostic stage. This dimension categorises the various behavioural determinants proposed in different theories mentioned earlier into three domains. In the paragraphs that follow, each behavioural domain or factor will be explained with an example of the concept being applied to a programme designed to combat Female Genital Mutilation (FGM). Additionally, a potential intervention activity or strategy will be discussed in the light of considerations for behaviour determinants.

According to this model, predisposing factors exist prior to a particular behaviour and serve as the rationale, or motivation, behind an action or actions. Individual behaviour change theories such as the Health Belief Model or Theory of Planned Behaviour are useful in illuminating different thoughts, attitudes or feelings that may lead to a particular behaviour. These are influences that, prior to intervention, will affect an individual's readiness or willingness to change or develop new behaviours.

Example: FGM Eradication Programme: A mother refuses to have her daughter circumcised because she is concerned about her daughter's health and feels that women have a right to control their own body.

Changes in knowledge and attitudes are often tackled through direct communication to the target population in the form of interpersonal and/or mass media strategies. For example, health worker conversations with mothers during regular home visits are an important method of informing them about the rights of women and children and health hazards of FGM.

Enabling factors refer to structural or situational influences that make it possible for predispositions to be realised and can positively, or negatively, affect behaviour. These factors can be external influences, such as available resources, supportive policies, assistance, and services or internal forces such as skills and capabilities. Two theories of interpersonal behaviour can provide insights about enabling factors – Social Network Theory discusses the role of structural relationships on behaviour and Social Cognitive Theory examines the influence of skill development.

10 ***Precede/Proceed Model (Behavioural Domains)***

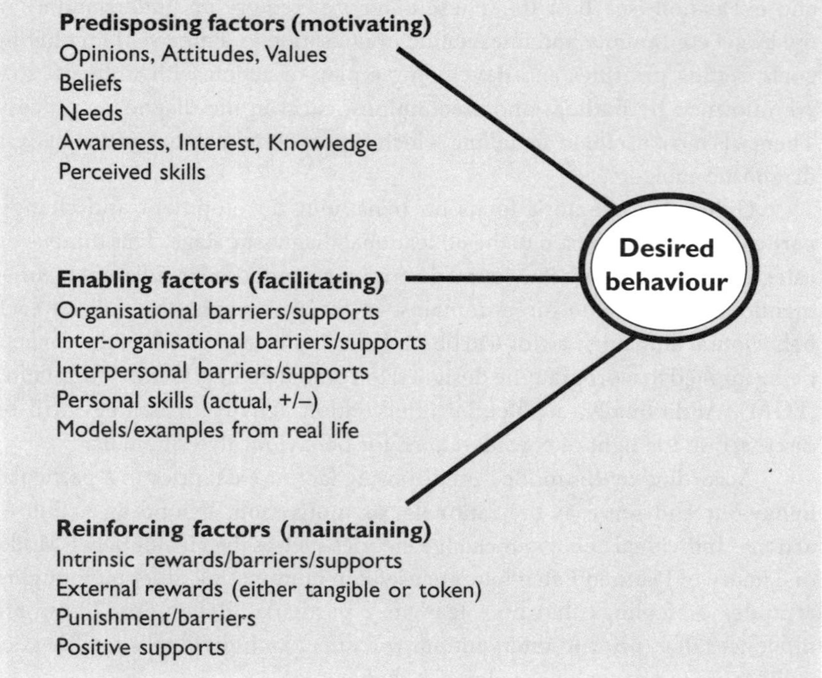

Example: FGM Eradication Programme: A family decides to circumcise their daughter because they live in a small community where everyone knows everyone else and where the operation can be performed safely by the local medical doctor, in the nearby health clinic.

Enabling factors are often changed through community organisation and participation; policy and training interventions. In each instance, identifying the most important causes for behaviour change and development allows the programmer to better tailor communication strategies, given the specific issue to be addressed. With reference to the FGM example, activities can be undertaken to organise women's groups and increase their skills in putting pressure against medical doctors who practice female circumcision.

Reinforcing factors are composed of the rewards, or punishments, that occur during (or after) a particular action and that influence whether the behaviour will be continued or maintained over time. They also refer to the positive, and/or negative, social effects of adopting new or different behaviours that influence whether or not an individual will sustain the new or changed behaviours, independently from the intervention. Theories of social or group behaviour such as Social Support, Diffusion of Innovations, and Community Empowerment are useful in clarifying social interactions and their role on behaviour.

Example: FGM Eradication Programme: A young mother who would like to protect her daughter from female genital mutilation is criticised strongly by her mother-in-law and other older, female family members. In an effort to reduce family tension, she finally agrees to the act.

When addressing reinforcing factors, programme focus tends to be oriented towards indirect communication to the target population, through parents, peers, teachers and significant others. In the above FGM example, efforts could be made to influence mothers-in-law or grandmothers who in turn would then influence young mothers and fathers.

BASNEF Model

Hubley (1988) expanded upon the work of Green *et al.* by placing a greater emphasis on the link between enabling factors and behaviour intention. As such, by incorporating concepts from the Theory of Reasoned Action into the Precede/Proceed planning framework, he has formulated the BASNEF (Beliefs, Attitudes, Subjective Norms and Enabling Factors) Model. This planning framework for behaviour change was developed to reflect special needs and realities in developing countries.

Hubley proposes that one's attitudes, or judgements, about a particular action combined with beliefs about the wishes and influence of "significant others", will determine the outcome, even if there is intent or a desire to act. Secondly and most importantly, this framework also suggests that individuals may intend to perform a specific action, but may not actually do so, due to factors beyond their control, such as lack of skills, money, time, etc. These enabling factors lead to an understanding that the onus of the problem (lack of performance) is not limited to the individual, but rather to mediating circumstances that intervene (see Box 11). In the example below, the application of this planning model can be seen in the recommendations for programmatic action.

11 ***BASNEF Model***

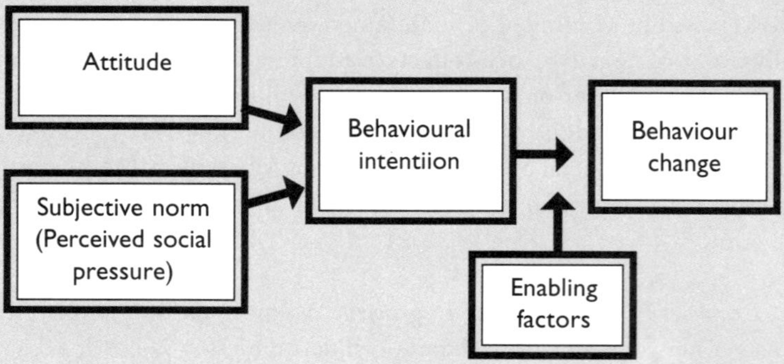

Example: Water, Environment and Sanitation Programme: A local community has a strong interest in building latrines in their village. After several months, they have not yet been built. Investigation shows that there is a lack of the necessary construction funds because a recent flood destroyed the crops and reduced the earnings of the villagers. In this situation, intervention might focus less on developing targeted communication interventions to promote knowledge about latrines and motivate community residents; and place more attention on community empowerment strategies that engage residents in solving their economic problems, instead of just building the latrines.

Programming for behaviour change

As a potential change agent, the development professional's understanding of behaviour has direct implications for strategy development. As evidenced in the examples above, theories of behaviour change/development can be useful tools in conceptualising situation analyses or problem diagnoses, planning feasible interventions, and shaping communication/change strategies. They contribute to programme planning by identifying and making explicit the assumptions behind intervention strategies and by helping to clarify the reasons why programmes succeed or fail in changing behaviours or even more difficult, in social environments.

These strategies vary widely and can be clustered into six main types (see Box 12) according to different theoretical frameworks. There is tendency among programmers to think that one strategy is better, or worse, than another one. Experience, however, shows that combined interventions are most useful when trying to reach a large and diverse target population. This means that arguments over the "correct" behavioural approaches are less important than adopting or adapting proven behavioural models or developing one's own

12 ***Summary of intervention strategies***

Type	Design emphasis
Cognitive interventions	designed to use both information and emotions to change perceptions
Structural intervention	designed to use changes in the behavioural environment/context to influence behaviour
Behavioural interventions	designed to provide incentives (natural or external) to reward desired behaviour
Policy interventions	designed to use social force or approval to influence behaviours and related determinants
Marketing interventions	designed to create exchange relationships with a specific target population to provide benefits with lower obstacles/costs
Participatory interventions	designed to maximize in the most feasible manner the active involvement of the target population in every programme stage on the premise that people ultimately know what is best for themselves and will sustain self-designed interventions longer than those externally imposed.

conceptual framework to explain a behaviour change process based on field experience. The focus should be on building an intervention strategy that is based on clearly-defined behavioural determinants and indicators (Steckler *et al*, 1995).

Most of our knowledge about successful intervention strategies and behaviour has focused on the individual-level change and has identified four key lessons learnt (Steckler *et al*, 1995: 310):

- a clear, operational and underlying, theoretical perspective informs most successful individual-level interventions;
- a wide range of educational and behaviour strategies are supported by these theoretical perspectives;
- the concept of social support appears to be important and frequently incorporated in these interventions;
- the combination of diverse strategies – educational, behavioural and communication, within multiple-component interventions lead to comprehensive programming.

They also found that a variety of community intervention strategies have been shown to be effective and thus have a great promise for development work:

- Mediating social structures (family, informal social networks; religious institutions, voluntary associations, communities, etc.);
- Linking agents (individual gatekeepers who facilitate access to community members and institutions);
- Community coalitions (alliance-building and partnership development);
- Citizen participation (civil society participation);
- Socio-ecological approaches (combined strategies directed at different segments of the community simultaneously).

In summary, there are a variety of theoretical models from which programme staff can choose. None of these have proven completely satisfactory in the field of international development. Many practitioners find that they can achieve the greatest understanding by combining more than one theory or developing their own conceptual framework. What follows in this book is such an attempt. It is not a theory, but it does offer insight in the form of a model which can be easily understood by professionals in many fields and it does answer some of the criticism sometimes made, that theories of behaviour are too Western and geared to the individual.

References

Aggleton, P. (1996) "Global priorities for HIV/AIDS intervention research", *International Journal of STD and AIDS*, Vol. 7.

Bandura, A. (1986) *Social foundations of thought and action: A social cognitive theory.* New Jersey: Prentice-Hall, Englewood Cliffs.

Bloomberg, L., Meyers, J. and Braverman, M. (1994) "The importance of social interaction: A new perspective on social epidemiology, social risk factors and health", *Health Education Quarterly*, Vol. 21(4).

Boot, M. and Cairncross, Ed. (1993) "Actions speak: The study of hygiene behaviour" in *Water and sanitation projects*. The Hague: IRC International Water and Sanitation Centre.

Earp, J.A. and Ennett, S.T. (1991) "Conceptual models for health education research and practice", *Health Education Research: Theory and Practice*, Vol. 6.

Fishbein, M. and Ajzen, I. (1980) *Understanding attitudes and predicting social behaviour*. New Jersey: Prentice-Hall.

Freire, Paulo (1970) *Pedagogy of the oppressed*. Baltimore: Penguin.

Gerschick, T.J., Israel, A. and Checkoway, B. (1990) *Means of empowerment in individuals, organisations and communities: Report on a retrieval conference*. Ann Arbor: University of Michigan.

Glantz, Karen, Lewis F. And Rimer, B., eds. (1997) *Health behaviour and health education: Theory, research and practice*. 2nd edition. San Francisco: Jossey-Bass.

Green, L.W., Kreuter, M.W., Deeds, S.G. and Patridge, K.B. (1986) *Health education planning: A diagnostic approach*. Palo Alto: Mayfield.

Green L.W. and Kreuter, M.W. (1991) *Health promotion planning: An educational and environmental approach*. Palo Alto: Mayfield.

Hubley, J. (1988). "Understanding behaviour: The key to successful health education", *Community Medicine*, July 1988.

Hubley, J. (1986) "Barriers to health education in developing countries", *Health Education Research*, 1986:1.

Israel, B.A. and Schurman, S.J. (1990) "Social support, control and the stress process", in Glantz, *et al. Health behaviour and health education: Theory, research and practice.* San Francisco: Jossey-Bass.

Israel, B.A. (1985). "Social networks and social support: Implications for natural helper and community level intervention", *Health Education Quarterly*, Vol. 12.

McLeroy, K. (1994) "Health education research: Theory and practice – Future directions", *Health Education Research*, Editorial.

Prochaska J.O., DiClemente C.C., Norcross J.C. (1992) "In search of how people change: Applications to addictive behaviours", *American Psychologist*, Vol. 47:1102-1114.

Rogers, E.M. (1983, 1995) *Diffusion of innovations*, 3rd edition. New York: The Free Press.

Rogers, E.M. (1986) *Communication of innovations.* New York: The Free Press.

Steckler, A.B., Israel, B.A., Dawson, L. and Eng, E (1993) "Community health development: An anthology of the works of Guy W. Steuart", *Health Education Quarterly*, Suppl. 1.

Steckler, A., Allegrante, J., Altamn, D., Brown, R., Burdine, J., Goodman, R. and Jorgensen, C. (1995) "Health education intervention strategies: Recommendations for future research", *Health Education Quarterly*, Vol. 22 (3).

Wallerstein, N. (1992) "Powerlessness, empowerment, and health implications for health promotion programs", *American Journal of Health Promotion*, Vol. 6.

Zimmerman, M.A. and Rappaport, J. (1988) "Citizen participation, perceived control and psychological empowerment", *American Journal of Community Psychology*, Vol. 16.

Dynamics of human behaviour

A STUDY BY MIRA B. AGHI

With an objective to understand the dynamics of human behaviour from the point of what people themselves think about their own behaviour and how it is determined, 30 people in New Delhi and areas bordering the Indian states of Haryana and Uttar Pradesh (selected at random with no special specifications in mind) were interviewed individually to respond to the following questions :

(1) Why do you think people generally behave the way they do ?

(2) Why do they sometime behave differently, like when they indulge in gossip, lies or doing any other action they normally consider not right ?

(3) Why do you think people behave differently than usual in front of those they respect, love or are in awe of ?

(4) Can people change their behaviour? Can they adopt new behaviour on a permanent basis? Under what circumstances is this possible ?

The responses to the questions appear at first to be disconnected, but when tabulated, categorised and synthesised, revealed compelling commonalities. Given below are the responses to the four questions :

(1) Why do you think people generally behave the way they do ?
Responses: "Our behaviour is not conscious. We just do things without thinking or contemplating . . . . I think I have imbibed certain principles and my behaviour flows from that. I usually behave the same way . . . . My behaviour is like a reflex action, automatic . . . . I have a philosophy of life and my behaviour is determined by that . . . . I have never thought about this question . . . . I behave in a particular way because that is how I am . . . . My behaviour emanates from what I am, as a member of society, as a human being: . . . etc., etc.

All these responses boil down to: every human being behaves the way he or she is made, he/she understands life, or views a particular situation. Every human being follows a particular pattern of behaviour which results from his beliefs, understanding, motivation and the circumstances present.

It was clear that not many people give a thought to this question. In fact the question, when first put, appeared very strange to most of the people, to the extent of sounding foolish. The above responses emerged after probing and requesting the respondents to deliberate on this.

The immediate response from most of them was "what?", "I don't know", "A strange question!", "Why do you ask this ?"

It can thus be said that understanding the circumstances the person is in, and the motivation that she/he derives from these, determine behaviour.

(2) Why do people sometimes behave differently, like when they indulge in gossip, lies or doing any other action they normally consider not right?
Responses : "Yes, we do indulge in lies, gossip, and tearing down people at times. But this is not because we think it is a right behaviour. In fact I do not approve of such behaviour on my part but I still indulge in it . . . . It gives me a strange satisfaction to do this . . . . It is one of those weird things where you try to hurt even the person you love. I guess it is the deviant in me who does it. I do it inspite of myself . . . . It is not necessary that you dislike the people that you gossip about. You gossip about friends as well . . . . I always decide I will not do this again but I do not stick to this decision . . . . Sometimes I do feel sad for doing it and once in a while it does not affect me much . . . . etc., etc."

Thus, the behaviour is not seen as always right by the individual. He/she may not approve of one's own behaviour at all times; but, in general, behaviour of an individual is in agreement with what he/she thinks or believes is right. Each one of us is born with or learns a certain predisposition to behave in a particular way, but the hues and colours change as the individual interacts with the people in one's family, community and country.

(3) Why do you think people behave differently than usual in front of those they respect, love or are in awe of?
Responses : "People inspire other people to behave in a particular manner. We behave differently in front of people we love or respect because we want to be liked by them . . . . I do this because I want to have an approval . . . . My reason for doing this is because I want to feel elated . . . . I want to feel good . . . . I behave deliberately. I think and as if chart out my action because I want to appear good . . . . I want to be liked, loved and respected likewise . . . . I want to impress him/her . . . . I want him/her to think highly of me . . . . I want him/her to be positive of me . . . . etc., etc."

Behaviour is not always automatic though largely it is. Special motivation improves behaviour in one's own eyes. Also, the situation is akin to a role model that induces a deliberation element into the behaviour. So the individual thinks before he/she acts. Here the behaviour is not automatic but deliberate, not intrinsic to the person, but it can change.

(4) Can people change their behaviour? Can they adopt new behaviour on a permanent basis? Under what circumstances is this possible?
Responses : "Yes, one changes one's behaviour. I have to have a reason for changing my behaviour . . . . The circumstances have to be different, they have to change before I can change my behaviour . . . . There has to be motivation, something new, something different, things have to change, they have to improve . . . . or else things have to somehow appear different, they have to be presented in a special way – this can only occur if the individual is called

upon to get involved in the new way of doing things from the point of why, how, where, etc. There has to be a seen advantage to changed behaviour, some kind of profit, financial or otherwise . . . . I have to be convinced that new behaviour will be profitable . . . . It has to improve my situation in order to be attractive . . . . It has to continue to be in keeping with my life. It has to fit in my life . . . . etc., etc."

Current behaviour has to be seen as disadvantageous, and the new suggested behaviour as profitable/ advantageous. However, the new behaviour cannot be basically alien, i.e. distinctly different from the existing life style. There has to be something, even though at a very micro level, which supports the new behaviour. It has to fit in the existing scheme of things, no matter how vaguely.

This research provides a backdrop to explain how behaviour can be modified or a new behaviour adopted. Any behaviour which rings a familiar bell in any corner of one's life style will have a possibility of being adopted. Something entirely alien will not have a possibility.

Let us now look at some cases where behaviour changes were the objective. Let us see how they were addressed.

The first is UNICEF's Meena Communication Initiative, which focuses on the problems and the issues of the girl child in the countries of South Asia. The goal of this project is to alter or offer stimulation to alter behaviour and attitudes of people towards concerns and issues of the lives of girl children. The changes sought are in the area of the treatment of the girl child. The girl child has the right to develop to her full potential; therefore the family, the community and the society has to provide enabling environments for her development. The girl child in South Asia is discriminated against when it comes to providing education, health, nutrition and many other such basic facilities. Growing numbers of people go for abortions after determining the foetus is female. This attitude towards the girl child has to alter, otherwise the logical conclusion of this would be extinction or total annihilation.

Research conducted to design strategies of communication to achieve these changes revealed that whenever people were called upon to identify the problem, its cause and eventually the solution, they saw the need to change. Involvement of the people in the total process allowed them to see the "faults" in their existing behaviour and many advantages to adopt the new behaviour. Somewhere, somehow the existing behaviour had a "flaw". The detection of this "flaw" and the realisation that there is a "flaw" seemed to be the first basic step in enabling one to move from a "faulty" to a "desirable" behaviour. However, the person should have heard or known about the "desirable" behaviour; or the desirable behaviour should be present somewhere else; or its description should make a lot of sense to the person to offer enough motivation to adopt it.

Meena: Dividing the mango

One of the films in the Meena series is on discrimination of food between the girl and the boy child. In the film the existing discrimination is in favour of Meena's brother, Raju. He gets more and better food than Meena. "This has been happening for ever . . . This is how it is, he always gets more . . . " says the grandmother. One day, somehow, the issues of workload and food come together in the family discussions. It dawns on the father that the food ought to be given in proportion to the workload a person has. The story, as it develops, allows for a realisation on the part of the grandmother, which the whole family sees as a revelation. The story writer very ingeniously brings in the element of growth of children and its relationship to nutrition. The new behaviour appeals to everyone and this lends itself to easy adoption.

This programme was telecast in Bangladesh on a trial basis. Women who saw the programme commented that after seeing the film they have become very conscious while serving food to their daughters. This demonstrates a view point expressed earlier that the new behaviour has to appear profitable and more positive than the existing behaviour. It has to be a familiar behaviour, for example, a boy is given more and/or better food etc. Given below are two more examples from the same series.

Meena: Saving a life

In this episode of the Meena series, "Saving a life", the issue to be communicated was care during diarrhoea and the message in focus was "increased fluid intake for a diarrhoea patient".

The concept research and pretesting of the storyline revealed that people seem to be aware of the information that the diarrhoea patient should be given plenty to drink. They did not seem to dispute that, but when asked if they were actually giving plenty to drink in case of diarrhoea, their answers were evasive.

Further, the research revealed that the people knew about this but did not adopt this behaviour, i.e., they did not practice giving fluids to a diarrhoea patient. The story involves Meena's family when her baby sister Rani gets diarrhoea and her condition is getting worse. As it gets late in the night, Meena, Raju and Mithu go to ask their teacher what should be done. The teacher says that it is important that they give her fluids, while Meena's old aunt represents the traditional approach that this should not be done.

The development of this episode, like all the other of the Meena series, was done in partnership with the people who are the target group for the film. It came from the people that they had been repeatedly told to give more to drink but they did not see any benefit in this because all the fluid came out and left the diarrhoea patient more ill.

The participation of the people revealed that the resistance point lay somewhere with not understanding why more liquids should be given and how they help the diarrhoea patient. A separate animatic was developed to explain the concept of dehydration, how repeated episodes of diarrhoea lead to acute water loss and could be fatal if the body fluids are not replenished. This animatic was separately tested with the people and refined upon to be finally incorporated in the film.

The resistance point to the acceptance of the message was overcome when the film clearly conveyed the information that is needed by the people to change an existing attitude, know the benefits of the newly proposed behaviour and the ills of the earlier behaviour.

This film was taken back to the people once again to pretest. It evoked very favourable responses from them. It was quite apparent on their faces and in their eyes that what was being said in the film was acceptable to them and satisfied a lot of their queries. This conviction is a prelude to positive behaviour change.

Meena: AIDS – A girl's story

This episode of the Meena series, "AIDS: A girl's story", attempts to put across to the people the messages on HIV/AIDS. This film is meant for all to view and seeks to provide basic awareness about HIV/AIDS, its prevention and control.

The concept in itself is very complex with a variety of dimensions. This had to be simplified to include enough relevant information that could be received even by the smallest unit of the society i.e., the family across all of South Asia. For this, an assessment of the present level of knowledge of the people across all sections of society was made, keeping in mind the social mores, cultural ethos and the traditional value systems of society.

The storyline that emerged from detailed discussions with people is built around Meena's family and her friend, whose father had died and whose mother and baby brother have HIV/AIDS. Meena and her family learn about HIV/AIDS from this experience and the HIV/AIDS messages are built into the health worker telling Meena and her friend about what AIDS is and how it spreads. The information that is relevant to children is given through the dialogues between Meena, her friend and her mother.

The field research at various stages of the development of this film revealed that it probes the people and urges them to question their own behaviour. A prerequisite to change in behaviour is the realisation of the wrong behaviour. It was clear from the reaction of the people who were shown the film, that it makes the viewer analyse his/her own behaviour as it relates to the potential risk of suffering, if one gets HIV/AIDS.

During the field test, the viewers across all test sites, were found to be captivated by the story and they were very anxious to know more about HIV/AIDS. They sought more information like, what does an AIDS patient look like? .... Where should one go for an investigative test? .... Young girls asked what should they do if they are being arranged to be married. Clearly the film had set people thinking in concern.

UNICEF/HQ95-1195/Giacomo Pirozzi

Watched by other villagers, a rural radio animator, wearing headphones, interviews another man on the importance of using clean water, for a radio broadcast, in the village of Bacaya, near the southern town of Kelo in Chad.

2

The age of information

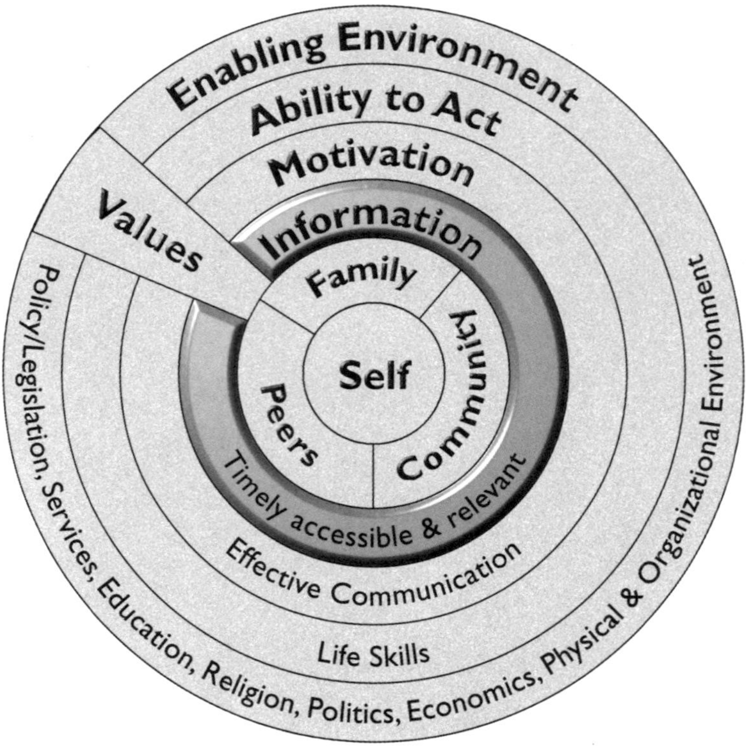

Enabling Environment
Ability to Act
Motivation
Values
Information
Family
Community
Self
Peers
Timely accessible & relevant
Effective Communication
Life Skills
Policy/Legislation, Services, Education, Religion, Politics, Economics, Physical & Organizational Environment

TWO

The age of information

Chin Saik Yoon

Introduction

The review of behaviour theories and frameworks in the previous chapter has identified a number of points concerning how we may launch initiatives aimed at developing and changing the behaviour of individuals and communities. A popular entry point among the many alternatives is the creation of awareness among the people whose behaviour has been identified for change. The conventional way of doing this is through information programmes which are designed to communicate new attitudes, facts and methods relating to the desired new behaviour.

This chapter will discuss the many ways in which information is formatted for communication, and various approaches used in processing information to support development activities. The chapter will then move on to review the principal development theories which have influenced the work of programmers, and how each theory assigned different roles and degrees of importance to information in facilitating behaviour change. It will conclude with a comment on the questionable trend amongst development agencies to use the words "information" and "knowledge" in an interchangeable manner.

Recent history

United Nations development programmes first committed significant resources to information and communication efforts in 1966 when then Secretary General, U Thant, Henry Labouisse, then Executive Director, UNICEF, and Paul Hoffman, then Administrator of UNDP, accepted Erskine Childers' arguments that communicating with the people was the key to the development process. This led to the joint funding by UNDP and UNICEF of the first project in the sector called "Development Support Communication Service (Asia)" in Bangkok in 1967. (Fraser & Restrepo-Estrada, 1998).

The type of information disseminated and the way in which dissemination is handled (since those early days in Bangkok) has changed significantly over the intervening decade. At the same time, the process of disseminating and communicating information has also grown in complexity and sophistication. This growth spawned relatively new disciplines and arts such as development communication and informatics, rural journalism, community broadcasting, street theatre, and so on. The next chapter will discuss them and review the techniques and methods which each has evolved. It will reveal how an important conceptual transformation occurred along the way which replaced the emphasis on informing people with one aimed at motivating them to action: or from a neutral reporting role to that of an active catalyst of behavioural change.

During the past decades of development programming, a number of important technological changes took place within the information and communication sector which affected the ways communicators and information specialists work. Programmers today have many more choices of media and formats than their predecessors of a decade ago. This broader range of options has contributed to a technologically more challenging environment in which development communicators must now operate. This is especially so since communicators and information professionals have yet to develop techniques for making astute matches between the type of information and the channels to be used in communicating the information to intended users so as to successfully meet the goals of information usage. Conventional wisdom and traditions guide most current decisions. A "multimedia" approach is often the choice because it deploys all the common types of media and theoretically provides for all eventualities. However, as the next chapter reveals, this assumption is not always correct.

Communicators in the private sector, and especially those working for advertising agencies, have developed scientific methods for making media selection (or in their jargon "media-buying") decisions. Almost all of these methods are based on scientific research to determine the information-seeking and decision-making behaviour of the "target audiences" and the popularity, credibility and reach of the different types of media available to a particular campaign. Media which reach the intended audiences at the right time, bearing an appropriate degree of credibility, and with the ability to present the information or "message" in a clear and attention-arresting manner, are selected on the basis of data on these important attributes gathered during field surveys among samples of the target audience.

A good body of research into the mass media has provided the sector with a comfortable theoretical base from which to base practice and professional training. It has also enabled disciplines, allied to the operation of the media, to win recognition and legitimacy necessary for advocating roles for their professionals in development programmes. However, this is not yet the case with the newer information technologies which operate on personal computers. The use of such new technologies in developing countries has attracted considerable attention in recent years. But a recent literature review (Sahay and Walsham, 1995) found research in this area largely fragmented and in need of consolidation. Inspite of the absence of a theoretical base, the new technologies are being promoted within development programmes and increasingly bigger budgets allocated to their deployment within projects. In another study (Velasco and Kowalski, 1996), researchers found that even within the print medium, which enjoys a strong theoretical foundation, practitioners are not drawing upon the rich legacy of their medium. The study found numerous departures from a checklist of best practices when it tested a number of recently published extension materials.

Since research costs are relatively low when compared to the total budgets of development programmes, project managers will find funds set aside for such research profitable investments for developing crucial project management information relating to the sector. Research funds should be invested in studying not only the social processes facilitated by the new information technologies, but also all other media as they are in a stage of convergence into hybrids with unknown potency. Research results will help build programmers' knowledge and wisdom in facilitating the most appropriate matches between people, messages, processes, formats and media.

Media and information formats

The process of taking information and "packaging" it into the different media for communication to target users is called the "formatting of information". The full range of media and formats which are at our disposal belong to four broad categories:

Interpersonal and group media: included in this category are personal counselling approaches such as telephone hotlines and personal consultations at clinics, talks given by subject specialists, and group meetings where all participants have the opportunity not only to seek and receive information, but also to contribute information and share their views.

Mass media: comprises print, radio, television and cinematic film. The availability of moderately-priced video-cassette-recorders, audio-cassette-recorders and compact-disc players has made possible the distribution of video and audio programmes in a non-broadcast mode. Such audiovisual equipment has gone a long way towards helping development workers schedule information sharing events at project sites to suit the convenience of the communities they are serving, rather than attempt (often in vain) to mobilize the people to tune into centrally-planned broadcast schedules. One of the most exciting pieces of recent innovation is the clockwork-radio which uses a wind-up mechanism to generate electricity to power a radio receiver. This has theoretically solved a several decade-old, power-supply problem for poor, isolated communities who cannot afford to buy batteries for their receivers. The technology has been adapted by its inventor to power lap-top computers and other equipment which operate on batteries. However, the initial cost of acquiring the clockwork radio remains beyond the reach of many communities in developing regions.

Folk media: songs, poetry, local forms of theatre, puppetry and dance are some of the common forms of folk media. Many communities also possess traditional media forms in addition to folk media. Traditional media often have fairly strict (even rigid) rules governing their performance, and artists are either prohibited or discouraged from improvisation during presentations. Development communicators have tended to avoid the use of traditional media to carry project information out of their concern for the corruption of such classical forms. Traditional media also tends to be performed as elements of larger cultural and religious celebrations or rites, which is another reason why they are avoided. However some innovative communicators, who have developed a deep understanding of particular traditional media, have successfully embedded project information even in such rigid media. They do this by identifying malleable aspects of the media which may be adapted to carry project information, without doing violence to the classical storyline or form: for example the court jester or clown in some classics are introduced to provide comic relief and their lines either are not rigidly scripted or may be adapted without inflicting violence on the particular performance or media form as a whole.

New ICTs: is the acronym for new "information and communication technologies". The majority of the new ICTs operate on personal computers. The computers are able to process, access and transmit text, graphics, video and sounds by converting them into a universal binary language which can be handled by all new ICT hardware. Examples of applications using these technologies include CD-ROMs (Compact Disc - Read Only Memory), DVDs (Digitally Versatile Discs) and databases of all types. The advent of affordable personal computers and data modems has popularised the use of networked databases for public dissemination of information. Internet's World Wide Web is the best known example of such a network. However the reach of the new ICTs within the developing world, remain limited because the effective functioning of networked databases depends on stable infrastructure such as local and international telecommunication connections, and power supply, which are not readily available in many developing countries. But inspite of these obstacles, the new ICTs have been adopted by a large number of development professionals based in developing countries because of their need to communicate with their headquarters and because of their personal desire to keep abreast with professional information posted on the Internet. Significant numbers of policy-makers and senior officials in developing countries also enjoy connections to the Internet as they have the resources and priority access to infrastructure which permit them to do so. So, although the new ICTs may appear on the surface to be inappropriate technologies, they are quickly evolving into important channels for reaching key members of the development community. They are potent media for policy-related information. In Sub-Saharan Africa, for example, new ICTs help in the dissemination of technical and policy-related, geographical mapping information on malaria. (Council for Scientific and Industrial Research, 1996).

A recent study (Pingree, Hawkins, *et al*, 1996) shows that members of disadvantaged groups will make vigorous use of the new ICTs if they are provided with access to these technologies. The research suggests that the main barriers to usage by poor communities is related to cost and not the people's inability to manipulate the technologies; and that if subsidized access is provided, members of these communities will learn to use the new ICTs and overcome other obstacles which may have hindered them in the past.

The development community must play a catalytic role in preventing the creation of "zones of silence" (Mansell and Wehn, 1998): ghettos of disconnected poor in the Internet who are denied the empowering benefits which new ICTs promises. They can accomplish this by facilitating the development and deployment of appropriate ICTs which meet the particular needs of Third World communities. Systematic discounting of the efficacies of new ICTs in developing settings will cause a new fracture in the sector which will quickly widen into another precipitous gap separating the rich from the poor.

One other reason why the new ICTs will probably become more accessible to disadvantaged groups is the growing momentum within the information industry to delink its technologies from the personal computer. A variety of dedicated, easy-to-use devices are being designed and manufactured to provide users with significantly simplified direct access to particular new ICTs (*The Economist*, 1998). These range from television "set-top boxes" to telephone sets with inbuilt screens, and from hand-held computers to cheap network computers which will enable users to surf the Internet, register their vote on public issues, send and receive e-mail, and perform other specialized communication functions.

Internet access centres, such as this facility at a public library in Ulaanbataar, Mongolia, allows children and adults who are otherwise unable to access the Internet, to log-on and obtain information from the network of databases making up the World Wide Web.

While the boundaries between the four types of media remain fairly obvious in most instances, they are beginning to blur in an increasing number of cases as each class of media tries to mimic and tap the best attributes of the others. A recent example of this would be community radio stations being accessed via Internet websites using special sound "streaming" technology. An earlier example would be television stations broadcasting folk media presentations, such as puppet shows. The evolution of these hybrids are aimed primarily at increasing the reach of the media, which are being fused. Many of these hybrids grew out of development projects.

Accessing information

The ability of development workers to disseminate a set of information to an intended audience depends partly on the audience's access to the media formats employed in packaging the information. Project managers will find that they are not always able to make scientific selections of media formats because accurate data on radio, television and cinema audience numbers and newspaper readership figures are often hard to obtain in developing countries. In those countries with a sufficiently large advertising industry, programmers may be able to subscribe to such data (usually at an exorbitant fee) from professional media research companies, who gather and sell such data to advertising companies, which rely on them to make "media-buying" or advertisement placement decisions. Even then, the data will apply only to that section of the population with the purchasing power which advertisers seek to tap. The poor communities of interest to development programmes are often not included in survey samples. Because of the difficulty of surveying dispersed populations in remote rural communities, such market research data is frequently focused on audiences living in urban centres rather than isolated rural locations.

Project managers and development communicators who find themselves without ready access to media research data may have to undertake their own research to determine the reach of various media. Such research should ideally be undertaken as a part of broader project development research, such as data-gathering activities aimed at collecting information to be used in designing projects, or establishing baselines to be used in project evaluation.

Summarised below are a practitioner's observations about the advantages and disadvantageous of the various types of media and technologies.

Interpersonal and group media

Advantages

- Theoretically one of the most accessible.
- Potentially participatory in nature; people can both receive and contribute information.
- A dynamic social process is readily available with the medium to act upon the information.
- Does not cost money to both share and receive information using this medium.

Disadvantages

- Opportunity costs may be high if people have to set aside long periods of time to participate in meetings.
- Members of developing communities may prefer not to participate in sharing their information or clarifying the information communicated to them.
- Information disseminated via word-of-mouth will rapidly decline in accuracy as they are relayed from one source to another.

Mass media

Advantages

• Information disseminated are packaged in the most stable formats and do not lose their original forms, even with repeated broadcasts.
• The "per head cost" of reaching a very large group of people with a given set of information is probably the lowest.
• This is the fastest way of reaching the largest number of people in a short time with the same set of information.
• Information disseminated via the mass media enjoys an endorsement of credibility, usually associated with these influential channels.
• Appropriately formatted information, effectively published or broadcast, may help to promote an issue as an important item for consideration and action by a country's policy-makers, senior officials, and community leaders.

Disadvantages

• The production process for mass media materials may be time-consuming; consequently, information may be dated by the time it is ready for dissemination or broadcast.
• Many media organizations now give priority to profitable entertainment programmes and give them the most popular time slots, and relegate development programmes and messages to off-peak slots when the least number of people are tuned-in.
• Information carried in the mass media tend to be formatted from the perspective of urban-based professionals. Most mass media organizations and their production facilities also tend to be "marooned" in the cities.
• Information tends to be generalised to cover very large geographical areas covered by the mass media. Such information may not be helpful to efforts aimed at promoting action of a very specific nature, or adapted to meet the particular needs of a locality.
• Government and commercially-owned media are often directed by their owners to promote their favoured interests. Such propaganda discredits the media in the long run, and taints even development information broadcast by them.
• Members of the audience have little influence on the workings of the media. As a result the "national agenda-fixing function" of the mass media tends to be dominated by politicians, senior officials, and influential entrepreneurs.

Folk media

Advantages

- Information disseminated is packaged in the culturally and socially most appropriate formats.
- Information can be quickly adapted to suit the needs and mood of an audience by experienced performers.
- The dissemination of information may be scheduled for the most advantageous moment and at the most appropriate venue.
- Most forms of folk media are entertaining and will hold the attention of the people.

Disadvantages

- Information disseminated may "not be stable" as performers may ad-lib and change meanings of messages from one performance to the next.
- Complex information and technical instructions may not always be successfully communicated by the medium.
- There is a limit to the number of performances which may be staged as gifted performers are in short-supply and the costs of staging performances may be high.

New information and communication technologies [ICTs]

Advantages

- Relatively "cheap" to setup compared to other media with a comparable "universal" reach.
- Information can be quickly updated.
- Information seekers can easily customise their searches to look for relevant answers to their questions.
- Facilities such as e-mail, chatrooms, and on-line polling, support participatory approaches.

Disadvantages

- People in the developing countries have limited access to the new technologies.
- The technologies are still in a state of rapid development and require frequent upgrades.
- The technologies are able to process only a limited number of languages written in the Roman alphabet and a few other scripts.
- The Internet has developed largely under the oversight of developed counties, and the special requirements of developing countries are rarely considered.

Creating information

Another important factor determining the effectiveness of information disseminated is the way in which the information is generated. As in most dynamic processes, there is no universally "correct" method to be followed. The challenge is to select the most appropriate method, or methods, for the task on hand, and for the audiences intended. Three ways of creating information are commonly used in development programmes:

Subject matter specialists (SMS): take charge of identifying the information which is needed and then proceed to draft or write the information for media practitioners to format into materials suitable for dissemination by the various media. SMSs are the "experts". They may be doctors in health campaigns, agronomists in agricultural extension programmes, and charismatic individuals in community projects. This is a top-down, expert-to-learner approach. Time and budgets permitting, prototype media materials containing the information may be pretested on a sample of the intended audiences to confirm the comprehensibility of the information, and the ways in which it has been formatted. This method was widely adopted by the early development projects and now considered overly top-down. However, projects working under time-constraint, such as to manage the outbreak of an epidemic, continue to resort to this approach. Systematic pretesting of information materials created via this approach will help in minimising the risks of people ignoring or rejecting information which they convey.

People-generated information: this is the opposite of the SMS approach. Here people determine what information needs to be created and then proceed to fill these needs for themselves. The Fogo Process, described in the next chapter, is an excellent example of this approach. Another example is the "photo-novellas". In this method people are provided with still-cameras and encouraged to tell "their story" through photographs taken, edited, arranged, and presented entirely by themselves. The product created here, the story book or board of photographs, while remaining meaningful and important, is less crucial than the process of creating it. In this case, information does not represent "the ends", but "the means" for facilitating self-empowerment amongst the people by their assuming control of information and communication processes normally controlled by "outsiders".

Partnership approach: is where people and SMSs get together to decide what type of information is required by the people, when it is needed, how the information is to be used, and in what ways the required information should be gathered and presented. This is theoretically the most appropriate method for projects with a participatory intent. It is also popularly considered to be the most robust and technically sound method.

Competing information

Programmers sometimes forget that they operate within highly competitive information environments. If they were to add-up all the commercial advertisements, messages of development programmes, principles being preached within places of worship, and issues being advocated within cooperatives and workers' unions, they will quickly appreciate how intense the competition is for the attention of the people.

This competition may be direct and obvious. A clear example will be the sleek advertisements published and broadcasted by manufacturers of infant formulas, competing against messages for breast-milk put out by non-governmental organizations (NGOs) and government agencies. The competition against the programmer is more daunting in this instance because the manufacturers often supplement their advertising campaign with a free-sample distribution strategy where mothers of newly delivered babies are given a free supply of formula by medical personnel of the maternity hospitals where the mothers are warded immediately after giving birth.

The competition could also be indirect, and it need not necessarily be between commercial interests and the development community. Development workers compete against each other all the time without realising it. For example, field workers of the Ministry of Health may approach a group of farmers to build proper latrines, while another team of workers from the Ministry of Agriculture may be busy promoting, to the same farmers at the same time, a method of terracing to minimise the erosion of fertile top soil. Although the two campaigns may appear to be discrete and non-competing, they are ultimately competitive because they concern the use of the limited number of spare hours available to the farmers.

However, most challenging of all is the subliminal competition presented by modern forms of entertainment. The competition here is strongest over cultural identity and societal values. Stars in popular entertainment programmes evolve quickly into role models who are often consciously or unconsciously emulated by the people who watch their performances. The situations portrayed in radio and television plays, the values cherished by the characters and the consequences of the plot, all subtly convey to the audience powerful subliminal messages about how their real lives should be lived. A television soap opera about how a young man makes the difficult decision about leaving behind his impoverished life as a farmer to work in a factory in the city, before striking it rich, is potent competition against information which is disseminated by development projects to promote new agricultural practices and farming as a desirable occupation. Children who watch capricious child stars effortlessly dispensing wit, and forever outsmarting adults, may begin to lose self-esteem or develop a rebellious attitude towards their own cultural setting which requires respect for one's elders, and restraint in social interactions. Paulo Freire, the famous Brazilian educator, viewed this competition as cultural invasion with far-reaching results:

> Cultural conquest leads to the cultural inauthenticity of those who are invaded; they begin to respond to the values, the standards, and the goals of the invaders . . . . In cultural invasion it is essential that those who are invaded come to see their reality with the outlook of the invaders rather than their own; for the more they mimic the invaders, the more stable the position of the latter becomes.
>
> (Freire, 1997)

The sleek advertisements which intersperse entertainment programmes broadcast by the mass media also bear powerful subliminal messages which aim to establish a new set of values and aspirations in their audience, serving the primary purpose of selling the product being advertised. For example, cosmetics advertised against background images of expensive clothes and jewellery does not just sell lipsticks to women in rural villagers but a radically different lifestyle. Programmers who plan to adopt the social marketing approach (see page 91) for motivating people towards change should be sensitive to the tendencies of media professionals to sugar-coat even development information in such subliminal cocoons which may hinder long-term goals.

Identifying information

Everett Rogers (1983), the conceiver of the once dominant Diffusion of Innovations Theory (see page 19 of the previous chapter), suggests that the process where a person makes-up her or his mind whether to accept or reject an innovation (and the behaviour associated with it) "is essentially an information-seeking and information-processing activity". He identified three kinds of information and knowledge involved in this process:

Software Information: which answers questions such as "What?" "Why?" and "How?". This information helps people to build "Awareness Knowledge" which lead them on to seek other information which helps them to build "How-to" or "Principles Knowledge".

How-to-Knowledge: is derived from information on how to use an innovation correctly. Complex innovations require more "How-to-Knowledge" than less complex concepts or ideas. If sufficient amounts of this knowledge are not developed by people prior to trying out an innovation, its rejection or discontinuation may result.

Princi ples-Knowledge: relates to the basic premises upon which an innovation is built or founded. An example of this would be the germ theory which underpins behaviour such as washing hands with soap, boiling water, and building and using latrines.

Rogers suggests that field workers (or "change agents" as he calls them) seem to concentrate their efforts in disseminating software or awareness information. He feels this is best done through the mass media. Field workers should instead dedicate themselves to helping people build how-to knowledge. He notes that it may be unrealistic to expect field workers to contribute in the building of principles-knowledge which may be more effectively addressed by formal and non-formal education programmes. However he cautions that a change agent's task may be rendered very difficult in the long-run if the need for principles-knowledge is not met.

Although Roger's theory has lost its dominance (because it is considered linear and non-participatory, and sometimes too simplistic in its description of complex social processes) his classification of the types of information needed offers us a good starting point from which we can proceed with our identification of the types of information needed by people in developing or evolving new behaviours.

The three types of information and knowledge identified by Rogers are actively processed by three elements of the behaviour change model proposed by this book. The "Information" element focuses on "Software Information" which is disseminated via the mass media. The "Motivation" and "Ability to Act" elements provide the processes to share and build "How-to-Knowledge", while the "Ability to Act" element strives to develop "Principles-Knowledge" as part of broader, long-term education aimed at imparting life skills.

The diffusion theory's limitation arises, in part, from its concentration upon the spread of innovations. It is ultimately pro-technology, and because of its technical focus, operates principally on the basis of subject-matter-specialists taking the lead in sharing information and skills with the people who are their students. This "experts' perspective" either deliberately ignores or accidentally misses the wealth of indigenous information and knowledge resident in any community. This ignorance is compounded by the pro-mass media packaging of information found in many development projects which recognises information as valid or valuable only when it is packaged in one of the mass media or new information technologies. The strong oral tradition of many developing communities is either not appreciated or mistakenly appraised as not of significant consequence. An information strategy which sets out to simultaneously reinforce indigenous information and external development information by blending the two, will significantly strengthen the validity and effectiveness of both types of information.

The highly competitive environment in which many development programmes now operate has created a need to disseminate not only positive information, promoting desired behaviour, but also critical information about the consequence of undesirable behaviour. Health and environment projects have a fairly well-established strategy of carrying-out "counter-marketing" campaigns against "bad" practices at the same time they are busy persuading people to accept "good", new ones. Information which counters undesirable behaviour may be broken down to the three categories which were identified for innovations:

Awareness information: about the consequences and dangers of undesirable behaviour;

How-to information: about the options available for ceasing the "bad" practices and ways of remedying any harm which may have been caused by the practices; and

Principles information: about the basis for deciding that the behaviour in question is harmful and undesirable.

Informing the informers

Because programmers see themselves primarily as sources of information, they often do not recognize that they are also important users of information. The information used by programmers relate not only to the behaviours of the people they plan to work with, but probably will also include data relating to their socioeconomic status. Information used by programmers have far-reaching consequences because it serves as one of the foundations upon which a project is designed. It ultimately helps in determining the behaviours targeted for change and the communities who will be involved. A major review of development projects selected from all regions of the world concluded that "the way in which (programme and project planning) information is sought and assessed can itself be exceedingly 'top-down' and nonparticipatory, and the value of the information is likely to be reduced accordingly" (Uphoff, 1985). It found that the conventional method of conducting sample surveys is liable to turn-up inaccurate information for programmers. The active participation of the people in gathering and analysing the information will go a long way in correcting misinterpretations of survey data.

The study also found that because many programmes and projects are planned and evaluated by economists, there is a tendency to think in terms of aggregate numbers and seek out averages and statistical distributions when gathering project-supporting information. This is contrary to real life where spatial distribution counts just as much or maybe even more than statistical distribution. The study found a worrying absence of maps in many projects. One of the lessons learned was that social and geographical maps were important information formats for development workers and their managers. These are maps which people should also take an active part in making.

The third important observation of the study was that project designers and managers tend to think that they are starting with a clean slate when they launch a new programme or arrive at a new project site. This is a false assumption as there is nearly always some legacy. The study remarks that "there seems almost a compulsion within development agencies to confirm the saying that 'history repeats itself'. Indeed, when projects 'reinvent the wheel' they usually end up in square one with a plan which has already failed". This experience advocates the gathering and usage of historic information by programmers. The best way of generating this information is through the involvement of the people the programmers hope to work with. The added benefit of considering "history" is that it will "greatly affect the willingness of the intended beneficiaries to take an active role in the proposed project" (Uphoff, 1985).

Development theories and the differing roles of information

The degree of importance assigned to the dissemination of information varies widely. One of the most important sources of influence on development specialists in this matter is the development theories or premises which underpin the operation of their organizations or programmes. Unlike the physical sciences, where one theory replaces another, the different development theories have coexisted through the past decades. Rather than replace each other, each succeeding "new" theory has evolved from earlier theories. A new theory would enjoy its period of dominance while the "older" theories continue to retain significant currency by supporting aspects of the new theory in vogue, or addressing a development issue which it is particularly well adapted to handle. This plurality has assigned information a range of roles in facilitating changes in people's behaviour, some placing it at the core of the change and development process, and others at the periphery.

This section of the chapter will briefly review the main development theories which have emerged over the past decades. It will also discuss the role of information prescribed by each theory and the core values which it champions. The classification of the theories used is by Nora Quebrel, a development communication specialist who helped in pioneering her field and who participated in a wide range of programmes which subscribed to the full range of theories described (Chin and Quebral, 1991). There is no complete agreement among development specialists on the exact number of theories driving our work, some have grouped the four theories described below into two, while yet others argue that there are three theories rather than four. The exact number is perhaps not as important here as the recognition that there is currently more than one way of looking at development, and therefore more than one view of what is desired or not desired in the behavioural change we aim to facilitate in our work.

Modernization: The "Modernization" Theory (sometimes also called the "Growth" model), influenced many early programmes in the developing world. It holds up industrialized countries as role models. Development is perceived as a process of economic growth. The poor countries are encouraged to adopt values, beliefs, institutions and technologies of the rich countries. The strategies recommended are capital and technology intensive in nature. The benefits of development are thought to reach private and public sector organizations first, before eventually "trickling-down" to the people.

Information played a central role in many of the projects driven by this model, partly because of the belief that people are trapped in their circumstance by their ignorance of doing things in the modern way. This belief often led to the strategy of dissemination of information obtained from sources outside the communities. It is a top-down process. There is unquestioning faith in the efficacy of mass-media to transmit information and change societies. Increased production of agricultural and industrial goods, and growth of macroeconomic numbers, are adopted as the criteria for measuring success in development and changes made in society.

This model has undergone significant modifications in the last decade. Instead of holding-up fully industrialized countries as models for change, many developing countries now turn to newly-industrialized-countries (NICs) for inspiration. The new role models were, until very recently, developing countries themselves. In Asia, the NICs being emulated include, Singapore, Korea, Taiwan and Malaysia. Malaysia is an interesting role model because it triggered its transformation into a NIC with a "Look East Policy" which focused on Japan as its model for development. Malaysia selected Japan because it felt that Japan has a history, a culture and values more akin to its own than to other industrialized countries in the West. In adopting Japan as a model, Malaysia hoped that it would achieve industrialization without sacrificing its cultural identity or losing its traditional values. The Asian economic crisis of

1997/98, which plunged many of these economies into steep decline, called into question the sustainability of this variation of the model.

Basic Needs: The Basic Needs Model is also known as the "Growth with Distribution" Model. It addresses a flaw in the Growth model by moving away from its previous preoccupation with growth of incomes. The new emphasis is on improving the quality of life of the people by addressing their health, nutrition and educational needs, in addition to issues of income and occupation. The focus is turned directly on to poverty issues. Priority is given to the rural areas and to agriculture as the chief source of employment; and strategies reorientated towards intermediate technologies and labour-intensive solutions. But most important of all, people are no longer perceived as obstacles to change – instead outmoded social structures are blamed for hindering change.

Information continues to be important in this model, however, the preferred mode of disseminating information has shifted from mass communication channels to formal and non-formal educational approaches. Major rural outreach initiatives are launched, including sophisticated agricultural extension systems, rural cooperatives networks, and continuing adult education programmes. The role of the mass media, which has been top-down and one-way in the past, changes from a central to a supportive one. Local or traditional media take on new importance for helping the people to express their needs. Interpersonal media (one-to-one discussions and group meetings) become indispensable to development action.

Dependency: Latin America is the source of this model. The modernization model had failed in the region, prompting reflection on its shortcomings. The analysis concluded that the cause of underdevelopment is the unequal relationships among countries. The on-going class struggle between the rich and poor is projected to the global level. The old East-West dichotomy becomes one between the North and South. The model has its strength in describing the relationships between the developed and developing countries, but suffers at the same time from a major weakness of not examining the inequalities within developing countries nor suggesting a direction for social change.

Information is highly politicized in this model. People in the South saw little important technological information trickling into the poor countries. They instead saw a strong flow of news and entertainment from the North that threatened to smother indigenous values and cultures. The attention then shifts to the workings of the international media and how news (and the views which come with it) is generated and distributed. Publishers and cinematic producers begin to monitor the predominantly North to South flow of books and cultural products. People in the South now see the need to defend their sovereignty and strengthen communication links among themselves to counter Northern information perspectives, cultures and values. Efforts are made to set-up South-South news agencies to avoid news being routed through the traditional hubs located in London, Paris, New York, Moscow, Madrid and elsewhere in the North. Cultural exchange within the South is intensified, while at the same time efforts are made to swap development-related information and experiences through the establishment of regional and international development information and documentation centres.

Southbound/Chin Saik Yoon/1998

The news editor (standing) and his subeditor (far right) of the United News of Bangladesh selecting the news reports and features to be distributed for the day. The news agency is an example of indigenous news organizations established by developing countries.

Participatory: The participatory paradigm is the most current. It is sometimes known as "another" or the "multiplicity" model (Servaes, 1989). It was spawned during the heated debates of the dependency era and retained the decentralist tendencies of the basic needs approach while innovating additional features. The conservation and enhancement of people's values, cultures and other "qualitative" attributes are stressed in the participatory approach. Antithetical solutions are proposed to a wide range of ills: e.g. violence–peace, destruction of the environment–sustainable development, injustice–social justice, repression–freedom.

The model recognizes that while all nations are interdependent at the global level, there does not exist a universal model for development. Instead, a multiplicity of approaches which draw on the indigenous resources, and social systems of communities should be applied to bringing about change and development in the respective communities. Each approach should pay careful attention to the values on which it is premised to ensure that they serve the long-term interests of the people who are active participants and stake-holders in the process of change.

Externally-generated information is given low priority, while information available within communities take centre stage. "Indigenous knowledge" (information, experiences and knowledge, often passed from one generation to the next via oral and other traditional channels) is highly valued. Information as a whole is given less importance than the processes used in sharing and using information. These processes ideally should be initiated and managed by the people themselves, the role of external agents (such as development workers) are as neutral facilitators whose chief role is to support social processes which enable people and communities to consider, decide and act on an agenda for conservation and change, determined by the people themselves.

The diversity of ideas which drives this model has created, in turn, a communication and information system of interpersonal channels and mass media which are loosely but extensively networked. The chief function of the system is to promote critical self-awareness to facilitate the empowerment of the people. The long-term goal is the full realization of the human being.

The information-based approach

The review of development theories in the preceding pages shows that approaches which stress only the provision of information by experts to the people are now largely considered to be inappropriate. However, this approach remains pervasive today, even though some of its chief proponents have long ago admitted to the limited validity of its underpinning theory. For this reason, it remains useful to review the information-based approach since development professionals will continue to come across projects designed in this way.

The information-based approach adopted by development professionals a couple of decades ago, subscribed to the Modernization Theory of development in both ideology and premise. It is derived from a concept of development, oriented towards economic growth and transfer of technology. The approach is essentially unidirectional – information and technology flows from an expert and informed source to an uninformed receiver. Early projects of this approach assigned central roles to the mass media for carrying this flow of information. When this purely top-down strategy proved to be ineffective in communicating the information to the intended audiences, two-way communication strategies were adopted and feedback loops introduced into the process. But the experts continued to decide on what was to be communicated, with feedback intended mainly to confirm if the audience was receiving the information clearly.

Early initiatives using this approach were marked by the high degree of emphasis given to the building of the mass media infrastructure which served as ready channels to convey information from the experts in the towns to the people in the villages. Radio and then television studios and transmitters were installed. At the same time, mobile cinema vans, public bulletin boards, posters, information brochures, and other mass media materials and strategies were introduced into development programmes. In order to ensure that radio and television broadcasts reached the poorer communities, public viewing centres and radio forums were set-up. The radio forum was an interesting innovation where small groups of the intended audience were provided with receivers and organized to meet in order to listen together to specific broadcasts at predetermined times. Each group would then discuss what they had heard and its leader would complete a questionnaire or postcard to feedback a summary of the discussions to the producers of the radio programmes. The producers were able to find out, in this way, whether their messages were "getting through" to their intended audiences. This approach was applied successfully to several agricultural extension projects and was the driving force behind farm radio programmes for many years.

Southbound/Chin Saik Yoon/1998

The chief engineer at the Louang Prabang Radio Station, Laos, studies an electronic circuit diagram in an attempt to extend the working life of a power transmitter, and other equipment from a variety of sources. They have been contributed by donor agencies over the past four decades. He faces a daunting challenge as spare-parts for the equipment are hard to obtain.

The radio forum feedback mechanism may have given programme producers a sometimes incorrect impression that there was a loyal mass of listeners in the communities. The reality, in many cases, was that development broadcasts were facing stiff competition from entertainment – popular music and "soap opera" programmes. The technical emphasis of development broadcasts, produced in boring formats, quickly lost its audience to attractive, sleek, entertainment productions made by the best talents in the business. The mass media, originally installed to support development, had been "hijacked" by the entertainment industry. Some development programmers made attempts to compete with the entertainment content by adopting production methods similar in style to those used by the entertainment industry. They tried to make development messages more "entertaining". More often than not, they failed. Social marketers then came up with the idea of doing the opposite: making entertainment more educational to support development and social change objectives. Producers of entertainment programmes were initially persuaded to weave development messages into "soap opera" or musical productions. At other times "stars" from the entertainment industry were commissioned to record "development songs" and stage specially written "soap opera" serials promoting a particular development project. This created a hybrid production style called "edutainment'".

As development professionals grew more experienced with the approach, they realized that information must be made available, together with the physical inputs needed to make it possible to adopt the behaviour they were promoting. This was especially the case in technology transfer projects which required the introduction of significant amounts of new, outside resources. A good example are projects aimed at persuading farmers to adopt new farming practices which are dependent on the availability of hybrid seeds, fertilizers and a stable water supply from an irrigation system. As the design of such agricultural projects became more sophisticated, other considerations such as pest management, crop storage, transportation of produce to markets, pricing of produce, and contingency planning for the occasional crop failure, became additional elements which were addressed. The sophistication of later project designs reflected the complexities of facilitating such change and put in proper perspective the role of information as a necessary, but not sufficient, ingredient for bringing about change.

The advent of the Internet and the new information and communication technologies appear to have revived the information-based approach. It has also resurrected development programmes to build urban-based communication hardware infrastructure – computer networks in this instance. Logic seems to suggest that this is all wrong. The poorest developing communities do not only lack computers and modems, but also telephone lines and electricity. Should we ignore the Internet and the new technologies?

The phenomenal speed at which the Internet, and particularly the World Wide Web, has developed, has prompted some development professionals to see a direct role for it at community-level activities. Titus Moetsabe, Communication Training Adviser, Southern Africa Development Community

(SADC), Centre of Communication for Development sees a direct role of the new technologies in promoting participatory approaches in promoting food security. He sees the possibility of "computer points" being established at either the district or village level. His vision includes information from the Internet being projected onto screens located at the village meeting venues for the "villagers . . . together or in groups discuss and strategize on what action to take next. Immediately they make their decision they could respond via the same way. Added to this is the possibility of the extension worker, the facilitator at village level, being an information worker too . . . (who) will play the role of decoding a lot of information which could be difficult to comprehend or respond to." (Moetsabi, 1997)

At the global level, international non-governmental organizations view the Internet as having a democratizing effect on global information flows in the context of the dependency model. The organizations have, for the first time, access to a medium which they can afford and control to communicate their views, information and news to the world at large. The Internet and World Wide Web has permitted these organizations to broadcast on the same platform, and to the same global audience which was previously the preserve of the richest international media corporations. These organizations are realistic in appreciating that the Internet does not reach the poor communities, and that it is principally a medium of the richer countries. The organizations therefore focus their communication over the Internet on audiences in the developed countries in information campaigns which aim to advocate, within these richer countries, improved global policy regimes which are fair and beneficial to the developing countries. Such campaigns have been conducted to advocate positions of developing communities in multilateral negotiations associated with the World Trade Organization, the environment, refugees and many other North-South issues.

Information as the only choice

Development professionals sometimes resort to an information-based intervention, not because they subscribe to the modernization theory or diffusion models, but because circumstances allow only for such an approach. The HIV/AIDS pandemic is a good example. When HIV was discovered to cause AIDS, the medical community did not (and still does not) have a cure for, or a vaccine against the virus. The information-based approach (usually launched simultaneously with health education programmes) has to serve as the front-line defence against the spread of HIV during the interim.

The case study which follows is of a similar situation when information and the mass media offered the only practical solutions to an urgent problem arising from armed conflict which discounted other methods of intervention:

Information shielding bullets: Red Cross information in areas of conflict

Three Red Cross workers, one African and two Swiss, were ambushed and killed in May 1978 when travelling in a clearly-marked Red Cross vehicle in then Rhodesia (now Zimbabwe).

Rhodesia was, at that time, the centre of high conflict, in which dissident black groups were bent on overthrowing the minority white government. The principal rebel factions operated from bases in neighbouring Mozambique and Zambia. Most of the rebel forces had only limited knowledge of English and were indistinguishable from the civilians of the rural areas.

All signs pointed to the guerrilla fighters as the attackers of the three Red Cross workers. In the aftermath, the Red Cross worked on the assumption that the attack was launched out of ignorance of the Red Cross's role in the conflict and not malice. Alain Modoux, then Head of Press and Information Division, International Committee for the Red Cross (ICRC) and his colleagues visited Rhodesia and neighbouring countries and found that the Red Cross was virtually unknown in the extensive rural areas of the zone of conflict. The team also discovered that black Rhodesians generally associated white Red Cross workers with the white government.

The only practical solution to the serious problem threatening the security of Red Cross staff, and the continued operation of their programme to care for battlefield casualties, was an information and education campaign. Modoux's division was put in-charge. In order to find out the communities and channels through which the fighters could be reached, Modoux conferred in Rhodesia and Zambia with sociologists, teachers, journalists and other communicators. Their advice was to enlist the help of African communication specialists and to keep the messages simple.

The target audiences were eventually identified as:

- political leaders of countries adjoining Rhodesia;
- guerilla chiefs;
- people in the refugee camps and areas bordering on rural Rhodesia, with an emphasis on schoolchildren.

A mix of communication methods and channels were used:

- the official mass media of the neighbouring countries;
- Rhodesian mass media;
- exhibitions;
- conferences;
- cartoon folders;
- tens of thousands of campaign gifts, e.g. pencils, T-shirts, calendars, first-aid scarves, note books for school children.

The emphasis was on radio and cartoon folders because the majority of the rural population was illiterate and also had no access to television.

Additional staff were recruited in Switzerland and information services established in Rhodesia, Botswana and Zambia. It took several months before the campaign began to make progress in the Autumn of 1978 through the support provided by African journalists and the hard work of Red Cross staff.

Newspapers in Rhodesia and Zambia were the most cooperative and supportive. Television was also deployed but since only the small privileged minority had access to the medium, its reach was limited. Radio posed some difficulties. The transmitters operated by the guerillas did not contribute any air time to the Red Cross. The Rhodesian radio system, because of its known affiliations to the white government, was not used until the Spring of 1979. Much of the broadcasts were carried by the Zambian national radio, which devoted 90 minutes each week to Red Cross programming in five different languages.

Posters were printed and displayed. One of them carried photographs of a Red Cross relief aeroplane and an ambulance, and urged in large type, "THE RED CROSS – RESPECT IT – LET'S HELP EACH OTHER". Another poster showed two Red Cross staff, one a black woman and the other a white man, helping a black woman.

The lessons learnt by the Red Cross in Africa were put to use in the design of labels such as the one on the left, which was pasted on thousands of food parcels distributed in the former Yugoslavia.

The cartoon folders or comics provided descriptions of the various services provided by the Red Cross. They were all of the same size and format. The front page featured the special Red Cross-in-Africa campaign symbol while the last page carried a letter to the reader which, in about 250 words, provided details about the messages conveyed by the illustrations.

The first comics was titled "Meet the Red Cross" and opened with the questions "Why is the Red Cross here in Africa? What can it do to help YOU? Look at these pictures and you will see!"

Initially, 19 comics were published. They illustrated the wartime services provided to people by the Red Cross – both combatants and civilians. A further seven comics were published in a later series titled "The Tenga Family". Each of these focused on the experiences of the father, mother, son, daughter, and their relatives with the Red Cross. The content dealt with the respect of soldiers for the Red Cross emblem, first-aid procedures, blood banks, tracing of missing persons, help for civilians in villages which had been bombarded, and saving lives of fighters wounded in combat. The comics were published in two African languages and English.

The Red Cross ran the campaign "by feel" because the conditions did not permit systematic evaluation of its effectiveness. The opportunity to evaluate the campaign finally came at the end of the conflict when surveys were conducted amongst people in refugee camps and with the black combatants who had gathered in preparation for demobilization after the Peace Accord had been signed. The survey revealed that the radio messages (even those broadcasted by the Rhodesian radio network), and the comics and posters, had been effective in reaching both the combatants and civilians. The effectiveness of the information campaign had been confirmed earlier by the cessation of hostile action against Red Cross personnel after the commencement of the campaign.

The experiences gained via the Rhodesian conflict became the basis for the design and implementation of very similar information campaigns in Angola, El Salvador and former Yugoslavia.

This case study is abstracted from two documents:

Case Study No. 1726
"A Communication Campaign Designed to Solve a Critical Humanitarian Problem" published in *PR News*, New York;
and
Zbiden, Eva-Maria (1981), "Red Cross Information in Areas of Conflict: Analysis of the Information Campaign in Southern Africa 1978–1980", unpublished report of the Information Department, International Committee of the Red Cross, Geneva.

However, it is not only in emergency situations that information-based approaches are appropriate or can be successful. In nation-wide programmes, such approaches may be the only way of imparting standard, validated information to a large population. The advent of satellite television has offered multi-channels of standard information and entertainment to the rich, around the world. But the overwhelming majority of the world's poor remain untouched by this development. As early as the 1970s, however, the Government of India recognized the power of television in educating that country's vast population. The case below demonstrates how information, which is well-researched and packaged in an interesting manner, can make an impact on the lives of children in thousands of rural villages:

Satellite Instructional Television Experiment (SITE) and behaviour change in children in India

A CASE-STUDY BY MIRA B. AGHI

Information/knowledge acquisition is believed to be a necessary step/ element in behaviour change or adoption of a new behaviour. What is not always realised, is that sometimes information alone is required for a new behaviour or to modify an old behaviour. Sometimes people are ready, adequately motivated to change a particular behaviour but they do not have the necessary information to do so. This does not undermine the presence of other elements, they have to be present. In fact if they do not continue to be present, the new behaviour is not sustained. The following case study illustrates how behavioural changes resulted merely by receiving information previously not available to the children residing in isolated rural areas.

During the decade of the seventies, the rural child in India was suddenly exposed to something unusual, almost miraculous. The child saw a moving picture which, at the same time, also produced meaningful sounds on a simple looking box called "television", placed in the village community hall/school by the Government, which was committed to usher a change in the lives of the rural folks, especially children. The child was able to see this picture daily in the morning as well as evening and it was free for all. All that was asked of the child was to watch and enjoy it. Educationalists believing that relaxation leads to learning, took this opportunity to give to the child what they thought was good for him/her.

The Satellite Instructional

Television Experiment (SITE) conducted in India during 1975-76 was a landmark experiment which offered a unique possibility for the entire country to receive television transmissions. This bold experiment was based on a memorandum of understanding between India and the United States of America in which a NASA Satellite (Applied Technology Satellite F) was loaned to India for a period of one year. The NASA satellite made it possible to provide "television signals" to far flung and remote villages via relatively simple antennas, designed to pick up the single transmitting channel from the overhead satellite.

Designing such a television system was an enormous multi-dimensional task. Realising that this service to the people was long overdue, particularly those poorly served by other means of communication, the Government took a bold step to provide educational TV programmes without the technology of ground based TV relay stations. This system was designed with the aim of addressing the needs of isolated villages throughout India. Based on the country's development needs, it was decided that there would be two types of TV programmes: one for providing information/knowledge on agriculture, health, family planning, national integration for general audiences and the other which would be enrichment oriented TV programmes aimed at school children between the ages of 5 and 12. The total programme time devoted to this age group was 1.5 hours, divided over six days. For two days out of a total of six the content of the programmes was science education.

The production of the science programmes was the responsibility of the Indian Space Research Organization (ISRO) which set up a studio in Bombay, totally dedicated to producing these programmes. Not all the programmes were produced in the studio, some had parts shot in the field. After a great deal of deliberation and country-wide consultations with educators and scientists, ISRO thought it was worthwhile to give the rural children an awareness of their environment; a curiosity for their surroundings and an understanding of how nature functioned. This, it was felt, would lead to a positive attitude of self discovery and learning of self, leading to the child adopting a set of new behaviours or modifying the existing ones.

For this purpose, and to provide a guiding principle, ISRO put forward what in India came to be known as the science "credo" – to make children realise that science is everywhere, that their immediate environment can be questioned, understood, explained and manipulated by them using the scientific method. It emphasises the learning of the scientific method, manipulating the information rather than mere transfer of information.

Looking at the topics for the programmes, it would appear that they were from the school curriculum but looking at the actual content, it was evident that they had an objective of enriching the child by positioning the information provided to him/her in such a way that he/she wondered and pondered over things of every day life, such as the "village pond" the "animals", "bicycle" and "kitchen".

Since the goal was to enrich the child by informing her/him, the programmes were designed by:

(1) keeping the specific objectives in view;

(2) utilising the content in the best way to achieve the objective;

(3) making the programmes relevant and applicable to the rural area; and

(4) including a question for the child to ponder over and seek an answer for him/herself.

Accordingly, production of all programmes utilised a variety of formats, always keeping in mind that unless programmes were interesting they would not hold the children's attention and unless they did so, they would not meet their objectives. Therefore, the programmes were produced in a special set up where a formative researcher-cum-developmental psychologist, a content specialist, a scriptwriter and a producer worked in collaboration with one another; a "formula" likely to be successful for generating and evolving user-relevant, user-useful information – information which can prompt adoption of new behaviours and/or modification of old ones.

Producing programmes for unfamiliar isolated villagers called for intense research into audiences and their characteristics, which was undertaken prior to programme production. However, experience indicated the need for rigorous formative research to fill the gaps of knowledge to produce quality and targeted programmes. Formative research was undertaken to seek answers to the following :

(1) What kind of language would be understood by the village children?

(2) What kind of visuals would be comprehended and would hold attention?

(3) What formats would be interesting and aid in children's comprehension of new ideas?

(4) How much content – bits of information – should be put in a programme of 10-11 minutes duration?

(5) How should the content be sequentially placed in a programme?

(6) What features enhance the credibility of a presenter?

(7) What kind of a presenter would be most effective?

(8) What kind of presentation would be most appreciated?

(9) What kind of characters and settings would have the most credibility for the rural children? And so on.

These questions needed timely feedback. Consequently they were researched on an on-going basis while production continued. Formative research activity dealt with the total programme from its inception to final production.

When information thus tailor-made was provided to the children, they immediately picked it up and

changes were observed during the experimental period. Children started doing many things for the first time:
(1) Dusting and sweeping their house, not only from inside but keeping the outside of the house equally clean.
(2) Stopped washing clothes at the well.
(3) Stopped drinking from the village pond.
(4) Insisted on eating before going to school.
(5) Washing hands and mouth before and after meals.

Summative studies undertaken later revealed the sustainability of these behaviours. However, what is very useful to remember is that information when presented in a form which is interesting, relevant and friendly, and stems from a recognition of needs of the person, is likely to contribute to behavioural changes. What is very significant to note is that children shared this information with adults which prompted them, as well, to change their behaviour, indicating spin-off effects. Information which by-passes the needs and requirements of people will fail to bring about any significant change.

Limits to information-based approaches

Accumulated experiences prove that the information-based approach is generally effective in increasing awareness about behaviours or techniques and technologies promoted by development programmes. However, they usually meet with only limited success in bringing about actual behavioural changes in the people on whom the approach is applied. The United States Smoking Cessation Guideline Panel recently undertook a systematic and exhaustive review and analysis of the available scientific research literature on anti-tobacco interventions. Its recommendations and observations on the impact of information materials (which the panel calls "self-help materials") in bringing about cessation of use of tobacco products among the targeted groups is interesting for its revelation of the potentials and limitations of such materials.

The panel made the following recommendations on various methods of disseminating anti-tobacco information on the basis of the ranking of each method derived from its study and summarised in the following table (Agency for Health Care and Human Services, 1996):

- Written self-help materials (pamphlets/booklets/manuals) when used alone do not increase cessation rates (of smoking) relative to no self-help materials.

• Videotapes and audiotapes when used alone do not increase cessation rates relative to no self-help materials.

• Provision of a list of community programmes when used alone does not increase cessation relative to no self-help materials.

• Hotlines/helplines (patient-initiated telephone calls for cessation counselling or aid) when used alone increase cessation rates relative to no self-help materials.

Efficacy of and cessation rates for various types of self-help formats when used alone (n = 12 studies)

Self-help format	*Number of arms*	*Estimated odds ratio* (95% C.I.)	*Estimated cessation rate* (95% C.I.)
No self-help (reference group)	8	1.0	7.9
Hotline/helpline	3	1.4 (1.1-1.8)	11.1 (8.7-13.4)
Video- or audiotapes	5	1.3 (0.6-2.9)	10.9 (3.6-18.2)
List of community programmes	2	1.1 (0.8-2.5)	8.8 (6.9-10.8)
Pamphlets/booklets/ manuals	22	1.0 (0.8-1.2)	8.1 (6.7-9.5)

Agency for Health Care and Human Services
Centers for Disease Control and Prevention (1996)

It is significant that the panel found that "cold" information, delivered via different types of mass communication channels and materials, does not increase cessation rates, whereas, hotlines seemed to be effective in promoting cessation. Part of this reason may be due to the patient-initiated nature of the calls to helplines which suggests active participation of the callers in the communication process, and their high degree of motivation in making a change in their behaviour. Both of these important conditions will be discussed in-depth in the subsequent chapters of the book.

The panel also reviewed the effectiveness of information delivered simultaneously through a variety of media or communication channels and concluded that: "The results suggest an increasing effect with an increase in the number of types of self-help interventions".

The findings summarised in the table below appear to support the multi-media strategies which aim to saturate the target audience with information which supports a particular public education campaign.

Efficacy of multiple types of self-help materials (n = 12 studies)

Self-help format	*Number of arms*	*Estimated odds ratio* (95% C.I.)	*Estimated cessation rate* (95% C.I.)
No self-help (reference group)	8	1.0	7.9
One type	15	1.0 (0.9-1.3)	8.1 (6.7-9.6)
Two types	7	1.2 (0.9-1.6)	9.6 (7.0-12.1)
Three types[a]	1	1.9 (1.2-2.9)	14.5 (8.9-19.1)

Agency for Health Care and Human Services
Centers for Disease Control and Prevention (1996)

The evidence that information materials and products on their own do not lead to behaviour changes does not suggest that information is not required for bringing about change. Information is an essential, though not sufficient, ingredient needed to bring about change. Information is often the first step of a long process in facilitating change. The information-based approach will work if the people have access to all the elements mapped in the behaviour change model proposed by this book, and all that is missing is information. This is often seen in private sector organizations, where management, production and marketing capacities are in place, and all that is missing is strategic technological information and market intelligence; and once such information is acquired the management and staff of these organizations are able to change and reinvent their organizations, if necessary. However, these processes and capacities are largely not built or are dormant in developing communities. The communities also face structural and systemic problems which prevent information, on its own, from catalysing change.

The case study on the next page illustrates how an information-based approach is necessary but not sufficient and where counselling and tobacco use cessation camps were instrumental in facilitating permanent behaviour change.

An intervention study of tobacco habits among rural Indian villagers in Kerala, Andhra Pradesh and Gujarat

A case-study by Mira B. Aghi

There is a great deal of consensus among health and behaviour professionals about how people acquire a tobacco habit. It is said that young people take up a smoking habit due to peer pressure or by watching adults smoke. They want to imitate those that they like, admire and hold high in esteem. At the same time, there is very little agreement on why some take to the habit and others do not. It has been observed that some children take to the habit of smoking and drinking practised by their parents, siblings and friends and others do not. In fact, some react in exactly the opposite direction by looking down on those habits and by determining never to take them up. It will be helpful to analyse both the behaviour of such individuals, thereby, gaining insight into the problems of taking up a tobacco habit, as well as, studying the habitués* for a possible strategy of weaning them away from this potent drug.

This case study provides an example of how the habitués of tobacco were motivated to give up their habit and accept a new life style. The case delineates how communication tactics were utilised to enable these people to realise that they were not being very smart in practising the tobacco habits, thereby motivating them to give it up.

Before undertaking this project, an attempt was made to examine if, indeed, people in rural India also take up the habit for the same reasons as in the Western countries – namely peer pressure, parental influence, media and role modelling. This investigation rendered very useful information. Villagers in India know of no health hazards connected with tobacco. In fact, if anything, they believe in medicinal and multi-magical properties of tobacco. Whereas for some tobacco is a panacea for all troubles connected with toothache (they actually are advised so by their friends, parents and neighbours), for others it is a means of getting rid of the foul smell in the mouth, for controlling ailments of the stomach (like gas, bloating, constipation, etc.), for postponing hunger, warding off sleep. The young boys see their fathers smoking/ chewing. They believe their fathers to be doing the right thing and they

---

* The tobacco habits include much more than smoking a cigarette, cigar or a pipe. There are a great variety of habits practised in India which includes smoking, rubbing, plugging and chewing of tobacco.

follow them unconditionally. These boys are usually sent by their fathers to buy *bidis* (indigenous cigarettes like tiny cigars) and commonly pilfer a few from the bundles purchased for their own surreptitious smoking.

Young boys find images in *bidi* advertisements very attractive. Often these advertisements have the pictures of movie stars and movie stars have a lot of charisma. Young men take to smoking, often to appear modern, open minded, tough, smart and, sometimes, to show they are educated.

Parents often send their young boys to work in the farms of other people, as labourers. The atmosphere there is conducive to smoking – "everybody smokes, so I should too". Many employers, such as the local tea shop owners or village grocery store owners, give free *bidis* to the boys to encourage and draw them to their shops. In addition, since much of the leisure time activities in villagers consist of getting together to chat, such social gatherings also become very conducive time for taking up the habit of using tobacco. A young boy who is not smoking is coaxed into it by his friends – "smoking adds glamour to get-togethers" they believe. "If you want to go to the city to work, you have got to learn smoking to look smart . . . It is a sign of being grown up, being independent and being carefree" – is the advice given to many.

Since the acquiring of the habit is so complex and intricate, the only strategy which is likely to be effective is one which takes into account a comprehensive understanding of the target population, not just their tobacco habits but their total life style, their beliefs, their level of knowledge of what tobacco does to people.

This intervention programme was carried out by professional dental surgeons and social scientists who were given special training in conducting in-depth interviews, approaching and interacting with the tobacco users in a considerate, sympathetic, warm and positive manner, without being condescending in any way.

The study population was selected from three districts of India. A large number of individuals from these districts were screened and about 12,000 tobacco users, aged 15 and over, were selected in each district. The tobacco habits practised in the study included smoking cigarettes, smoking *bidis*, smoking *chutta* (indigenous hand rolled cigars) in conventional and reverse manner and chewing tobacco with or without betel quid (Aghi 1989).

A programme of intervention was developed after appropriate pilot and pretesting surveys. In-depth interviews of the participants were conducted to investigate:

(1) reasons for their starting and continuing the tobacco habit (such as when and how the habit started, who encouraged it, was it a peer or a parent?);

(2) the perceived implication of the habit in its social, economic and health aspects; and

(3) possible reasons for giving up their habits (Aghi, 1987).

In addition, pilot surveys were conducted to assess the communication media facilities available to the target population that could be used to convey the intervention message. The intervention programme outlined a timetable for employing different media of communication and regulating the flow of information so as not to overwhelm the target population. The pilot study also helped to modify the messages, whenever necessary, with a view to making them easily understandable. The intervention lasted for 10 years, with a follow up every year. Each follow up used strategies of communicating messages to the target population which assisted and enabled them to give up the tobacco habit by motivating them sufficiently to ask for ways to give it up.

Breaking the habit involved
(1) elimination of the old response;
(2) acquisition of a new response.
The new response was a tobacco-free life. Depending upon whether it was a group or an individual whose tobacco habits had to be dealt with, it was required that a series of graded tasks, leading to a tobacco free life, be set. The steps recommended required a therapeutic person to work on graded tasks remembering:
(1) the consellor's attitude had to be accepting and understanding; that the subject was a human being rather than somebody with a bad habit; and the habit should be regarded as a health and not a moral problem;
(2) to relieve discomfort or pain from minor complaints, medication was administered;
(3) tools of understanding, encouragement and support were used;
(4) all the steps were user-based/user-driven by involving the habitués completely.

The first and foremost task of the interventionist was to make the habitué become aware of the structures within the oral cavity and the concept of oral health. The link between tobacco habits and oral cancer was explained through the oral precancerous lesions. (It should be mentioned at this juncture that the overall motivating factor for this project was the high prevalence of oral cancer among the Indian population. One-third of all cancer cases are oral cancer.)

When the relationship seemed to be convincing, people were urged to think about their tobacco habits. Various possible ways of giving up the tobacco habits were discussed. Withdrawal symptoms were explained as real, but emphasised as a temporary phenomenon. General benefits of giving up the tobacco habits, e.g. financial, health and aesthetics were pointed out. Further support and encouragement were given to those who attempted but failed to give up their tobacco habit. Reinforcement, in terms of reminding them that it is a harmful habit and that they have done the right thing by giving it up, was provided to those who succeeded and a model and leadership role was suggested to them. It is to be noted that for different individuals and even for the same individual at different times, there was an interplay and exchange between various stages of the intervention.

The intervention used two approaches: personal communication and mass media. Personal communication involved one-to-one contact with the target population with a view to helping them sort out doubts and learn behaviours that would result in abstaining from tobacco. The steps in personal communication were worked out in a logical order, recognizing the dynamics of human psychology and what it takes for people to make decisions and change their attitudes and behaviour. Certain visual aids were used in the personal communication.

Two films were produced specifically for this phase of the study. The objective of the first film was to give information and create awareness of the relationship between tobacco habits and oral cancer. The objective of the second film was to point out how habits are taken up and developed. In addition, this film presents ways the habits can be given up. Film is a very powerful medium for creating awareness and, when effectively utilized, works to motivate behaviour changes.

Posters were displayed to remind the target population that they ought to be reconsidering their tobacco habits. Two kinds of posters were used, one with a written message only and the other with a visual display along with a written message. Slides were prepared from the posters and were projected in movie theatres in the vicinity to serve the same objective. In addition,

Stages of intervention

- Information regarding association of tobacco habits and oral cancer was imparted.

- This information was further strengthened by visual reinforcement through flipcharts, posters, films, etc., and a small amount of fear was deliberately induced.

- Information of the health benefits and other advantages of quitting the habit were conveyed; for example, regression of lesions and saving of money.

- Various possible methods of discontinuing the tobacco habit, such as "cold turkey", gradual reduction, postponing the first smoke or quid, etc., were described and the most appropriate one for the subject was suggested, depending on the psychological profile of the subject and characteristics of the habit.

- Withdrawal symptoms were explained and emphasis placed on their temporary nature.

- Appropriate praise and reinforcement were given and leadership roles suggested for successful quitters.

handwritten posters summarizing the findings about the particular village were left behind to remind subjects that they had been examined for oral cancer.

Articles were published in newspapers to inform and educate people about oral cancer. It was known that many members of the target population do not read; nevertheless, the articles could be read by some, including school children, who have been found to be important agents of change in rural India.

There were folk drama enactments with the objective of talking about the prevalent superstitions and misconceptions about tobacco. In addition, radio programmes were designed to motivate people to give up their tobacco habits as they may lead to oral cancer.

The programmes were used to create an environment to help the target population think about their tobacco habits.

In the last two follow-ups, we held cessation camps to address the demand of our target population, who told us that they believed what we said about tobacco being harmful and that they would like to give it up; they wanted to know how to do it. In the cessation camps, detailed discussions were held to suggest the solutions to the problems encountered in discontinuing the tobacco habit. Regular daily follow up was maintained for a few days after the camps were held.

In addition to the above methods, clinics were run to address dental complaints and thereby try to eliminate at least some of the reasons given by users for practising the habit. Also, exhibits and group meetings were conducted to show common lesions and hold discussions that might help the target population to ask questions and express their feelings and doubts.

The various methods of communication were assessed individually, through carefully designed questionnaire-based sample studies, for their impact relative to their objectives. Since all of the communication methods could impinge on an individual's decision to quit or reduce tobacco use, it is hard to ascertain which actually led to the decision. A rank ordering of the various inputs (see table on page 79) by the target population revealed that subjects have been helped the most by one-to-one interaction; cessation camps had also aided them immensely.

One-to-one communication helped the participants the most. The reason given for this was that they were able to ask all kinds of questions on their minds. It gave them the opportunity to resolve their doubts and misunderstandings and develop a rapport with the programmers. The cessation camps were conducted only in Andhra Pradesh where they were rated on the same level as one-to-one communication. The camps also succeeded in providing participants with a sense that they were not alone in facing their problems.

The statistics in the table on the next page may appear insignificant those unfamiliar with tobacco intervention campaigns. But these numbers do indicate permanent cessation – not a small achievement considering that people usually revert back to their habits.

The cessation of tobacco use in successive follow-ups: Percentage stopping tobacco use

Follow-up	Bhavnagar	Srikakulam	Ernakulam
1st	4.1%	2.0%	4.9%
2nd	7.6	4.4	10.9
3rd	10.5	6.4	14.2
4th	11.6	7.6	15.4
5th	12.5	9.4	16.6
6th	14.1	11.2	17.0
7th	11.5	11.6	17.3
8th	12.2	12.3	17.4
9th	12.7	13.1	18.1
10th	13.6	14.0	18.8

Tobacco has been declared as addictive by WHO. It is to be noted that it is extremely difficult to over come addiction. The people in this project were able to achieve this because the education/communication that was provided acted as a motivator to change their life style.

References

Aghi, M.B. "Psychosocial aspects of acquisition and cessation of tobacco habits in India" in *World Smoking and Health Journal* 12(2) : 4.7, 1987.

Aghi, M.B. "The tobacco tradition in India" in *World Health,* January-February, 1989.

Producing effective information materials

The review of the effectiveness of various types of information materials and methods, discussed in the preceding section, makes generic references to categories of materials and methods. However, development workers know from their field experience that the effectiveness of a particular leaflet, poster, video or radio programme can vary greatly. The difference rests on the superiority of the design, and production skills and techniques employed for each material or method. Only effectively designed and produced information materials will harness the full potentials and powers of the medium in which they are formatted.

What are the attributes of effective design and production? First to come to mind are the obvious professional norms which have been distilled from decades if not centuries of professional practice of the particular medium. In print, this involves deft wording of messages, the astute use of type faces, and the preparation of informative illustrations. In film and video, it requires the preparation of interesting scripts and screen plays, sensitive creative direction, good camerawork, a sound track which enhances the visuals, appropriate sound and visual effects, and first rate editing and post-production. And in folk media, it is the astute selection of performers, the development of an interesting presentation, creative direction, adequate rehearsals, the making of attractive costumes and sets, good staging, appropriate choice of venues, dates and times for performance. These are the variables which are relatively easy to identify and address through the cooperation and services of experienced media professionals. While these professionals may be the experts in designing and producing media, they are not the authorities on the effectiveness of particular information products. Nor are the development professionals. The jury in this case has to be the people for whom the media materials are intended. Only they can tell us if the materials and information successfully engages them in the process of the change intended by the messages formatted in the materials.

A study on audience recall of HIV/AIDS public service announcements (PSAs) among US and overseas college students revealed the complex assortment of variables existing in the mindset of members of the audience, which ultimately contributes to their ability in recalling the PSAs (Lee and Davie, 1997). It found that emotionally crafted messages were more effective than rational ones and that such messages worked more effectively with women viewers than they did with men. The study also showed that US students demonstrated a higher recall level than their overseas counterparts. It concluded that overseas students were unable to find relevant cultural cues in the PSAs and found it difficult to understand both the visuals and audio elements of the HIV/AIDS messages even though more than 50 percent of those who participated in the study had lived in the US for more than five years. The study also found that US female students responded better than US male and overseas students of both sexes to PSAs which featured a US female (of the same age group as the students) as the central character and narrator. In a similar way it found that US male students responded better than US female and overseas students of both sexes to PSAs which featured a US male as the central character and narrator.

The study clearly showed that the cultural backgrounds, gender and the age of the students all affected their ability to recall the PSAs which were tested on them. The results of this study, while interesting, cannot be extrapolated to other audiences as their characteristics will differ, as will the content of the messages and the manner they are formatted. The only way to find out if a set of information materials is effective is by pretesting the materials on members of the audience for whom the materials are intended. Some communicators go a step further by involving the audience in the process which precedes media materials production. Through formative research, they establish the information needs of the audience first, before embarking on message and information design, and production. This ensures that the information is not only clear, but relevant.

Knowledge, not information

A part of that process which brings about changes in people's behaviour takes information and converts it to knowledge. "Information" and "knowledge" are two words which are currently often taken within the development community to mean the same thing. There is a trend to replace the word "information" with "knowledge" in the preparation of programme and project documents. It is a worrying trend because it suggests a lack of appreciation for the complex processes involved in converting information into knowledge.

Information is the raw input used in creating knowledge. Information is created once it is spoken, printed on paper, recorded on tape, or broadcast over the airwaves. The person or group with the strongest capacity to disseminate information is usually in a better position to influence action and changes in a community. Whether the person or group succeeds in doing this depends on their ability to disseminate their information in a way that people can use it in creating knowledge, essential for catalysing the desired action, which is the final confirmation that a change has occurred in their behaviour.

The process of taking information and converting it to knowledge is a complex one which will be described in the later chapters of this book. It begins by people choosing to receive the information and taking note of it. The success of this first step depends on the information being presented in a language and media format which the people understand and can remember. It also depends on the information being communicated in a medium to which people have access. People must trust the source of the information as credible. They should next decide that the information is related to their needs and lives, and in what way this relationship connects. Finally, the people should be able to remember or record the information which they have sieved through, in a way which can be accurately retrieved or recalled when the opportunity arises for them to apply the information (or by now, knowledge) to an action.

This process is better facilitated in an interative manner, with plenty of opportunity for the people (who are the intended receivers of the information) to dialogue with the senders of the message for clarifications and confirmations. It is possible that for this reason the hotlines studied by the smoking cessation panel reported above, are more effective than the unidirectional publications and audiovisual materials. The hotlines are also significantly different in that calls are initiated by the people, confirming their active participation in the process which they are also better placed to influence and control. This supports the current views of most development professionals that participatory approaches are the most effective in bringing about change and sustaining them on the long-term. In the participatory approach, the differentiation between the provider, sender and recipient of information is deliberately blurred. Everyone taking part in this approach (members of the community, development professionals, government officials, etc.) can both provide, request and receive information. The approach also encourages the group to vet and process the information in a participatory manner so that the knowledge which is created is shared and validated by the community – a meeting of minds – which provides a shared foundation on which to take collective action and bring about communal (rather than isolated individual) behavioural changes, which leads to the collective development of a community.

Iteration and participation ultimately contributes to the creation of meaning out of cold and often alien information. For facilitating change, this meaning has to be within the local context. The making of meaning progresses through four levels of "knowing" (Dixon, 1993):

Data: Awareness of data which we perceive through our senses of sight, smell, sound, touch, and taste.
Information: Organised data is information which is disseminated using language, sounds, graphics and numbers. For data to be useful it must be sorted, analysed and displayed or presented.
Knowledge: Information takes on meaning and becomes knowledge only after it has been explored in the context of our lives. We know something in a useful sense when we are able to create meaningful links between information and its application in a specific situation.
Wisdom: Is our ability to make correct inference from incomplete information and knowledge.

The participatory approach has a superior edge over unidirectional media channels in processing information related to important intangibles which are increasingly recognized as the driving forces to change: communal priorities, family values, cultural heritage, etc. In developing communities, these important social fundamentals are seldom chiselled in "stone". They are in a state of slow but constant evolution. There is rarely a single source or credible provider of such information which usually resides within the community in a subliminal way. Experience has showed that the most effective approach of gathering and processing this information is by facilitating a highly participatory process within a community to define the information sought, then collect and sort the information required, and finally process it into communal knowledge essential for making the changes desired. One of the reasons why the participatory approach is superior is its ability to motivate people to take part in the process and subscribe to its results. This is truly a transition from information to knowledge.

References

Agency for Health Care and Human Services, Centers for Disease Control and Prevention (1996) *Smoking cessation.* Clinical practice guideline number 18. Rockville, USA: U.S. Department of Health and Human Services. pp. 44-46.

Chin, Saik Yoon and Quebrel, Nora (1991) "Project for broadcasting in development": Evaluation report. Canadian International Development Agency.

Council for Scientific and Industrial Research (1996) *The use of information and communication technologies in the health sector in Sub-Saharan Africa.* Ottawa: International Development Research Centre

Dixon, Nancy M. (1993) "Report to The Conference Board of Canada on organizational learning". The Conference Board of Canada, pp. 36-37

The Economist, 12 September 1998 "The future of computing: After the PC". pp. 67-68.

Fraser, Colin and Restrepo-Estrada, Sonia (1998) *Communicating for development.* London: I.B. Tauris. pp. 43-48.

Freire, Paulo (1997) *Pedagogy of the oppressed.* 20th anniversary edition. New York: Continuum. p. 134.

Lee, Jung-Sook and Davie, William R. (1997) "Audience recall of AIDS PSAs among U.S. and international college students" in *Journalism and Mass Communication Quarterly*, Vol.74 No.1, Spring 1997. pp. 7-22.

Mansell, Robin and Wehn, Uta (eds.) (1998) *Knowledge societies: Information technology for sustainable development.* New York: Oxford University Press/United Nations. pp. 196-197

Moetsabi, Titus (1997) "Participatory approaches in promoting food security through rural connectivity and Internet: An exploration of issues". A paper presented at the Virtual Conference on Participatory Communication: One Approach to Sustainable Development? http://www.PanAsia.org.sg/conferen.htm

Pingree, Suzanne.; Hawkins, Robert P.; Gustafson, David H.; *et al.* (1996) "Will the disadvantaged ride the information highway? Hopeful answers from a computer-based health crisis system" in *Journal of Broadcasting and Electronic Media*, Vol.40 No.3 Summer 1996. pp. 331-353.

Rogers, Everett M. (1983) *Diffusion of innovations*. Third Edition. New York: The Free Press. pp. 167-168.

Sahay, Sundeep and Walsham, Geoff (1995) "Information technology in developing countries: A need for theory building" in *Information Technology for Development*, 6, 1995, pp. 111-124

Servaes, Jan [1989] *One world, multiple cultures: A new paradigm on communication for development*. Leuven, Belgium: Acco

Uphoff, Norman (1985) "Fitting projects to people" in Cernea, Michael M. 1985. *Putting people first: Sociological variables in rural development*. New York: Oxford University Press. pp. 382-384

Velasco, M.R.; Kowalski, R.; Lowe, J.C. (1996) "Technology transfer materials: Are we learning the technology of transfer?" in *European Journal of Agricultural Education and Extension*, Vol.3 No.1. pp. 35-46.

UNICEF/HQ98-0485/Alejandro Balaguer

University students shovel mud to clear a public park and playground in the city of Choluteca, capital of the southern department of Choluteca in Honduras. In 1998 following the hurricane, university students spontaneously organised volunteer work groups to help clean and rehabilitate public and other spaces.

3

Motivation to act

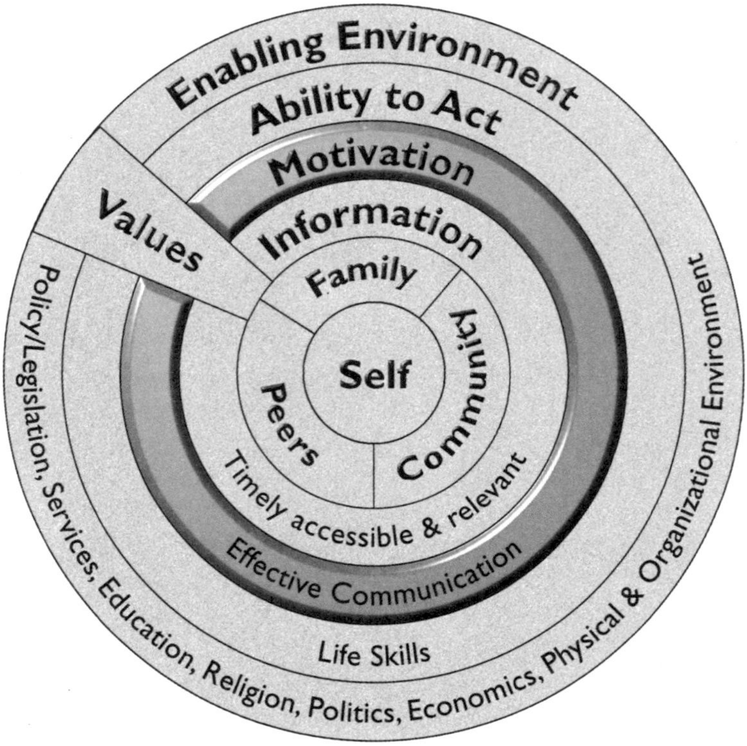

Enabling Environment
Ability to Act
Motivation
Values
Information
Family
Self
Community
Peers
Timely accessible & relevant
Effective Communication
Life Skills
Policy/Legislation, Services, Education, Religion, Politics, Economics, Physical & Organizational Environment

THREE

Motivation to act: Effective communication

Neill McKee

Introduction

This chapter is a basic overview of methodology of using communication channels as strategic tools for motivating people to develop positive behaviour or change unhealthy or antisocial behaviour. It also deals with the issue of motivating individuals, communities and other social actors and forces to work together in bringing about positive change through participatory research and planning, taking into account existing attitudes, beliefs, perceptions, values and practices.

As is shown in the preceding chapter, information is basic to any social or behavioural change. However, information has to be packaged and delivered in a form which is motivating. Finding the keys to motivation, that spark of energy which spurs people to change and consolidate those changes, has become increasingly difficult. There are many factors which prevent people from taking action, in spite of what would appear to be clear evidence that their behaviour may have drastic consequences. This is most evident in complex social and medical problems such as the HIV/AIDS pandemic (see Boxes 1 & 2). People, including young people, often have sufficient facts needed to make a considered decision. In spite of this, their actions are often dangerous to their own health and well being.

Motivation to act or change may be derived from different sources such as financial incentives or legislation, for instance a public health act, as discussed in Chapter 5. It may also be stimulated by role models and peer groups. However, motivation should not be viewed as something that is entirely driven by factors which are external to the individual. Motivation may be intrinsic, coming from within one's life experiences. Although there is no clear boundary between extrinsic and intrinsic motivation, in this chapter we will be addressing the extrinsic, the methods and means of galvanising people into action. In the next chapter, we will be dealing with the intrinsic, psychological and social skills and abilities which are essential for sustaining behaviour change.

Perhaps the most sustainable, externally-driven motivation is derived from human interchange, from communication through interpersonal and mass media channels. This chapter is concerned with the methods and means of converting information into forms of communication which are motivational. It explores:

- Planned approaches to communication
- Communication research and values
- Message design and positioning
- Selecting channels
- Interpersonal communication
- Using natural networks
- Participatory communication
- Social mobilization and communication definitions
- Community mobilization
- Media-based mobilization

1 ***Motivating adolescents in an HIV+ World***

Studies conducted in Thailand, Zimbabwe, Malawi and Brazil – countries that have been hard-hit by the HIV/AIDS pandemic – revealed that adolescents are generally knowledgeable about AIDS. Males and females know how the disease is transmitted and that it is fatal. But many young people interviewed did not think they were at risk of HIV/AIDS. For example, 86 percent of 300 girls surveyed in the Malawi study said it was not likely they would get AIDS despite the fact that 56 percent of the sample reported being sexually experienced. In Nigeria, one-fourth of the young university women surveyed agreed with the statement "young people cannot get AIDS". Instead of feeling vulnerable themselves, young people tend to believe that AIDS is a disease of "outsiders" – bar girls, prostitutes, homosexuals and truck drivers. According to one young woman from Mauritius, "AIDS is only for bad people. They have sinned and are most likely to die". Sexually active girls in rural Malawi reported they did not feel they were vulnerable to HIV infection because they knew the boys with whom they developed relationships. According to one girl, "My mother knows his mother", so this boy could not be infected. Unmarried female and male factory workers in Chiang Mai, Thailand, also reported they believe that good people do not get AIDS. According to one male worker, "If she asks me to wear a condom, I tell her there is nothing to worry about – I am a good boy".

Weiss et al. (1996, pp. 12-14)

2 *Traditional practices and the spread of HIV/AIDS*

In Eastern Uganda and Western Kenya, the Luo community continues to practice widow inheritance in spite of what appears to be clear evidence that the practice contributes to the spread of HIV/AIDS. The tradition requires that widows marry one of the surviving brothers, or another close male relative of the deceased husband. The act of intercourse with the new partner is seen as a "cleansing" right. It is required to seal the new arrangement. The original purpose of the tradition was to provide protection for the widow and her children.

This tradition has continued, but it appears that rather than a protective arrangement, it is often used to access the wealth and property of the deceased. In spite of this abuse of the traditional motivation behind the arrangement, and consequent mistreatment of women and children, women often adhere to the practice for fear of social sanctions and curses. These fears are strong. In cases where it is believed that husbands have died of AIDS, widows sometimes hire outsiders who may be professional "cleansers", to perform the sexual rites instead of exposing the brother or other male members of the deceased man's family. Of course, the risk of HIV transmission grows through such transactions and relationships.

Agyie and Midadde (1995, pp. 47-60)

Planned approaches to communication

The field of development communication is evolving. We use a wide range of terms to describe what we do as communicators: information, advocacy, IEC (Information, Education and Communication), programme support communication, programme communication, social communication, social marketing, social mobilization, health promotion, etc. . . .

Since the 1970s, there has been a call for planned rather than *ad hoc* approaches to development communication. Experience has shown that comprehensive communication planning, including the proper use of formative research, can maximise impact and reduce costs. In spite of this, communication professionals are often driven by organisational priorities and expectations to produce materials which do not relate to an overall planned strategy, and which have not undergone proper pre-testing with clients or service providers. Much money is wasted each year in such product-driven efforts which have little or no connection to positive behaviour development of young people or sustained behaviour change (see Box 3).

Why is it difficult for us to change our behaviour? As illustrated in the adoption process in the Diffusion of Innovations Model (see page 19), the process of behaviour change is a complex one, involving a series of steps such as awareness, interest, trial, decision and adoption. To address this

3 *Information without process*

The Expanded Programme on Immunisation (EPI) has been a priority for many developing countries, throughout the 1980s and 1990s. The communication components of the drive to achieve Universal Child Immunisation (UCI) by 1990 provided many lessons. In some countries, a plethora of materials was produced to support EPI. For example, television and radio spots, flash-cards, flip charts, posters, bill boards, sign plates, rickshaw plates, matchboxes covers, banners, hats, flags and special kits for religious leaders. By 1990, such materials had been produced by UNICEF and distributed through governments and NGO channels.

In Bangladesh, operational research in 1990 and 1991 revealed some deficiencies in this approach. It was discovered that many of the posters and kits had hit bottlenecks in government storage facilities and had not been distributed to their intended users. In addition, interviews with intended users often revealed that even if they did receive the kits through "orientations" – usually one-day events – they did not know how to use them or what their duty for EPI entailed.

It was found that when posters did reach health facilities, they were often placed in doctors' offices, or high up on walls for damage control, out of the line of sight for most clients. Research on flip-charts further revealed that few health workers actually carried them to the immunisation sites because they did not fit inside their kit for vaccines and syringes. They were a burden on bicycle or on foot. Nor had health workers been trained how best to use such materials.

The above approach is probably typical of many of the first approaches taken in EPI and other programmes in the 1980s and early 1990s. Indeed, such approaches continued in the 1990s in many programmes, such as the drive to "Kick Polio Out of Africa". The push to produce glossy, highly-visible materials, without due attention to the process of their development, dissemination and utilisation, is endemic in the social sector of many developing countries and is sometimes driven by international organizations.

Author

complexity there have been many efforts to adopt a more planned and professional approach to communication in the social sector. These have come from a number of fields, including social marketing. However, there has been a great deal of controversy over the meaning and intentions of this latter approach.

One of the original definitions of social marketing is as follows:

> Social marketing is the design, implementation, and control of programs calculated to influence the acceptability of social ideas, involving considerations of product, planning, pricing, communications and market research.
>
> (Kotler and Zaltman, 1971)

This definition spells out a marketing, research-based approach. However, the terminology of social marketing has not found wide acceptance, largely because it is understood by many as a top-down approach which emphasizes products through mass media. Social marketing has been viewed with suspicion by many who work in the social sector. Consequently, it is often more productive to drop the language of marketing and look instead at what social marketers do, or what they say they do.

Another term for a planned approach to communication endeavours is "programme communication". This term has been adopted by UNICEF and other organizations and is seen as more acceptable:

> Programme communication is a research-based, consultative process of addressing knowledge, attitudes and practices through identifying, analysing and segmenting audiences and participants in programmes and by providing them with relevant information through well-defined strategies, using an appropriate mix of interpersonal, group and mass-media channels, including participatory methods.

Effective communication depends on a number of steps through which our programmes should be planned (see Box 4). As with all programme interventions, review and analysis of the existing situation is required before beginning: Who are the audiences and participants? What are their present knowledge, attitudes, beliefs and practices? How can they be reached most effectively? What are the main environmental factors which can hinder or facilitate? Setting communication objectives with in-build knowledge, attitude, practice and beliefs (KAPB) components is also a step which is difficult to do and often overlooked. Without objectives, there is no way to measure success or failure.

Formulating, implementing, monitoring and evaluating communication strategies (see Box 4) is an essential part of effective communication programming. The tendency is to jump to materials development, as noted above. Seldom do we take the time, or are given the time, to carefully plan strategies in a logical way. Very often, *ad hoc* efforts are taken in order to increase the visibility of our programmes. Although we must remain pragmatic and opportunistic, we should not lose sight of the planning steps mentioned in Box 4; Assessment/Communication Analysis/Design/ and Action (ACADA).

4 **Communication Planning Framework (ACADA)**

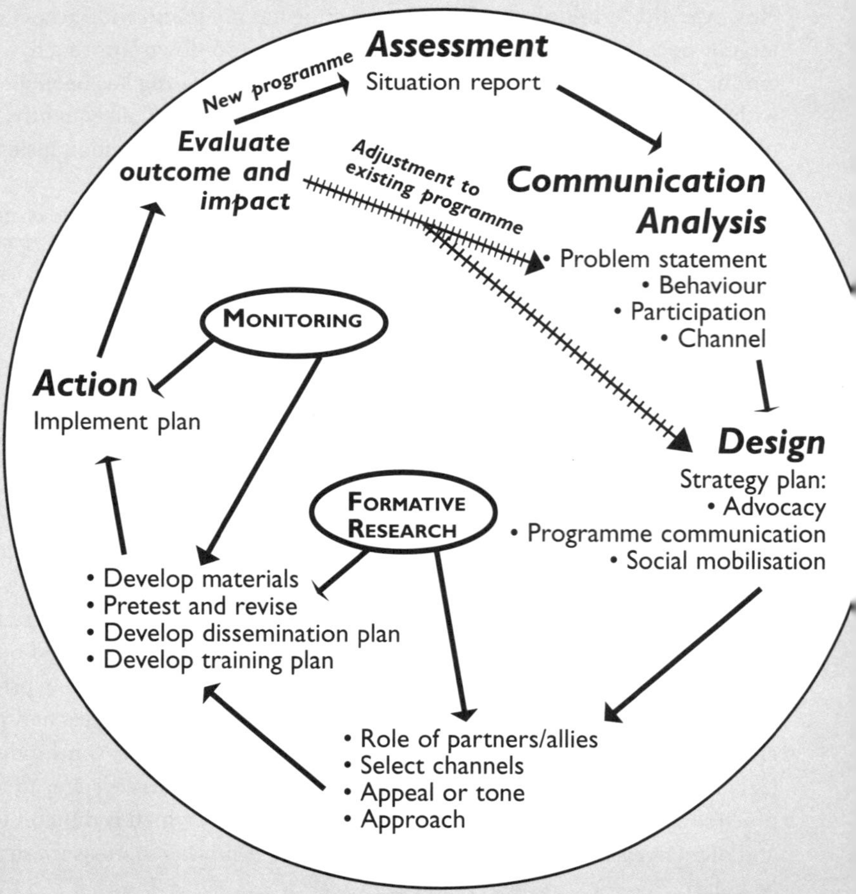

Communication research and values

Some of the basic steps most often skipped or performed at a minimum level, but which we can least afford to overlook, is the baseline analysis and formative research required to define what we should communicate to whom, through which channels. This research may be both quantitative and qualitative. (This is elaborated in Chapter 6).

Through quantitative research, such as survey methods, potential audiences can be classified in terms of their media access and use. Very often this information is already available for review, thanks to large-scale studies which have been undertaken by governments or media and marketing research firms. However, one criticism often levelled at quantitative researchers is that by imposing a structured set of questions, they are in fact imposing a reality which may not exist in the minds of the people. The answers given may validate the researchers' reality but not that of the participants. Quantitative research, therefore, should be backed up by qualitative methods.

As visualized on the behavioural model proposed in the introduction, values are cross-cutting. They influence all aspects of human life. Our values, shaped by the cultural and family context in which we are raised, are one of the main determinants of our behaviour. Beliefs, attitudes and perceptions are, in large part, influenced by value systems. Through qualitative research, we are able to uncover the basic values which shape a "world view" and give meaning to people's lives. This information can then be used in the formulation of messages. These can be designed to align with those values, striking a common chord of understanding instead of clashing with them.

Obviously, the use of such information puts a great deal of responsibility on the shoulders of the communicator. Such information can be used to sell a product or an idea in a manipulative way. This is the often-heard criticism of the social marketing approach, since marketing and advertising are often understood to mean manipulation to acquire goods which may not be needed, instead of meeting felt needs.

The onus is on the programmer to use the research findings in a fair and consistent manner without hiding essential facts. The information uncovered about positive values can be used to strengthen communication messages. Those values and practices which appear to be detrimental to the improved health and well-being of people, have to be addressed openly. Of course, there is a value judgement in deciding what is detrimental and what is positive. This, the communicator cannot avoid. The situation is similar to the conflict between pure and applied anthropology. Do we simply study and understand traditional cultural systems without intervening in any way or do we use the information to improve the situation of people? Who makes the judgement on what an improvement is in a given cultural system?

One of the other main areas of concern is the apparent clash between modern and traditional values. Although they are difficult to dichotomize, traditional values are those which are passed on from generation to generation in relatively isolated cultures or subcultures, whereas modern values are those which are penetrating all cultures of the world today through the fashions, concerns and life-styles transmitted through mass media, due to rural-urban migration and population mobility. There does, indeed, appear to be an "international youth culture" which has a very wide appeal. People may have the ability to live in both cultures at once or to switch between them easily and either cultural system may be harmful or helpful in the context of a particular social programme.

Message design and positioning

We can motivate through appropriate messages. Good message design and positioning are essential components of effective communication. On the other hand, communication with poor design and positioning can have absolutely no effect, or even a negative effect, on attitudes and behaviour. Radio and television programmes, spots, posters, booklets, drama and interpersonal communication sessions can be cluttered with too many messages, or messages which are confusing or unclear. Messages are usually most effective when they are creatively delivered and are short and to the point. Often they need to be repeated, but not to the point of message fatigue.

In the commercial world, messages are designed to motivate purchasing behaviour. In the social sector, they are designed for many purposes: to increase the chances people will buy subsidised health products; adopt an innovation; change unhealthy behaviour; contribute to a social cause, etc. As such, messages are never neutral. They implore people to act. They may be balanced, or at least appear balanced, to allow people to make up their own minds. But the preferred option of the sender is usually transparent.

There are many choices in the types of messages to deliver. A message may be emotional or very rational in tone, humorous or serious. A whole range of options are open to us: joy, anger, sadness, fear, urgency, sarcasm, patriotism, family values, brotherhood and sisterhood, youth appeal, etc. This is part of what is called positioning of messages. Sophisticated advertisers spend thousands of dollars analysing the most effective positioning of their products for their various consumer groups.

Messages can be positive or negative. Generally, it has been accepted that fear, or negative motivation, has less impact than positive positioning. However, this must be qualified. Much depends on how fear is used and who the target audience might be. Fear may have little effect on those who think of themselves as invulnerable. However, it may have a direct effect on others, and it may have a direct but harmful effect on children. Much depends on the characteristics of the receiver.

Then there are other options: mass appeal to the social conscience or appeal to the individual; direct appeal versus indirect, or giving people apparent choices through two-sided messages instead of one-sided, or delivering messages that are open in their conclusion or conclusive or very definite. The choice of effective message appeal will depend, very much, on the target audiences' characteristics and social context, as well as the nature of the programme. For instance, direct appeal may be very effective in one society or age group, whereas indirect appeal may be effective with others. Humour may be effective in communicating sanitation and hygiene messages but not in communicating HIV/AIDS messages, in different cultures.

Another key aspect of positioning is the source. The credibility of the source for the intended audience is very important. Youth may respond best to messages from youth, a youth leader or a celebrity rather than an authority figure. Authority figures may be effective for particular issues, such as avoiding heart disease, or for an environmental clean-up. But use of authority should not be overdone. People sometimes "turn off" if the message is so top-down that it appears they are not being allowed to make up their own minds. Very often, people respond best when they see themselves in the messenger, someone with approximately the same values and perspectives.

Qualitative research methods are often used in the selection and creation of messages. Through such techniques as in-depth interviews and focus group discussions (see Chapter 6), social scientists can obtain information on what people think of a product or a service, their fears and frustrations, their hopes and aspirations. Information on their attitudes, perceptions and values can then be fed back into the formulation of messages. This is the programmers's most powerful tool. It can be used responsibly or irresponsibly. Irresponsible use is manipulative and may be destructive to long-term development goals.

A further risk is an over-emphasis on message design, as opposed to strategy formulation. Messages are only a small part of the communication process. Messages are delivered in a context, for example, a television soap opera or in a song. If we concentrate our efforts on messages or facts without researching the most effective context for our messages, we will be wasting our time. Too often communicators churn out lists of messages which they try to deliver through posters or booklets. Most often these instruments miss the mark. Their rapid production and distribution fulfils work plans and satisfies bosses. But that is usually as far as the satisfaction goes. There are many factors to consider in choosing appropriate communication channels or media (see Box 5). In strategy development, formative research can offer vital information on how best to make selections. Audience access to, and actual use of, the media is of prime consideration.

There is often a tendency to rush to the use of mass media because of its visibility, especially television. However, in many developing countries or communities, television may be only useful in reaching decision makers or the middle class. Radio may be a better option because it has a wide reach. Quantitative research may indicate that 60 percent of households have radio receivers which are functioning in a given area at a given time. However, qualitative research may reveal that in some societies children and women have little control over the actual use of radio, including times of listening and programme selection. If children and women are the target of a communication programme, clearly, in such societies more operational research will be needed to determine the most effective way to use radio to reach these target groups. It may be decided that interpersonal communication channels are the main option open to communication programmers and that this has to be backed up by radio programming at specific times on specific days, or programmes targetted at men, asking them to support the intervention for women and children.

5

Key factors in working with the media

- There is no one "super-medium" that can do all things;
- A mix of media is usually more effective than a single medium;
- Media selection is important, but production quality and method of use are also key determinants of success;
- Effective media production requires appropriate skills and equipment;
- Passive audiences learn little, active audiences are more receptive;
- Media can reinforce and extend face-to-face communication but cannot replace it.

Adapted from "Mobilising messages: Appropriate use of media for rural development", Cambridge: International Extension College

Interpersonal communication

Mass media may be only a part of an overall communication strategy. An effective strategy should also focus on processes between people – one-on-one and group. When communicators formulate plans to motivate behaviour change, they often forget that the major changes and developments in their own lives were not triggered by external sources which suddenly broke through psychological barriers. Such events can occur. However, our behaviour is largely determined by interpersonal relationships, beginning when we are infants. Interpersonal communication (IPC) is a key feature of these relationships. The quality and depth of communication will often determine whether new information is received at all, whether it is persuasive, or whether it facilitates a decision to change and to sustain new behaviour.

Very often communication professionals rush to produce posters and pamphlets, radio and television spots without thinking of the above (or in order to demonstrate a tangible output as quickly as possible). Little thought is put into how these products will support IPC processes.

In spite of many attempts at reform, formal education systems around the world are founded on top-down lecture or "chalk-and-talk" methods in which the student is seen as an "empty vessel" to be filled. There are too few teachers, or role models, who can relate and communicate well, engaging in a two-way process. Instead of emulating those few individuals, most accept the predominate "expert culture". Unfortunately, the expert is often one who spends more time lecturing than listening.

We pass on information to supervisors of field workers and expect them to pass it on to field workers who will, in turn, pass it on to the clientele of our programmes. What could be more simple, especially if we can distil it into some basic facts for life? Unfortunately for those who would like simplicity, human communication and learning does not work in such a mechanistic manner. We are challenged with the task of trying to make people effective, two-way communicators and helping them unlearn bad habits.

The essentials of good IPC are also the essentials of good counselling (see Boxes 6 and 7 developed for family planning). Communicators may be involved in providing a social service, such as family planning or clinical services for sexually transmitted diseases. We may also speak of "counselling" people in hygiene and sanitation, diarrhoea prevention and treatment, or in nutrition, although professional counsellors would hold that this is a misuse of the term. Any social or health programme can benefit from good IPC or counselling methods. Numerous manuals and guides, including facilitators' guidelines, exist to illustrate these.

When devising a new programme it is important that communication programmers do not attempt to "re-invent the wheel". IPC training modules can be made relevant for just about any programme because, stripped of the technical information, they are essentially the same. In fact, some countries have begun to develop generic modules. For instance in Bangladesh, it has

6

GATHER

G - Greet the client warmly and politely.
A - Ask the client about his or her needs.
T - Tell the client about choices available.
H - Help clients choose methods.
E - Explain how to use the chosen method correctly.
R - Return visits to be planned before the session is over.

Adapted from: Population Reports, Series J, No. 35, November 1987.

7

Good interpersonal communication

Empathy – the ability to see the situation from the client's point of view.
Respect – for the client's feelings and attitudes which may be different from your own.
Honesty – in addressing the client's concerns.
Active listening – listening to what the clients say and mean through verbal and nonverbal behaviour.
Attending behaviour – greeting clients politely and making them feel comfortable with verbal and nonverbal behaviour.
Questioning – asking questions to encourage clients to talk about themselves.
Summarising and paraphrasing – restating what the client has said to demonstrate active listening and understanding.
Reflecting feelings – by observing and listening in order to communicate how providers think clients feel.
Giving information – instruct, explain and describe, simply, clearly and accurately.

Adapted from: Population Reports, Series J, No. 35, November 1987.

been recognised that each technical health programme should not attempt to expand its own technical training module to include an IPC component. Since the same field workers are responsible for delivering a variety of services at the community level, a generic IPC module for health and family planning worker training was devised (see Box 8). Other countries are experimenting with IPC modules in the same way. In fact, it has been suggested that for integrated management of childhood illnesses (IMCI), IPC should become the common denominator or hub for all health personnel training and that the technical programmes be considered the "spokes" in the wheel of training (see Box 9).

Traditionally, health personnel training is not organized in this generic way. This is because courses are often designed and organised by medical

8

A generic curriculum for IPC

In Bangladesh, the Expanded Programme on Immunisation (EPI) had achieved 62 percent coverage by 1991. However, statistics indicated that dropout levels were still very high. A large-scale, qualitative study revealed that much of this was due to the poor quality of communication between service-providers and clientele. Vaccinators allowed relatives and people with higher status to jump places in lines. They seldom counselled on possible side affects and treated poorer people rudely. It was found that, on average, they spent 21 seconds with each child and caretaker. Very little use was made of the thousands of flip charts and flash cards produced to support interpersonal communication. A more in-depth analysis of the same data indicated that there was little difference in performance between those field workers who had undergone training programmes and those who had learned on the job. This led to the formulation of an interpersonal communication training strategy for field workers and their supervisors. Source: EPI, (1991); Griffey-Brechin, (1993); MOHFW (May 1994)

However, at the same time, those responsible for other health and family planning programmes in Bangladesh were searching for a way to increase the quality of IPC in their programmes. The goal was to create a generic IPC curriculum which could be used in all programmes. Since the same health and family planning field workers are trained to undertake different programmes, confusion and repetition was predicted if they were subjected to different IPC training modules for a variety of technical programmes. In this way, IPC was made a unifying force in training and programming and a schedule was set up to arrive at a generic training manual for the health and family planning sector.

Author.

9 A new conceptual framework for integrated management for childhood illnesses (IMCI)

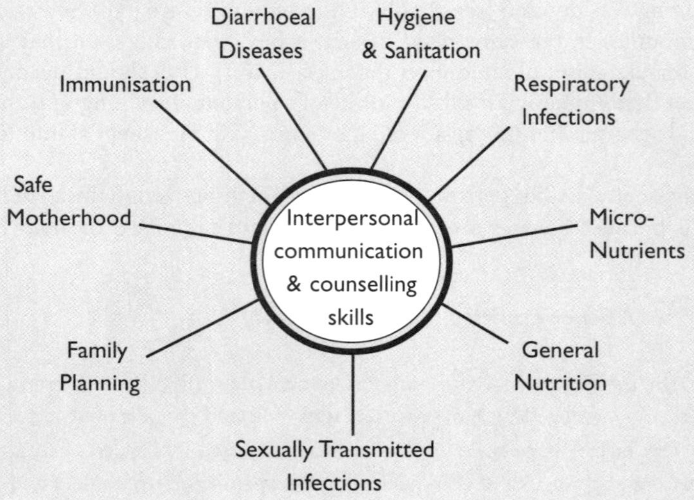

Author

personnel who specialize in different programmes, with little involvement of communication professionals.

In addition, acquiring effective skills in IPC can require a complete change of educational approach. Whereas the dominant method in health education has been one of information giving, through lecture or "show and tell", we now know that learning new skills such as counselling and communication requires the learning of new attitudes and perceptions of oneself and one's relationships with others. Participatory training methods are required to transfer such skills. This often entails retraining the trainers, or revamping the training team with people who have the right skills and attitudes for such approaches.

Participatory training methods often run counter to the educational conditioning and the formal "seminar culture" most people have grown used to. It is a great challenge to design training methods which are effective and culturally appropriate. An even greater difficulty is to prevent "systems loss" when the training programme is taken through a number of hierarchical layers to the community. Systems loss is a loss of energy, focus or intent, when an innovation is diffused through various levels. Methods may become so diluted that they are no longer recognisable and have little effect. The only way to prevent such loss is to ensure that sufficient resources and checks are built into the training programme at every level. This is easier said than done, especially when those deciding on the programme priorities and budget have little exposure to IPC concepts or the need for participatory training methods.

The other main consideration is the need for training at all levels. There is no sense in training field-level staff in new communication methods if those who supervise them are not supportive. Supervisors' training should be integrated with that of field staff, so that the problems in communication throughout the system can be addressed and remedied at the same time. This presents a great challenge to organisations and systems which have evolved in hierarchical, non-participatory forms.

Interpersonal communication for adolescent health and development is another area that needs a great deal of attention. Very few countries have special services for youth. Yet, around the world, this age group is becoming increasingly vulnerable to health threats such as HIV/AIDS and other Sexually Transmitted Infections (STIs), as well as early pregnancy. Counselling services for young people cannot be easily integrated with such services for adults. The assurance of privacy and anonymity is important to youth, though this is a controversial issue. Some organisations take the point of view that it is unethical to offer adolescent sexual and reproductive health services without parents' knowledge and consent. Regardless of policy, services should be offered in places where young people congregate, not in locations which will be psychologically or physically difficult for them to access.

Finally, if a programme is serious about IPC, a great deal of attention has to be paid to budgetary and staffing requirements, well-developed support materials for service-providers, the provision of an environment and working space which is conducive to counselling, as well as personnel policies and staff communication mechanisms which promote an open and respectful interchange on important concerns. In other words, the organisation which promotes IPC must "practice what it preaches" or the employees will soon become disenchanted with the new programme thrusts. This is a challenge to any large-scale organisation, such as a government health department, and it may require a revamping of organisational structure and reporting relationships.

Some may say that we are asking the impossible. However, large organisations have already demonstrated success in this domain. This will be taken up in greater detail in Chapters 5.

Using natural networks

Interpersonal communication is not limited to doctor and patient or service provider and client. People learn from their peers and neighbours. The debate over how innovations are, or should be, diffused and adopted in developing countries continues to rage in development communication circles. As mentioned in Chapters 1 and 2, Rogers (1983) devised a Diffusion Model which describes a one-way flow of knowledge, leading to adoption or non-adoption. In comparing early adopters to late adopters, the results indicate that early adopters are likely to be more educated, literate, upwardly-mobile, empathetic, rational, intelligent, and motivated to achieve.

However, this model has long been attacked, particularly from Third World writers (e.g. Beltran, 1976). The criticism is centred around the fact that much diffusion research has had a pro-innovation bias; the notion that innovations come without values and, by their very nature, are good for people and should be disseminated as widely as possible. Scholars have also pointed to the model's individual-blame bias; the implication that the individual is at fault for not adopting an innovation. The world is divided into "laggards" and "adopters". "Laggards", by implication, are backward people. The model overlooks what might be very important societal, or economic reasons for not adopting an innovation and, in some cases the so-called "laggards" may turn out to be the most far-sighted.

In spite of the criticism waged against the diffusionists, there is considerable evidence to suggest that diffusion theory can be useful and applicable in some settings. What if natural networks are intentionally used to diffuse innovations or healthy behaviours? There is good evidence that the reduction of HIV sero-positivity in homosexual communities in Western countries is due to more than receiving and acting on messages received over the media. It is mainly due to the informal and formal networks, as well as the counselling and support mechanisms which these groups set up as a result of watching friends and colleagues die of AIDS. However, on a global scale, gay men in Western countries are above average in education and socio-economic status and often have access to the latest information on AIDS on a daily basis. This has obvious implications for developing countries where many people have little education and access to information.

The case study in Box 10, however, indicates that existing interpersonal networks are very useful, especially when they are reinforced through peer education. Education by people of the same social standing and age group has been found to be very effective in the dissemination of new information and in reinforcing required new behaviours, especially amongst young people and high-risk groups who are otherwise marginalised by society. People are usually more confident in modelling the behaviour of someone with whom they can identify. Behaviour change seems more possible to make and sustain. It seems evident, then, that diffusion theory has its place in development communication programmes. Natural networks and peer groups can be used to disseminate an innovation or a preventive action.

10 *Jiggasha family planning approach, Bangladesh*

Jiggasha is a community network approach to family planning, which originated in Trishal Thana, Bangladesh. *Jiggasha* means "to inquire" in Bangla. Through this method, the reach of family planning field workers is extended by identifying and building networks of women, who meet in the homes of local opinion-leaders, to discuss family planning matters. The opinion-leaders, or link persons, are chosen according to the following criteria: they must have unquestionable respect in the community; be married and satisfied contraceptive users; be able to read and write; be centrally located with available meeting space; and have a zeal for voluntary work. They should also have family approval for involvement.

The networks identified in such communities are complex (see diagram on the next page). Facilitating women to meet in this way, in a traditional Muslim culture, has proven to be a powerful tool for their sense of empowerment. Satisfied users of contraceptives share experiences; newly-married women learn about family planning; and non-users, and those who have discontinued, discuss their reservations. These components, plus multimedia initiatives which may include local performing arts, cassette-listening in groups and client-provider materials, encompasses the social support that leads to behaviour change. Men have also formed *jiggashas* to address their own concerns and to increase male support for family planning and related health issues. Highlights of a report (World Bank, 1994) include the following on the results of the approach:

- Contraceptive use jumped from 38 percent to 56 percent between 1990 and 1992 among women visited by a field worker and who also attended *jiggashas*;
- In the initial 12 villages having *jiggasha* groups, 58 percent of women surveyed said they had heard of *jiggasha* meetings and 28 percent attended; of those, 63 percent discussed family planning with their husbands and 31 percent adopted modern contraceptives;
- Several other NGOs are replicating the approach in the context of their own programmes.

As is evident by the diagram on the next page, natural networking between clusters of human settlement, or *bari*, in Bangladesh, does not form a predictable pattern or order which can be easily understood. Links between groups of settlements are often weak. Programmers wishing to harness such networks for development purposes, therefore, must invest a great deal of time in analysing and understanding the community before introducing innovations. Devising a methodology which is transferable between communities, therefore, is a great challenge. The approach is "input-intensive" and its replicability on a national scale has still to be demonstrated.

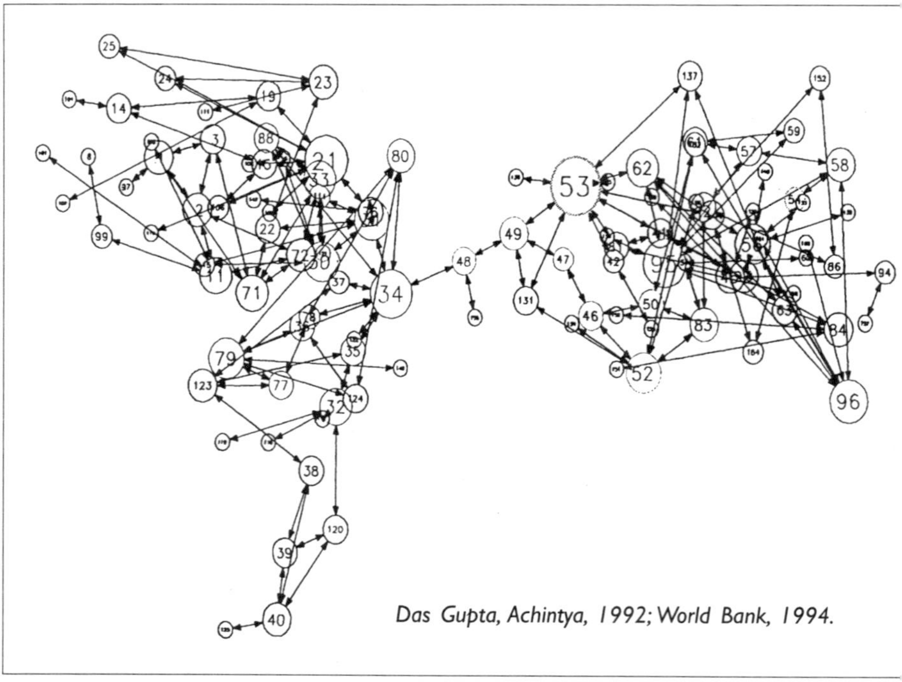

Natural networking between clusters of human settlement, or bari in Bangladesh, does not form a predictable pattern or order which can be easily understood

Purposely using opinion-leaders to influence the behaviour of slower adopters or "laggards" and the less informed or less resourceful, can be successful. However, this does not overcome the original criticism of the diffusion approach. It is time to ask once again, who decides on the action or innovation to be adopted and who judges a person a "laggard" if they do not take up the prescription?

Participatory communication

In the past 20 years or more, development communicators have been searching for a more participatory mode, or model, of communication. Diffusion theory, social marketing or planned approaches to communicating innovations which go by other names, may be viewed by their promoters as essentially apolitical theories. They are devoid of concern over the question, "Who controls?" There is an assumption that the innovations, chosen from above, are for the benefit of the people. However, others would argue that taking such a position is not at all apolitical. It is yet another attempt to foist alien premises and values on developing communities or countries. Assuming that new ideas will benefit all, or that planning and implementing communication strategies will create demand for innovations which people never demanded before, can be viewed as a political act, anchored in a set of assumptions about power.

11

The Fogo Process

What has come to be known as "The Fogo Process" began on Fogo Island, off Newfoundland, Canada, in the 1960s. The government wanted to resettle unproductive fishermen and their families onto the mainland, to cut down on the cost of social services. Instead, with the involvement of Memorial University's Extension Education Department and The National Film Board of Canada, the fisher-folk began a process of reflection and debate concerning their values, sense of community and their future. Film footage of themselves was used as a "mirror" to spark such debate in the community. Seeing themselves on camera, talking about their problems, gave the community a sense of self-esteem not experienced before. Some of the same footage was used to start a dialogue by showing film of the islanders and then recording the reactions of policy-makers who came to see that the objects of their resettlement plans were thinking, feeling people. After much dialogue and planning, the resettlement plans were scrapped and a fishing cooperative, and other community initiatives, were founded.

Such processes have since been taken up in other communities in Newfoundland and throughout the developing world. There has been a big push towards the use of inexpensive video for dialogue between communities and policy-makers. Participatory video has been used to establish dairy cooperatives in India, through electronic dialogue between farmers and bankers. It has also been used to establish other income-generation activities, including women's cooperative movements.

Radio and print can also be used in a similar fashion. The Catholic Church has used radio stations as community development centres in many countries of Latin America. Where radio licences are possible, underprivileged sectors have established communication systems through radio, producing their own programmes which address community needs and aspirations, resulting in a sense of solidarity and vision which was previously lacking. Similar experiments have been undertaken in Africa. Also, there have been parallel approaches with community newspapers in many developing countries.

Williamson, 1994 and White et al, 1994.

Social marketers will reply that their careful, formative research is designed to reveal the real needs of people, as opposed to their wants, and that such groundwork contextualizes the innovation being offered in the culture and experience of the client. However, critics would reply that this is just a more sophisticated approach to manipulating people into accepting what they may not need. They argue further that people should be allowed to set their own agenda through participatory processes which are truly democratic. This is the only way to ensure that innovations will truly meet the needs of people. They should propose and prioritize the changes they want.

Communicators have attempted experiments in participatory communication through interactive film and video (see Box 11), through community radio and newspaper, as well as other media. Excellent results have been attained in empowering people to make their own decisions. A *conscientisation* approach (Freire, 1970) showed how people will galvanise themselves into action to address their priority problems. However, there have been few good experiences in replicating grassroots participatory processes to address district or national health or social problems. How do you scale up such processes without a great deal of systems loss? Should we attempt to take such experiences to scale?

How then do we reconcile our innate desire to make our programmes more in touch with the needs, desires, perceptions and values of the people we wish to serve, and the necessity to scale up our work? How can programmes have an impact on a wide enough front to make a marked difference to a people's health and well being? The answer probably lies in our ability to do the best possible job with the tools we have, to increase the quality of our research and consultation processes so that we do not compromise when it comes to sounding out, respecting and reflecting the value systems which we discover at work. We shall continue the considerations of people's participation in communication programmes in the next section of this chapter, where social mobilization is discussed.

Social mobilization and communication definitions

Unhappy with the apparent lack of impact of other approaches, and aware of the need for greater participation in programmes, in the early 1980s UNICEF began to experiment with and evolve an approach called "social mobilization". There are numerous definitions of social mobilization, a process which goes much beyond a communication campaign or social marketing plan. (See pages 108-109 for two definitions.) The longer definition on page 109 comes from an overall programme point of view. It entails little recognisable communication language and methodology. In a number of countries communication professionals have adopted a more precise definition (see shorter definition on page 109) which, when combined with the overall strategies of advocacy and programme communication (see Box 13) have formed a new model for development communication (see Box 12).

12 ***Communication for Development Model***

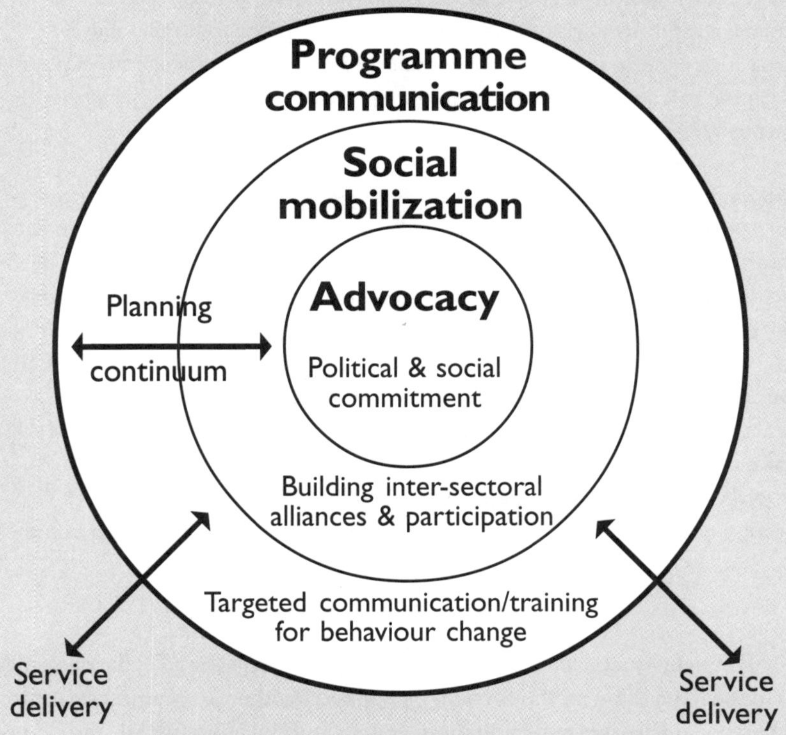

McKee (1992)

Social mobilization within this model denotes the idea of "partnership-building" – accelerating programmes through the involvement of partners from governments at different levels, non-governmental organisations (NGOs), service clubs, religious and social groups, communicators, artists and entertainers and leaders at the national, sub-national and community level. Such involvement was at the root of successful child survival programmes in the 1980s and early 1990s, especially EPI.

13

Communication: Some definitions

Communication for development is a researched and planned process which is crucial for social transformation, operating through three main strategies: advocacy to raise resources and political and social leadership commitment for development goals; social mobilization for wider participation and ownership; and programme communication for changes in knowledge, attitudes and practices of specific participants in programmes. When combined with strategies for the development of appropriate skills and capacities, and the provision of an enabling environment, communication plays a central role in positive behaviour development, behaviour change and the empowerment of individuals and groups.

Advocacy is a continuous and adaptive process of gathering, organising and formulating information into argument, to be communicated through various interpersonal and media channels, with a view to raising resources or gaining political and social leadership acceptance and commitment for a development programme, thereby preparing a society for its acceptance.

Social mobilization is a process of bringing together all feasible and practical inter-sectoral social partners and allies to determine felt-need and raise awareness of, and demand for, a particular development objective. It involves enlisting the participation of such actors, including institutions, groups, networks and communities, in identifying, raising, and managing human

Following successful social mobilization processes for EPI, the challenge was to see if the same methods could be applied to other programmes: Control of Diarrhoeal Diseases and Sanitation, Nutrition, Education for All, and others. The description in Box 14, below, makes it evident that the concepts and methods are transferable to other social programmes.

The combination of these three concepts is synergistic in application because it provides a comprehensive approach to the use of communication channels and actors for different purposes, beginning with advocacy for political and social will and to stimulate partnership development; social mobilization, the selection and activation of partners, bringing a communication endeavour from a technical programme to a social movement when necessary to do so; and programme communication: the more targeted and planned approach to sustained behaviour change or behaviour and material resources, thereby increasing and strengthening self-reliance and sustainability of achievements.

Programme communication is a research-based, consultative process of addressing knowledge, attitudes and practices through identifying, analysing and segmenting audiences and participants in programmes and by providing them with relevant information and motivation through well-defined strategies, using an appropriate mix of interpersonal, group and mass-media channels, including participatory methods.

UNICEF Global Communication Team, 1998, unpublished.

Social mobilization is a broad-scale movement to engage people's participation in achieving a specific development goal through self-reliant efforts. It involves all relevant segments of society: decision- and policy-makers, opinion-leaders, bureaucrats and technocrats, professional groups, religious associations, commerce and industry, communities and individuals. It is a planned, decentralised process that seeks to facilitate change for development through a range of players engaged in interrelated and complementary efforts. It takes into account the felt needs of the people, embraces the critical principle of community involvement, and seeks to empower individuals and groups for action.

UNICEF, 1991, unpublished.

development. The two-directional arrow indicates that planning advocacy, social mobilization and programme communication is not a one-way process. Strategies must be continually evaluated and changed as a programme matures.

These three concepts, when strategically employed, can make a big difference. They also help other programmers understand the role of communication in social programmes, giving clarity to the sometimes imprecise language of information and communication.

Community mobilization

An essential part of social mobilization is community mobilization. Very often, however, this is all that is understood by social mobilization, whereas the latter term may be inclusive of all levels – national to the community.

14 *Mobilising for Education for All in Bangladesh*

A year after the World Conference on "Education for All", held in Jomtien, Thailand in 1990, not a great deal had been achieved in Bangladesh. There was a great deal of rhetoric and disagreement over the strategies required to bring education to a population of 110 million which was less than 25 percent literate. UNICEF was still giving emphasis to the provision of educational materials, curriculum development and teacher training. There had been much energy and concentration on mass education in the past, with little progress. The Government, academics and NGOs were at odds as to the reasons for the lack of progress, each tending to blame the other. Compulsory primary education was declared by the President at Jomtien, but no one believed that it was enforceable or achievable. The call for "Education for All" remained a hollow cry.

Participatory planning

A breakthrough came in April 1991. UNICEF organised a participatory planning workshop using a method called Visualisation in Participatory Programmes (VIPP) (See Chapter 5). High-level government, NGO staff and academics attended, along with participants from UNICEF and UNESCO. In three days, participants worked through the essential steps to be taken in mobilizing for Basic Education in Bangladesh and developed a multimedia and multi-partnership plan of action for advocacy, social mobilization and programme communication.

This initial planning workshop was followed by training in VIPP facilitation for key Government, NGO and UNICEF staff involved in education. This training initiated a whole sequence of participatory planning processes, right down to the lowest administrative level. For the first time, people in lower-level posts had a say in what was needed to mobilize the educational bureaucracy, social partners, parents and children.

In addition, there has been a great deal of emphasis on community mobilization or community participation, a related but separate concept, in many social programmes. Unfortunately, very often the emphasis is on getting the community to participate in a programme which has been designed from above. This is, in reality, the lowest form of participation. If people are not active members in the design, implementation and evaluation of community-based programmes, the whole concept of participation becomes corrupted.

There are numerous methods of community mobilization and a plethora

Determining the value of education

A qualitative research study was carried out on the perception and value of education. After a great deal of discussion, it was decided that before launching a major communication initiative for accelerating the provision of educational services and quality of services, more should be known about what parents and children think and believe about schools and school personnel, revealing deep-seated perceptions, beliefs and values. The information from this research was used in the formulation of mass media, traditional media and interpersonal communication messages aimed at various stake-holders in the educational process.

Launching a movement

In 1992, the Prime Minister launched the "Education for All" movement in a major national conference attended by people from all relevant sectors and all parts of the country. The conference was a lively affair, with a great deal of debate, which sparked new initiatives. At the above event, a communication symbol for "Education for All" was unveiled. The final symbol above, with the girl slightly ahead of the boy because of her historic disadvantage, was adopted as the best concept to promote basic education for all in Bangladesh. Today, it is used by all major partners in the movement and can be seen throughout the country. It is easily recognisable and communicates a message, even to illiterates.

Author

of participatory packages and tools which go by different acronyms – Participatory Action Research (PAR) and Participatory Rural Appraisal (PRA) are two of the most famous. These may involve visualisation methods such as village mapping on the ground, rank ordering of issues with stones, and problem identification using the ranking of pictures in a problem area, such as hygiene and sanitation. These tools bring people very much into the process of identifying problems and formulating action themselves. As such, they are both a research technique and a group communication strategy which has the potential of being very participatory and perhaps even empowering in nature.

However, limitations arise when we employ one set of tools for, say, sanitation and hygiene, and the process unearths needs and perspectives in a different programme area, such as HIV/AIDS. This is the essential dilemma in the way we often work with communities. We may go in with the best of participatory tools, but with one intervention in mind, and the process unearths the need for other interventions, which we have no power or resources to implement. It may be the mandate of another agency with which we are not connected.

Perhaps the best solution to this dilemma is to start with an intervention in an inter-sectoral area, such as nutrition, water and sanitation or HIV/AIDS and facilitate a process which allows the community to Assess, Analyse and take Action – and then move back to Assessment (Triple A Approach). This involves a process of reflection, action and reflection. The actions taken in the original area of intervention often have a spin-off effect in other areas of development, as defined and prioritized by the community. For instance, beginning with nutritional status, a community may come to realize that sanitation or AIDS is a major problem for them.

This approach takes us beyond the realm of communication for development, per se, but group communication methods and tools are an essential part of such processes. Community mobilization, otherwise, may quickly become coercive and a danger to long-term development.

Media-based mobilization

Another popular strategy in motivating people to act is the use of entertainment for education, sometimes called "enter-education" or "edutainment". Programmers have used grassroots theatre troupes and musicians, poets, youth choirs, popular singers, rap groups, movie stars and animated films in an attempt to send social messages and set norms of behaviour. The fight against HIV/AIDS in the 1980s and 1990s has increased the use of such strategies. Around the world, popular youth music stars have joined the cause, promoting sexual abstinence and safer sex. Entertainment channels have been used because they have a number of the following "P characteristics" (see Box 15).

The actors on this stage have helped to foster a transnational revolution. Sexual and reproductive health education was traditionally pedantic, unimaginative and failed to reach youth. The edutainment artists, on the other hand, have aligned with the values of their audiences, be they villagers, slum dwellers, suburbanites or street kids.

15 *Enter-Educate or Edutainment*

Popular: People like it; they choose to look at or listen to it, they enjoy it.
Pervasive: It reaches people everywhere.
Personal: It may be more personal and intimate than much of daily interpersonal communication.
Passionate: It rouses emotions such as fear, hope, love and hatred and such emotions may be more powerful than rational arguments in motivating people to act.
Persuasive: Entertainment can depict role models. It can show how healthy behaviour is rewarded and unhealthy behaviour punished.
Practical: Often it can be arranged at little cost through the willingness of professional entertainers to cooperate.
Profitable: It is cost effective and people will pay to watch or listen to well-produced programmes, if required.
Proven: It has been proven effective in disseminating information and new attitudes and values.

Johns Hopkins, 1994

In Uganda, the artist, Philly Lutaaya, a person with AIDS himself, took up the cause (Kyenkya-Isabirye, 1990) and made AIDS an acceptable subject to talk about. In Latin America, a young singing couple, Tatiana and Johnny, reached 12 countries with songs and videos highlighting sexual responsibility. Their songs topped the popularity charts in Peru and Mexico. Most important, the intended audience, especially girls, talked to their female friends and mothers about the issues, indicating they were seeking more information and guidance on sexuality. The programme was acclaimed by parents and community opinion leaders. (Johns Hopkins, 1994)

A similar project in the Philippines took a much more planned approach which involved working with youth specialists, linking the media campaign to interpersonal services, such as a dial-a-friend telephone hot-line, and a referral service for counselling, building corporate support into the project. Essays and art contests and school tours were supported by popular singers. The programme generated a great deal of free television and radio time and many thousands of column inches in newspapers and magazines (Johns Hopkins, 1994).

The soap opera format on both radio and television has been used to inform and motivate people to change behaviour. The *Hum-Log* programme

16 Soul City

In South Africa, approximately 92 percent of the population has access to radio, 76 percent to television and 55 percent to newspaper. This makes the country ideally suited for an "edutainment" approach to communication on health and social issues. The Soul City initiative grew out of the Alexandra Health Centre in Johannesburg, a community hospital which continues to service Alexandra, a township within the city which refused to be moved throughout the dark days of apartheid.

The initiative has as its flagship a series of half-hour soap operas for television, using popular South African stars. Through corporate sponsorship and bargaining with authorities as apartheid was crumbling, the organisers were able to gain prime-time access on South Africa television's main channel. The first series of 13 programmes emphasised the themes of safe motherhood, breast feeding, infant nutrition, immunisation, diarrhoea, respiratory illness, child abuse and accidents. These themes were woven into the stories in an entertaining way with love affairs, comical incidents and common issues in community life. A number of sub-themes were also addressed throughout: empowerment of women and communities, pro-social issues such as co-parenting, family values and nation building, and the growing pandemic, HIV/AIDS. It was decided not to address AIDS head-on in the first series. The credibility and popularity of the characters, and the series, was to be established first.

Besides television, a parallel radio drama was also developed called "Healing Hearts", following a similar story-line. The project also utilised newspapers to publish serials on the issues addressed in the soap operas, synchronised with the time of broadcast. These inserts were later developed into a 36-page booklet. An educational audio, video and print package was developed to facilitate learning at

in India addressed such themes as family harmony, the status of women, alcoholism, family planning and health in a series which was addictive for television viewers in India (Singal and Rogers, 1989). In Egypt, two television soap opera series, "And the Nile Flows" (Underwood *et al*, 1994) and "Family House" (Elkamel, 1994) have proven very popular in putting across sensitive issues concerning family planning methods and choices, child marriages, birth spacing and HIV/AIDS, as well as health issues such as acute respiratory infections, home accidents and drug addiction.

In the United States, comprehensive communication approaches, aligned with youth entertainment values and media, have also been used to address the problems of inner-city youth (*The Mee Report*, 1994). In South Africa, a the community level. It was recognised that face-to-face communication is the most effective catalyst of sustained behaviour development and change.

Soul City is based on substantial formative research. Following story-line development through concept testing, a pilot programme was produced and tested. It was found to be too full of messages on different issues, but it did validate the potential of the TV programme. An extensive script development and research process followed.

Following the launch of the first series, an evaluation was carried out, showing wide-scale reception and great popularity of the programmes. In addition, those exposed showed significantly greater knowledge levels on health care issues than those not exposed.

An independent, impact evaluation of the second series has revealed even more information on knowledge gained, attitude shifts and self-reported behaviour change compared to a baseline study:

- 95 percent of respondents claimed to have learned something new
- 78 percent stated they had used the information
- significant shift in attitude to the statement "AIDS sufferers should be moved away" and "It is cool to smoke".
- Reported change in behaviour on using condoms, multiple partners, smoking.

The Soul City project moved to a second, third and fourth series which address, more directly, the issues of HIV/AIDS, tuberculosis, smoking, housing and banking - all major concerns of the formerly excluded majority in South Africa. There are also plans to build on the popularity of the series through competitions: search for stars, primary health care worker of the year, school and youth club "Soul Citizens" – all for a visible commitment to a healthy society at all levels.

CASE, 1994 and 1997.

popular approach has been taken following the opening of the airwaves with the downfall of apartheid. The *Soul City* series is a real breakthrough in a country which previously subverted and concealed most discussion of social problems (see Box 16).

If entertainers can sing of sexual abstinence and of modifying sexual behaviour, while generating income for spreading health messages even further, then social and commercial marketing become one. Considering that so much of popular culture supports unhealthy and at-risk life styles, the edutainment movement is one of the greatest communication revolutions of the 20th Century.

However, the glare of the lights may blind us from the difficulty in developing healthy behaviours, or changing unhealthy ones. Edutainment can use, as its flagship medium, a popular form such as the television or radio soap opera or the animated film. However, there is a need to align these efforts with what is actually happening at the grass roots. They should be linked with interpersonal and community-based approaches, as has been done in UNICEF's Sara and Meena projects (see Chapter 4). This has been achieved through the development of a strong set of characters and entertaining stories which serve as a vehicle for a set of values and messages. They serve as a "springboard" for interpersonal and group processes, backed up by users' guides and facilitation manuals, together with training on their use. Without such comprehensive approaches to behaviour programming, our efforts with "flagship" media may constitute only advocacy, an important, but insufficient first step.

Conclusions

This chapter has stated that communication can be a powerful force in the motivation of behaviour change and development. However, we must avoid *ad hoc* initiatives and strategy design without adequate planning and research. Occasionally we can make a correct, educated guess about what people may be thinking. However, more often, we will be wrong. Our communication initiatives need to be firmly grounded in research on the values, attitudes, perceptions and behaviours of the people they are meant to address. They may have to be multimedia in nature, if we really want to affect sustained change. Good interpersonal communication is essential, and often the most difficult to achieve. The use of communication symbols and edutainment approaches may be very effective, if used properly and comprehensively.

Communication channels can be further extended to the development of partnerships and alliances for social causes. Reinforcing communication efforts by broadening the base of support for social programmes through social mobilization is essential for sustainability and institutionalisation in many programmes. Participatory research and planning have a great role to play in gaining wide-scale ownership in plans and in changing the context of the organisational environments in which we work. This will be addressed in greater detail in chapters 5.

However, motivating children and adults to develop positive behaviour or change unhealthy behaviour is not enough. Very often people may be motivated, but lack the abilities or competencies to act. These life skills are taken up in great detail in Chapter 4.

References

Agyie, W. K.A. and Midadde, M. (1995) "Demographic factors influencing contraceptive use in Uganda". *Journal of Biosociology*. Vol. 27, pp. 47-60.

Beltran S., L.R. (1976) "Alien premises, objects and methods in Latin American communication research". In *Communication and development: Critical perspectives* pp. 15-42. E. M. Rogers (ed.) Beverly Hills: Sage Publications

CASE. (1994 and 1997) *Soul City evaluation reports*. Braamfontein: Community Agency for Social Enquiry

Das Gupta, Achintya. (1992) "*Jiggasha:* Community networks for family planning". A paper presented at South Asian Population Conference, February 8-11, 1993, Dhaka.

Elkamel, F. (1994) "Soap operas may be good for health". Paper produced for UNICEF workshop on mass communication and mobilization technical support group, Game Valley, South Africa.

EPI. (1991) "Needs assessment study of field workers involved in the Expanded Programme on Immunisation". Directorate General of Health Services, Ministry of Health and Family Welfare, Government of Bangladesh.

Freire, P. (1970) *Pedagogy of the oppressed*. Baltimore: Penguin

Griffey-Brechin, S.J. (1993) "Evaluating health worker performance: The relationship between knowledge and practice of counselling-related activities of field workers in the National Expanded Programme on Immunisation in Bangladesh". New Orleans: Ph.D. Dissertation, School of Public Health and Tropical Medicine, Department of International Health and Development, Tulane University.

Johns Hopkins. (1994) *Promotingsexual responsibility in the Philippines through music: An enter-education approach*. Baltimore: Population Communications Services, Johns Hopkins University,.

Kotler, P. and Zaltman, G. (1971) "Social marketing: an approach to planned social change". *Journal of Marketing*, 35(3), pp.3-12.

Kyenkya-Isabirye, M. (1990) "The life and times of Philly Lutaaya, Ugandan Singer". *Development Communication Report*, No. 71, p. 12

McKee, N. (1992) *Social mobilization and social marketing in developing communities: Lessons for communicators*. Penang: Southbound

MOHFW (Ministry of Health and Family Welfare). (May 1994) "Generic curriculum: Interpersonal communication and counselling training". Interpersonal communication and counselling training forum, Generic curriculum task force, MOHFW, Government of Bangladesh.

Population Reports. (1987, Nov.). Series J, No. 35.

Rogers, E. (1983) *The diffusion of innovations*. (3rd ed.) New York: The Free Press/ MacMillan Publishing

Singal, A. & Rogers, E.M. (1989) *The Hum-log story, India's information revolution*, pp. 88-121. New Delhi: Sage Publications

The Mee Report. (1994) "Reaching the hip-hop generation". Philadelphia: Research Division of MEE Productions, Inc.

Underwood, C., Kemprecos, L.F., Jabre, B. and Wafai, M. (1994) "And the Nile flows on: The impact of a serial drama in Egypt". Baltimore: Johns Hopkins Center for Communication Programs

Weiss, E., Whelan, D., and Rao Gupta, G. (1996) "Vulnerability and opportunity: Adolescents and HIV/AIDS in the developing world". Findings from the Women and AIDS Research Program, International Centre for Research on Women.

White, S.A., Nair, K.S. & Ascroft, J. (1994) *Participatory communication: Working for change and development*. New Delhi: Sage Publications

Williamson, H.A. (1991) "The Fogo Process: Development support communication in Canada and the developing world". In Casmir, F.L. (ed.) *Communication in development*. Norwood, New Jersey: Ablex Publishing Corporation. pp. 270-287.

World Bank. (1994) *The determinants of reproductive change in Bangladesh*. Washington, D.C.

UNICEF/HQ97-0069/Jeremy Horner

As a part of an AIDS education and awareness project, girls sit on the floor around a large poster, drawing lines to connect groups at risk of contacting HIV/AIDS, at the Pang Lao School, in the northern town of Chiang Rai, Thailand.

4
The ability to act

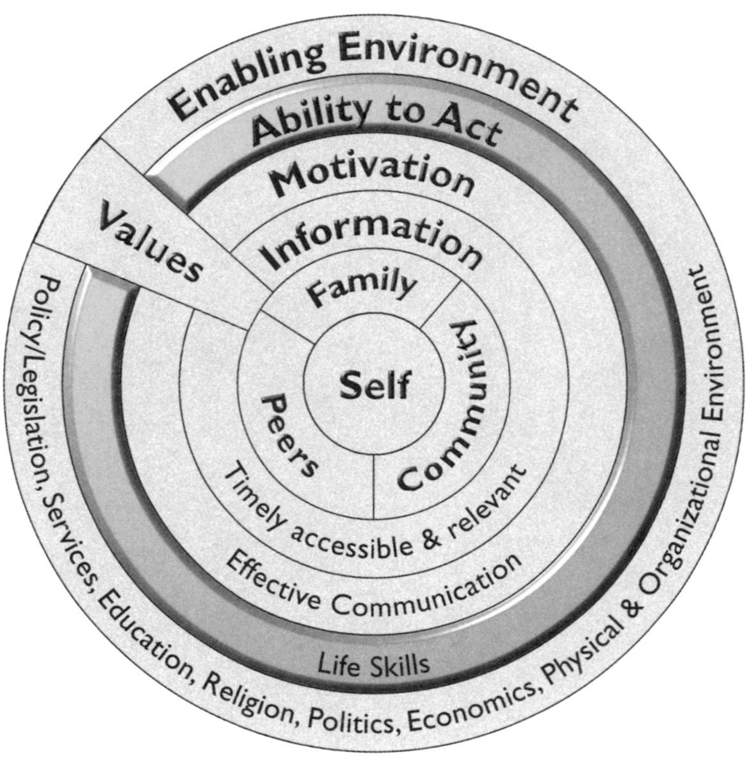
Enabling Environment
Ability to Act
Motivation
Information
Values
Family
Community
Self
Peers
Timely accessible & relevant
Effective Communication
Life Skills
Policy/Legislation, Services, Education, Religion, Politics, Economics, Physical & Organizational Environment

FOUR

The ability to act: Strengthening people's life skills

Rachel Carnegie and Rhona Birrell Weisen

Introduction

Paulo is 11. He lives in a very poor village. His father drinks a lot and hits him when he comes home. His mother looks after the younger children and doesn't seem to care whether he is there or not. He cannot see what he can do to improve his situation. Some of the other boys his age have left home to seek a better life in the city. He hears mixed stories about their life. Some of it sounds good. These boys are independent and have some kind of work. He is tempted.

Kurt is 7 years old. His parents moved to another town to look for work and he has just started at his new school. The other children know each other well and he, as a shy newcomer, makes an easy target for their bullying. He doesn't know how to cope with this and the problem gets worse each day. The children even steal the money for his lunch. They rip his clothes and push him to the ground to make him dirty. His parents get cross about this but he is too afraid to tell them what is happening. The bullies warn him that if he tells anyone they will kill him. Life at school is miserable and he is not able to concentrate on his school work.

Tanya is 8 years old. Her mother and father are busy with the family business and they do not notice the way that Uncle Marc plays with her. He likes to touch her in private places and tells her to take her clothes off. She does not like these 'games' but she does not know how to stop him and she is afraid to tell her parents. Tanya is tired and tearful much of the time.

John, 9 years old, is confused. He has learnt at school that smoking damages your health and yet he sees cigarette advertisements around the city which show sporty and glamorous people smoking, suggesting it is part of the good life. John doesn't know which message to believe or indeed what to do next time his friends offer him a cigarette. He thinks that his friends will reject him if he refuses to smoke with them.

Sonal, a 15 year old girl, is distraught. Her parents, who were not educated themselves, have decided to pull her out of school to get married. She enjoys studying and longs to complete school and try to get a job. It seems her life choices are not her own to make. What should she do? She doesn't know what to think or how she should act.

Sheila, a 15 year old girl, is also anxious, but for different reasons. She is desperate to get a boyfriend, to be like her friends at school. A boy has asked her out on a date, which might or might not lead on to sex. She is not sure what she wants. And should she go prepared with contraceptives, or will the boy despise her for planning to have sex? She doesn't know what to do. How can she avoid being labelled as either 'frigid' or 'easy' by her school mates?

Fatima, a young mother of 18, has a baby with pneumonia. Fatima had learnt at school how to recognise the disease and knows that without antibiotics the child may die. Yet her mother-in-law does not think that the situation is serious and refuses to let Fatima go out to the health centre. How can Fatima convince her mother-in-law? To whom should she turn for support?

Stella is a 22 year old sex worker. She was taken from her village home 5 years ago. Through the government AIDS campaign she has learnt that the only way to protect herself from HIV infection is to use condoms. Yet her 'manager' refuses to allow her, saying that talk of condoms will put off her clients. Stella enters each new sexual encounter with dread: will this be the one to infect her? If only she had the confidence to stand up for herself; if only she knew how to convince her clients that condoms would keep them safe too. Last week her closest friend, a fellow sex-worker, tested HIV positive.

The above scenarios illustrate real-life situations where people find themselves oppressed by circumstances which they feel unable to control or cope with. The last two chapters have discussed information and motivation as key ingredients in the process of behavioural change. Yet even with the right information and the motivation to act, people may still feel powerless and believe that they lack the *ability to act*, including the skills to communicate their needs, to solve their problems and to follow through their decisions. In this chapter we reflect on the needs of individuals within their family and community and consider the life skills that they require to cope effectively with the daunting demands of living in contemporary society.

As highlighted in Chapter 2, the structure of societies across the globe is changing at an unprecedented rate, with an explosion in access to information and exposure to other ways of life. People often have to cope with conflicting values and behavioural expectations, as they confront the clash between traditional and modern cultures. To deal competently and positively with these challenges, children and youth, and indeed adults too, need to be supported and encouraged to develop and enhance their life skills.

In this chapter, we will first examine what is meant by the term "life skills" and then explore how people, in particular young people, can be enabled to develop these skills through participatory, active learning methods. This will lead into a debate on issues of quality in teaching and learning processes for life skills and an analysis of how life skills contribute to empowerment. The discussion will focus mainly on life skills programmes with children and young people, in formal and non-formal schooling and in various kinds of youth groups. Some examples are also given of how these concepts have been adapted for work with adults, particularly those most marginalised by society, such as sex workers.

What are life skills?

The term "life skills" is applied in a variety of ways in the context of different programmes. In some cases it is taken to refer to practical, technical skills, such as mixing oral rehydration solution or putting on a condom. In other cases, it refers to entrepreneurial or livelihood skills, necessary for economic survival. In the school context, it is sometimes taken to mean the essential skills of basic education, including literacy, numeracy, and technical skills in health education.

In this chapter, however, the discussion of life skills focuses on what are often termed psychosocial competencies. These are the skills which enable individuals to think and behave in a pro-active and constructive way in dealing with themselves, relating to others and succeeding in the wider society. Life skills are required both in everyday circumstances and, particularly, in specific risk situations.

1 *Five Main Areas of Life Skills*

Decision making	Critical thinking	Communication	Self-awareness	Coping with stress and emotion
Problem solving	Creative thinking	Interpersonal relationships	Empathy	

The most accessible way to explain life skills is perhaps to provide a list of life skills which have been identified by different programmes around the world. The Mental Health Promotion Unit of the World Health Organization in Geneva has analysed the content of numerous life skills programmes in schools around the globe, and has found that there are five basic life skills areas which frequently appear (WHO/MNH, 1994). These life skills areas (see Box 1) provide a starting point. Later in this chapter we will examine whether life skills have a cross-cultural relevance and the ways in which they can be adapted.

2 **Examples of life skills in context**

Decision making	• A group of children living on the street decide, with support from a street educator, to help each other to give up glue sniffing. They set goals to motivate themselves; try to anticipate the potential problems and consequences of their decision; and encourage self-respect and mutual motivation to try to see their decision through.
Problem solving	• A school child knows that his baby sister should be immunised, but his parents are unwilling. The child considers the advantages and disadvantages of different ways of dealing with the situation. The child solves the problem, working out whose support to enlist to help him persuade his parents.
Critical thinking	• A group of children are able to analyse critically the negative and deceptive influence of advertising which shows smoking by sporty and successful people. They are able to see the connection between such images and young people's desire to take up smoking. • A girl is able to assess the risks potentially involved in accepting an invitation from a male family friend, or a stranger, to take a lift in his car to school.
Creative thinking	• A young person is able to envisage options for his or her future and to think independently and constructively on how these options could be pursued. "What could I do if I . . . stayed in school . . . took a technical training course . . . etc.?"

Each basic life skill area leads to a multitude of other skills to be developed and practised. For example, developing critical thinking skills can strengthen people's ability to clarify their values and assess risks more effectively. After developing basic communication skills, young people can go on to learn about negotiation skills, assertiveness and resisting peer pressure. Learning decision making skills can be further refined with additional activities to practise setting realistic goals for the future.

Clearly, different dimensions of life skills are appropriate for different age groups. For example, in the case of communication skills, while young

Communication and interpersonal relationships	• An older child is able to discuss his or her concerns about puberty and growing up with the appropriate family member or other adult. • A female worker is able to communicate clearly and confidently what she considers to be appropriate and acceptable behaviour from a male colleague. • A sex worker is able to negotiate effectively with her client to use a condom for safe sex. • A parent is able to listen supportively to an adolescent's concerns and to help the young person to come to her own decision. • A young man is able to be assertive and to resist peer pressure when his friends ridicule his refusal to drink excessive alcohol. • Neighbours are able to resolve conflict over a land dispute peaceably.
Self-awareness	• A young person develops awareness of his or her own sexual feelings and the way such impulses can override rational judgement. This self-awareness helps them to avoid situations where they could risk unsafe sex.
Empathy	• A student makes regular visits to a young person living with AIDS and comes to understand his feelings and perspective. • A group of school children conduct a joint project with children living on the street. This enables both groups to understand the strengths and needs of each other.
Coping with stress and emotion	• Refugee children learn how to cope with the trauma of leaving their homes and with the psychological stress of life in a refugee camp. • A family of orphans, whose parents have died of AIDS, is helped by teachers and social workers to learn how to cope with their grief and fear, how to support each other, and how to call on the help of other adults.

children might aim for clear expression and the ability to speak and listen in turn, older children need more advanced skills in negotiation. Adolescents, and indeed adults, could refine this still further and should be able to combine communication skills and problem solving skills for conflict resolution.

To make these concepts more concrete, some examples will show how life skills are required both in daily life and in specific risk situations (see Box 2). These are grouped in the skill areas set out in Box 1 and give a number of cases to illustrate the range of skills related to one area.

Interdependence of life skills

Of course, in many of the scenarios given in Box 2 people will actually be drawing on a variety of life skills, because, in practice, they are all interrelated. The selection or relative emphasis given to different life skills depends on the needs of individuals and groups, and the particular situations they have to deal with. While life skills are listed and described as separate skills, they remain interdependent, strengthening the holistic development of the individual.

For example, problem-solving skills need to be combined with development of other skills such as communication and coping with stress, to strengthen the individual's belief in his or her ability to take effective action. At the same time, being able to think critically and creatively about situations can help in making and following through decisions. Likewise, a person needs to be able to cope with emotions and manage conflict when such personal decisions are resisted by others. Each skill, therefore, reinforces the use of other skills and together they enhance the individual's self-esteem and feelings of competence and control.

To illustrate the interdependence of life skills, we can take the example of a 14 year old girl from a poor family in Africa. She is being harassed by an adult neighbour, who is offering her money and gifts in exchange for sexual favours. To handle this situation, she will require a range of life skills, including:

Critical thinking:	to analyse the risks involved in such a relationship, including risks of STD and HIV infection and of unwanted pregnancy.
Self-awareness:	to be clear what her personal values are and to recognise how such a relationship would affect her self-esteem.
Decision-making:	to decide how to respond to the neighbour's advances and to follow that decision through with confidence and determination.

Communication: to discuss the issue with a supportive adult and to convey her decision clearly and assertively to the neighbour.

Problem-solving: to work out whose help to enlist if the harassment continues.

And so on . . .

All of these skills, if fully internalised, could give the girl greater confidence in her ability to take effective action. However, as the following chapter will examine in detail, it is important to take into account the context in which people act: the complex economic, social, cultural and other factors which can constrain people's behavioural choices. If, to the above scenario, further contextual detail is added, we may discover external pressures which could limit the girl's options. For example, the girl may need money to pay her school fees; the neighbour may also be her school teacher, threatening to mark her exams as failed if she does not comply; or the girl may be an orphan, struggling for her very survival.

While this chapter examines the scope of an individual's ability to act within his or her environment, Chapter 5 looks at the environment from a programmer's perspective and explores strategies by which it can be made more supportive and enabling of positive behavioural choices.

3 ***Model illustrating the interdependence of life skills***

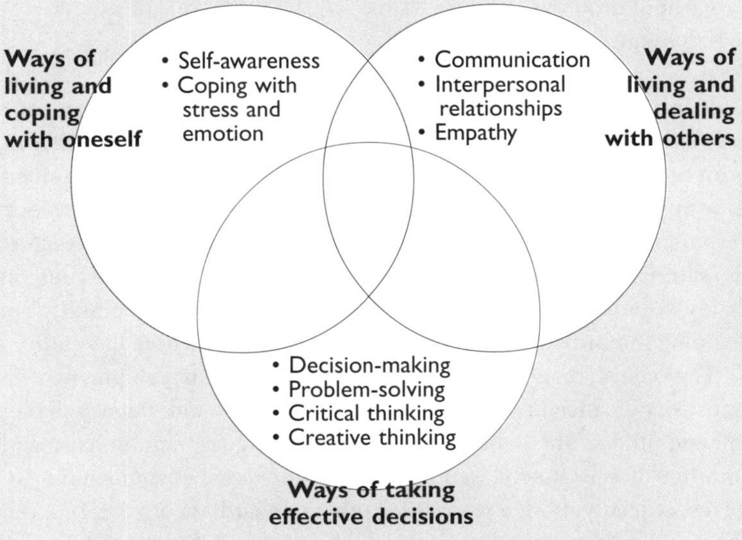

Adapted from UNICEF Kampala (1997)

Why are life skills required?

The skills listed in Box 1 have been termed generic life skills because they are required by all people for their healthy development:

- to acquire a sense of self-worth and self-efficacy;
- to build supportive relationships with family and friends;
- to promote healthy living;
- to cope with the stresses and pressures of daily life;
- to deal with conflicting values and norms for behaviour.

All of these are essential conditions for mental and physical health. Life skills education should therefore be seen as an entitlement for all young people.

At the same time, life skills are vital to all to prevent specific problems, to avoid risks and to overcome particular barriers to healthy development, including:

- drug, alcohol and tobacco abuse
- exposure to Sexually Transmitted Infections (STIs), including HIV/AIDS
- adolescent pregnancy
- child abuse
- injury from accidents
- depression and anxiety
- bullying and violence
- suicidal behaviour
- gender and racial discrimination
- school drop out
- delinquency.

In practice, many life skills programmes take one or more of these priority "problem areas" as their entry point. Because many of these concerns require similar life skills, more recent initiatives aim to create a unified and holistic approach to life skills learning. Two such programmes, developed by government and NGO consortia in Uganda and Namibia, have designed life skills materials and training which integrate the various issues of youth health and development. This integrated approach builds sequentially on the developing maturity and related health and social concerns of youth.

The acquisition of life skills is clearly linked to the development of values. Of most significance are the attitudes relating to the individual's perception of self and others. The enhancement of life skills goes hand in hand with the promotion of self-esteem, self-control and personal responsibility. It also involves, crucially, both a respect for others, regardless of race, sex, religion or life style, and a sense of the individual's responsibility for the group, be it family, friends or community.

These general attitudes need to be combined with efforts to clarify one's own set of values. In many regions, vast population growth, urban migration and exposure to alternative values through new information channels, have challenged traditional family and community structures which formerly raised young people within their own particular cultural system. In many cases, the social and sexual mores of the modern world are in direct conflict with traditional values. Within societies there is often moral ambivalence, when what is practised contradicts what is preached. All these factors lead to feelings of confusion and alienation for young people attempting to make sense of their world, feelings which may manifest themselves in risky behaviours.

Cultural expectations of the role of adolescents are frequently at odds with their actual levels of competence. In many societies in the South, the idea of "adolescence" may not even exist, as young people, especially girls, are expected to move abruptly from childhood to adulthood at the onset of puberty. Young people may be expected to behave like responsible adults and yet will often be treated like children. It can also be argued, however, that other young people, especially those in industrialised societies, are not being given enough responsibility. "Adolescents are often frustrated and angered by the ambiguity in their status and the level of responsibility society accords them." (WHO/MNH, 1992:12)

Where are life skills programmes conducted?

The problems described above are particularly acute for adolescents, although by no means confined to that age group. The focus of life skills programmes is usually on children and adolescents, since they are in their formative years and can be helped to develop positive, healthy ways of behaving. Many programmes, which initially worked with youth over 13 years, have now included primary school-aged children, recognising the needs of younger children as well as the value of intervention before typical adolescent risk situations arise. Young people need skills to adapt to the social, economic and political realities of their world, to make decisions which will enhance their opportunities. Life skills education should be seen as an entitlement for all young people. Life skills are clearly of equal value to adults, who require them to feel enabled to make constructive behavioural choices in their own lives.

While taking one of the above groupings as their primary focus, the more successful and sustainable interventions have often extended their outreach work to other members of the family and wider community in order to create a more supportive environment. For instance, the "Skills for Adolescence" programmes, developed by Lions-Quest (USA) and "Skills for the Primary School Child", designed by TACADE (UK) (see Box 5), both work principally with school students, but also emphasise the need for

4 Examples of groups involved in life skills education

- primary and secondary school students
- non-formal school students
- out-of-school youth groups
- children in preschool education
- children and youth from ethnic minorities
- girls where gender discrimination exists
- teenage parents
- street children
- refugee children
- working youth
- sex workers
- unemployed youth and adults
- women's groups, including women who have been abused
- youth and adults in reform school and prison
- parenting education groups

workshops with parents and involvement of community members in the activities.

The aim is to develop young people's personal autonomy and responsibility within a supportive and consistent environment. Furthermore, these programmes have been designed to guide the learning and practice of life skills progressively, and in different contexts, over a number of years. In this way, the life skills programme goes beyond a discrete training intervention and is concerned with a more global approach towards an education in psychosocial skills for life.

Life skills learning process

What most clearly defines a "life skills approach" from other health promotion initiatives is the teaching and learning approach. In life skills programmes the emphasis is more on process rather than on content; on how something is learned, rather than what is learned; on how to think, not what to think. Life skills are not a set of technical skills that can be taught on the basis of information transferred from the teacher to the pupil. Nor should life skills be taught in isolation. They need to be dealt with holistically, taking into account the social, cultural and economic context of the learners' lives, with application to real life concerns.

Considering the health and social issues addressed within life skills programmes, the information content is, of course, significant. However,

5 *Skills for the primary school child*

TACADE is a British NGO working in the field of health, life skills and substance abuse prevention education. Its activities include materials development, training, and advising on project development in Britain and overseas.

One of the resource packages developed by TACADE is "Skills for the Primary School Child" (SPSC). SPSC is a life skills programme promoting the health and protection of children. Following TACADE's work with secondary schools, it was realised that life skills education needed to begin earlier, so that children adopted positive behaviour patterns before adolescence began. It was also apparent that children were starting to experiment with alcohol and some other substances, particularly solvents, while still at primary school, and they have knowledge of a wide range of illicit drugs.

SPSC promotes a 'whole school' approach to child protection, in which all those working in school, including children, work together to plan and implement policies on issues such as avoiding drug and other substance abuse, dealing with bullying and contributing to the prevention of child abuse. It stresses the importance of partnership between home, school and community, developing the child's autonomy within a supportive environment. The SPSC package contains three units: one for workshops with teachers, health personnel and community members involved with the school; one for parents to gain their support for the programme and enhance their parenting skills; and one for children, containing lesson cards, detailing learning activities for children to develop their life skills. These emphasise group work, cooperative learning, listening and sharing to enhance children's self-esteem and self-confidence to make healthy and safe choices. According to TACADE, "young children can be taught skills of critical thinking, choosing and deciding. They can learn to recognise, express and deal positively with a range of feelings. They can develop and practise strategies for keeping safe in a variety of situations. They can explore attitudes and values and their effect on behaviour, and learn to value and respect themselves and others." (Moon, 1992)

Evaluation studies conducted on SPSC in Britain have indicated the impact that the materials can have on developing children's personal and social skills, particularly their attitudes. They showed the impact on improving the culture and practice of classroom and school. However, the studies also revealed the limitations of time and other pressures which prevent schools from organising parents' workshops, needed to gain parental involvement, although it was found that parents and governors were usually at least informed of the activities. The evaluation demonstrated the importance of life skills education being developed as a 'whole school' initiative, rather than conducted by individual teachers without any reinforcement in the wider school community. (Lloyd, 1994)

Tacade, 1990

6 *Life Skills Learning Methods*

Group discussion

- group discussion using trigger materials, designed to introduce life skills concepts: e.g. videos, pictures, stories, poster scenarios, problem-page letters, stories stopping at the "decision point", etc.
- group work using tools (e.g. problem solving steps) that could be used to facilitate the practice of skills
- debates
- brainstorming of options and solutions
- using mass media to discuss positive and negative role modelling: especially youth culture media: films, pop videos, song lyrics, comics, soap operas, magazines, advertisements, problem-page letters, etc.

Surveys – Participants as researchers

- self-assessment questionnaires to promote self-awareness
- case studies to develop empathy and understanding of others' lives
- opinion and behaviour surveys
- interviews with peers and others
- projects to learn about own community

Role play

- modelling of life skills
- guided practice of life skills, with role cards to resolve particular situations
- role plays: to act out situations to see what behaviour is effective or not and why
- playing "devil's advocate": to gain insight into how people can be persuasive on risky behaviour

Games and exercises

- games: e.g. communication games, team trust-building games
- structured group exercises: e.g. exercise to illustrate different listening styles; value clarification exercises on, for example, gender issues

Creative expression

- illustrating and exploring life skills through drama, storytelling, mime, puppets, dance, art and songs

Homework assignments

- practice of skills in real life situations at home and in the community environment

Feedback and reinforcement

- feedback sessions to discuss real life experiences of using life skills and to practise skills to analyse what went well or went wrong in each situation effective learning is likely to depend more on the methods employed than on the information component of the programme. “The methods used are what most clearly distinguishes life skills programmes from information dissemination initiatives, such as teaching ‘facts for life’.” (WHO/MNH,1994:3) This educational approach involves participatory and active learning methods. The objective is to create an environment conducive to experiential learning of life skills.

Defining knowledge as a “process of inquiry” (Freire, 1973: 46), in which the learner is the active agent in creating knowledge, is the key issue which demarcates active learning in life skills education from conventional, didactic approaches. “The central, and indispensable, component of active learning is the ‘inner’ activity in which the learner constructs and reconstructs his system of knowledge, skills and values. It is this structure which enables him to order new experiences, and thus to attach meaning both to the outside world and to his role in it.” (Somerset, 1988: 151)

However, at this stage we need to be careful to distinguish between skills based, active learning and what could be termed “activity-based teaching”. Life skills programmes use a range of methods, as listed in Box 6. These are all useful and valid teaching methods, but they do not automatically involve participants in a process of active learning. When used in isolation, they could tend to become teacher-directed activities, with little effective, internal learning taking place. Rather, these methods should be used as part of a process to facilitate experiential and self-directed learning (see Box 7).

Model of active learning process

Through reviewing a range of life skills and health promotion programmes, the following model has been developed to demonstrate how the separate learning activities listed in Box 6 can be incorporated into a broader process of active learning. Life skills education is likely to have limited value if taught in an abstract way, unconnected to a context. A lesson on the elements of problem-solving, without consideration of a real-life problem, would be a purely academic exercise. Life skills education has to be related to the actual needs and experiences of learners. This process model can be applied to any issue, from substance abuse to gender discrimination, HIV/AIDS prevention to teenage pregnancy. The learners are thereby exploring both the issue and the life skills involved. In this process the learners are led through the stages outlined in Box 7.

It is important to stress that this model is not envisaged as a single linear process, but as a continuous cycle of learning, action and reflection, since such learning takes place in response to actual situations encountered. Each skill area also needs to be addressed, not in isolation, but in relation to others.

For example, a programme would be inadequate if it sought to teach decision making skills purely as a rational thought process, ignoring wider factors influencing behaviour, such as conflicting value systems, peer pressure, emotional responses, etc. Such an approach to teaching decision making skills might provide a step by step guide, which "implicitly assumes that a rational procedure for appraisal of situations with review of options will result in

7 *Model of Active Learning Process*

Learning stages	**Example activities**
Understanding the issue (e.g. risks of drugs) and life skills required	Using trigger materials to stimulate discussion, e.g. videos, problem-page letters, picture stories, pop songs, soap operas, etc.
Relating to their own lives	Pair and group discussion; creative expression; anonymous personal experiences; self-assessment questionnaires; peer interviews; community projects; etc.
Practising in a safe, supportive environment	Role play; playing "devil's advocate"; games; structured group exercises.
Applying to real life situations	Both *pro-active*: i.e. planned action in personal life or in outreach activities (e.g. avoiding risks at next Saturday's disco), and *reactive*: in response to situations arising at school, at home, in social groups, etc. (e.g. being pressured by schoolmate to take drugs).
Reflecting on experience gained	Peer debriefing, group discussion, listing problems encountered and brainstorming possible solutions.
Strengthening life skills for further use	Further role play, and so on . . .

Author, principally adapted from the Child-to-Child approach to active learning (Bailey et al., 1992)

prudent choices" (Hamburg, 1990: 13). However, as Hamburg points out, young people tend to appraise situations and take decisions based on their emotional response. "Even for adults who have mature cognitive abilities and skills and substantial life experience, decision-making has been shown to be far less rational than once believed" (Hamburg, 1990: 13-14). While this comment clearly highlights the need to teach decision making skills, it also, however, illustrates the importance of teaching and practising decision making alongside other life skills. It reminds us of the fact that life skills education should not be restricted to children and youth, but should also be made available to adults.

It must be acknowledged that, for learners of all ages, their experiences will not always be easy or positive. Applying life skills to their real life involves taking risks. If young people refuse to smoke, take drugs or alcohol, they might risk ostracism from their social group. If a person, concerned about his or her partner's sexual history, insists on condom use, he or she might risk rejection. This is why life skills education should always include time to practise skills in a safe learning environment. This is an opportunity to test out other people's reactions to new behaviours.

Obviously all efforts should be made to create as supportive an environment as possible, through parallel work with parents and the community. However, it must be acknowledged that use of life skills is, in itself, a risk-taking venture, since it potentially alters the individual's relationship with others, challenging their values, roles and power relations. This underlines the importance of life skills education as a long-term, sequential and developmentally appropriate intervention. To support the learning and practice of life skills, they should always be taught first in the context of low risk, non-threatening situations, to provide opportunities for positive feedback from the application of life skills. The skills should then be explored and practised in progressively more challenging or threatening situations over time. It is the confidence gained in the practise of skills in low risk situations which helps people to persevere with their intended action when people do not respond favourably to their behaviour.

For example, if a young girl has practised assertive communication for some time in her daily interactions with her peers, when the occasion arises where she has to resist pressure to engage in an unwanted sexual relationship, she is more prepared. Based on her previous experience, she is able to be assertive in what may be perceived as a threatening situation. Of course, practice of life skills in low risk situations does still imply some level of risk, in terms of the reactions of other people. Frequently, even assertively stating an opinion which is contrary to that of the peer group implies taking a certain degree of risk, in terms of how this action will be received. Taking such risks, even small ones, is an important part of life skills education, since the learner's sense of self-efficacy is strengthened by taking on new challenges. "To succeed at easy tasks provides no new information for altering one's sense of self-efficacy, whereas mastering of challenging tasks conveys salient evidence of enhanced competence" (Bandura, 1977: 201). However, since risk is such an important concept in life skills education, it is essential that the practice of skills is facilitated in a supportive, "safe" learning environment, as demonstrated by the sample lesson given in Box 8.

8

Planning your life

The Mexican Institute for Family and Population Research (IMIFAP) developed a health and family life education programme which facilitates the learning of life skills. The programme, called *Planeando tu Vida* (Planning your Life), provides young people with the necessary tools to make informed decisions about sexuality, reproduction, as well as other health and life issues, including substance abuse.

Evaluation of this programme has shown that, if it is provided before the sexual debut of adolescents, it is effective in promoting responsible contraception use (Pick de Weiss *et al*, 1990; 1991).

Planeando tu Vida has reached approximately 3,000,000 adolescents, parents and instructors in Bolivia, Chile, Colombia, the Dominican Republic, El Salvador, Greece, Guatemala, Honduras, Peru, Uruguay, and the United States.

Sample lesson on verbal communication: assertiveness

Principles of assertive communication:

- Identify what you feel, what you think and what you want.
- Accept your own thoughts, feelings and beliefs.
- Control any feelings which prevent communication.
- Look for the opportune moment and situation to say what you want to say. Remember that being assertive also implies consideration for others.
- Be specific and say what you really think and feel, speaking in a clear and direct manner without being vague or ambiguous.
- Clarify the situation and say what you want to say. It is important to give clear and concrete replies at once.
- Communicate what you understand to be the other person's position and make it clear whether or not you agree with what they are saying.

Objectives of the session:

By the end of the session young people should be able to:

- express what they want in a direct, open manner;
- defend what they want;
- understand the importance of effective communication;
- identify assertive behaviour.

Role of teacher/facilitator

Aiming to emphasise how life skills education is learner-centred and experiential, practitioners are often sensitive over the title given to the adult leader. "Indeed, because the term 'teaching' is so often associated with passive learning, some practitioners in the life skills field prefer to avoid reference to teaching at all, and talk in terms of 'facilitating the learning' of life skills"

Process of session includes:

- Explaining the principles of assertive communication; the difference between assertiveness, aggressiveness and passivity; and the problem of interpretation in communication.
- Various learning exercises, including:
  "Learning to be assertive". This exercise requires young people to practise assertive communication from instructions selected randomly from a box, e.g.
  - Say something which expresses disagreement with the teacher.
  - Say who in the group has been honest in discussion and why.
  - Constructively criticise the course.
  - Express your opinion concerning having or not having sexual relations.
  - Express your opinion about male adolescents having sex with sex workers.

  At the end of the exercise the group discusses the difficulties they had in expressing themselves and how to overcome these. The exercise may make the young people tense, but it is part of the objective for them to practise expressing their opinions in daily life, even when it is not easy.

  Discuss and analyse questions asking: "Is it true that ...?" e.g.
  - Is it true that a way to show maturity is to hide your feelings?
  - Is it true that a woman who expresses herself assertively is less feminine?

- Discuss application of learning:
  - In what situations will adolescents apply what they have learned?
  - Do they understand the difference between assertiveness, aggressiveness and passivity and the implications for each one?
  - How assertive do they believe they are and how can they be even more assertive?
  - What can young people do at home to emphasise the importance of positive and assertive communication?

Extracted and translated from Pick de Weiss et al, 1988

(WHO/UNICEF, 1994: 3). In reality, the leader of a life skills activity has to be able to alternate between the teacher and facilitator modes. With his or her pedagogical experience and access to resource materials, the "teacher" is best placed to design and set up structured learning exercises, while maximising the students' autonomy within that structure. The learners need a safe and supportive environment in which to practice and to which they can return to reflect on their experiences of applying life skills to real-life situations.

A life skills approach, whether in schools or in community contexts, marks a radical departure from traditional forms of didactic teaching, in which the teacher transfers information to the passive learner. Life skills education can undeniably present a stimulating challenge to the status quo, especially when introduced to the formal school system. "It encourages pupils to explore, question, come to decisions and take responsibility for their actions. How often are these things genuinely encouraged?" (Dixon in Campbell, 1987:137) The development and empowerment of learners can either be welcomed or resisted.

This brings us to the crux of the matter when introducing a life skills approach to the formal education system. Teacher education presents the greatest challenge to implementing life skills programmes. In school systems where child-centred, active-learning methods, and acceptance of the school's role in the socialization of young people, already characterise mainstream education, life skills learning can be incorporated with relative ease. Where didactic teaching styles predominate, for life skills education to succeed a transformation is required in the teacher's role and the teacher-student relationship. The Zimbabwe School AIDS Education Programme has made a bold attempt to address this teacher education issue (see Box 9). According to the programme design, "the teaching methods used are participatory and student-centred. The teachers' role is that of a manager, a non-judgmental facilitator who creates situations in which students explore problems . . . and come up with their own solutions

An illustration dealing with "bad touches" extracted from a Grade 5 student textbook disseminated by the Ministry of Education and Culture, Zimbabwe, 1995.

9 *Zimbabwe School AIDS Action Programme*

The School AIDS Action Programme in Zimbabwe provides an interesting example of an attempt to take a life skills approach from small scale intervention into a national programme, introduced through the formal education system. With HIV/AIDS prevention as its primary objective, the programme has a broad foundation in the development of life skills.

The programme has been developed by the Ministry of Education's Curriculum Development Unit in partnership with UNICEF. Its main impetus has been on the research, development and dissemination of student textbooks, teachers' manuals and supplementary materials, combined with teacher training.

The programme targets all students from primary Grade 4 to the highest secondary class. It is compulsory in the school curriculum and has one weekly period timetabled. The text books are graded and incremental. As the students mature, so the topics move from "bad touches" to actual rape, from making friends to physical relationships. "The textbooks used are issue-oriented and pose a series of scenarios requiring students to explore feelings, examine alternatives, think through situations, take decisions and make judgements. The books avoid talking down to students and do not prescribe answers to problems. The material provides situations that help students confront issues that enable them to make decisions about their own sexual values and interpersonal relationships." (UNICEF, Harare, 1994) This approach demonstrates how HIV/AIDS education can be planned around life skills development, rather than pure information transfer.

The greatest challenge lies in teacher education, in being able to transform didactic teachers into facilitators. In-service teacher training is provided through a "cascade" model (each level training a lower level), from national down to school level, although this inevitably tends to get weaker as it moves downwards. To provide further stimulus and support to teachers and to promote school interaction, "demonstration" schools receive targeted training and serve a local cluster of schools. However, established teachers have found it difficult to transform their conventional approaches, fearing that greater student participation could lead to a loss of control.

Pre-service training is conducted in all teachers' colleges. This incorporates factual information on HIV/AIDS as well as training in the participatory, life skills approach used by this programme. It also targets the college students themselves as a group at risk.

In a preliminary evaluation study on the text books and implementation in Grade 7, students "were unanimous in viewing the book as useful, enjoyable, appropriate and in the main relevant to their experience," although many expressed embarrassment at having to discuss these issues with adult teachers, who were themselves also uneasy with the material (Chisuo, 1995:30-31). However, the study highlights the difficulties which participatory methods present to teachers. Rather than introducing the books as a separate lesson, many teachers have tended to integrate the lessons into other core subjects, returning to their conventional, didactic approaches. This necessarily inhibits the development of life skills. Future development of the programme will focus on teacher training and monitoring mechanisms.

UNICEF Harare, 1994: 1-19

and conclusions . . . It is clear that teachers need a lot of support in adopting a non-directive teaching style. They feel they are losing power and control." (UNICEF Harare, 1994: 18)

However, active, learner-centred methods are not necessarily non-directive. The facilitator, trained to be aware of group dynamics, has arguably more, rather than less control of the group than the teacher using traditional methods. In the school context, for example, greater understanding of the group dynamics should result in better classroom management. This theory has been confirmed in practice. Life skills programmes in schools are often associated with better classroom management and better relations between teachers and pupils.

It is, nevertheless, important not to underestimate the challenge presented in introducing life skills approaches to formal education systems, especially when planning national programmes. High quality training is crucial to establish teachers' belief in the approach and their competence to facilitate life skills learning. It is necessary to consider how far and how fast schools and communities are able to move in accepting and assimilating life skills programmes. There is a danger in trying to move too fast, rather than building incrementally from didactic to participatory learning methods, thereby losing credibility with teachers and failing to provide a supportive environment for learners. Learning environments for out-of-school youth groups and adult education groups may initially present an easier ground for introducing life skills approaches.

Life skills and empowerment

Although increasingly questioned, the supposition underlying most health education programmes still suggests that, given the necessary information on health, people will act rationally, perceiving the associated risks and benefits, and will change their behaviour accordingly. It presupposes that health is a matter of individual habits and life styles. It thereby removes individuals from their social context, assuming that they live in a void, free from all external pressures and barriers to health. Yet people do not systematically operate as rational beings, who, on receiving "public health warnings", will do as they are told. Nor are they necessarily free to do so, given other constraining factors in their environment.

Underlying the information-centred approach is the questionable assumption that some people have lifestyles that are "unhealthy" or "inadequate" and that these people should be made to see the need to adopt "healthier" habits and attitudes. This can lead on to a sense of blaming individuals for their ill-health, since they chose not to adopt a healthy lifestyle. It does not take into account the social, economic and environmental pressures that can determine people's behaviour. This kind of "victim-blaming" can also be internalised, resulting in feelings of guilt and a diminishing of self-esteem. It undermines people's sense of "self-efficacy" (Bandura, 1977, 1982): their belief in their ability to take positive action. This approach can, in effect, disempower the very learners it seeks to educate.

It is significant that life skills programmes are gaining most impetus now in areas of health where information transfer alone has most patently failed to make an impact, i.e. programmes with youth on substance abuse and on sexual and reproductive health, including HIV/AIDS education. Life skills education is now being promoted globally by UNICEF, WHO and other agencies as a vital strategy for tackling the HIV/AIDS pandemic, and for the prevention of other behaviour related health and social problems.

Life skills education can be designed to equip people to think critically about the social, cultural and economic context of their lives, and the way in which this influences their health choices. With this critical consciousness, the learners are then supported in strengthening their problem-solving and decision making skills, their communication and coping skills. This aims to give them the ability to act, and, as importantly, to gain a *belief* in their ability to act upon their environment, rather than feeling passive victims and incapable of influencing their life circumstances.

This sense of ability and autonomy cannot be developed in individuals in isolation from the context of their lives. It matures in people through participation in a complex learning process. This stage is reached when the learners understand the wider context of health; when they have an objective awareness of the varied forces – economic, social, cultural, political – which shape their experience, and a belief in and accurate assessment of their own power, as individuals or as a group, to transform those circumstances. In planning life skills interventions, it is necessary to define the wider determinants of behaviour and design interventions in this context.

For example, a life skills programme for a group of inner city youth could focus on prevention of drug abuse. It would promote critical thinking, by reflecting on the underlying, root causes for this behaviour – the social, cultural, economic and political factors which spur them to turn to drugs as a coping mechanism. This could give the learners a critical distance from the experience, helping them to consider the causes and effects of their behaviour, and identify feasible, less risky, alternative coping strategies. The programme would seek to help young people to develop their interpersonal skills, self-awareness and empathy for others, to enable them to build a supportive peer group network.

Life skills programmes represents for many an "education for empowerment". However, if we link life skills to the concept of empowerment, it is necessary to clarify exactly what we mean by that term. For life skills education to be empowering it needs to meet the learners' needs both as individuals and as part of a wider group.

> Empowerment Education . . . promotes health in all personal and social arenas. The model suggests that the participation of people in group action and dialogue and in group efforts directed at community targets enhances (their) control and belief in (their) ability to change their own lives.
>
> (Wallerstein *et al.*, 1988: 379)

As a term, "empowerment" has lost the force and precision of its original meaning through over-usage. However, there is general agreement that the concept involves a process of growth and development in the learners, leading to deliberate efforts to transform the situation of their lives. This transformation in individuals, in relation to their social group and their environment, can also be defined in terms of the outcomes of empowerment.

Wedeen (1991) defines empowerment as both a process and an outcome in terms of the life skills acquired and practised. She has established a flexible framework for measuring empowerment, which is offered as nine interrelated components:

> *Ways of thinking*: knowledge of the environment and its resources; critical consciousness to question the status quo; aspirations to strive for a better life; skills in problem-solving.
>
> *Ways of feeling*: feelings of competence; feelings of self-esteem; feelings of control over the events of one's life.
>
> *Ways of behaving*: autonomy; determination to make decisions and follow them through.
>
> (Wedeen, 1991: 4-5)

These ways of thinking, feeling and behaving are therefore prerequisites to individual and group empowerment to take effective action for health and development. Life skills education is crucial to building people's confidence and competence to act, but such learning must be based on a realistic assessment of the political, economic, social and other forces which can limit the actions of individuals and their choices in life. People can become empowered to influence some of these forces, but, for those beyond their control, complementary interventions which work at a structural level, are essential to create an environment which promotes safe and healthy behaviour. The next chapter will consider some strategies for creating an enabling environment.

Peer education and life skills

Some practitioners believe that a life skills programme can have greater impact by incorporating a peer education approach. Young people, as well as adults, can be trained and supported to work with their peer group. People feel more confident in accepting, as a role model, the behaviour of someone from the same socioeconomic background. It demonstrates that the same set of barriers can be overcome and that changes can be made and sustained. The Peer Education Programme amongst Commercial Sex Workers in Zimbabwe (see Box 10) provides an example of this. Clearly, such activities require peer leaders to model good communication, listening and other interpersonal skills, which will also be strengthened through participating in these activities. Peer education approaches are also being employed in programmes for youth sexual and reproductive health. Peer-led education may be more effective in raising young people's knowledge levels and perceived susceptibility to HIV infection than adult-led education.

Are life skills cross-cultural?

Life skills programmes covering similar issues and skills are proliferating worldwide. Existing programmes, like the Lions-Quest "Skills for Adolescence", have already been adapted for use in over 25 countries. Other

10 ***Peer education amongst sex workers in Zimbabwe***

The Sex Worker Peer Education Programme carried out by the Department of Psychology, University of Zimbabwe, is one of the more successful HIV/AIDS programmes in Zimbabwe. It has reduced the transmission of STIs in programme areas by 50 percent in a very short time. The focus is on the free distribution of condoms and the promotion of the use of condoms in licensed beer halls. Peer educators advocate and educate on the use of condoms, targeting both fellow sex workers and their clients.

The peer educators live in the communities where they work. They are therefore credible communicators, to whom their audiences can relate. The peer educators operate within associations of sex workers, established to provide social and material support to their members. At their meetings the women also discuss AIDS and related problems. They view videos and other materials, discuss personal experiences, and work collectively to strengthen their assertiveness and negotiation skills to bargain for protected sex. They also practise putting on condoms. The inclusion of life skills development is critical, particularly with this group of socially-marginalised women. Life skills training can improve the women's sense of self-efficacy, which is central to their adopting safer sex practices themselves and demanding this from clients. "On a collective level, these women develop the belief in their power to effect change" (Wilson, 1994:58).

Wilson (1994)

countries have pioneered new ground. Across these different programmes, similar life skills concepts are found. While, initially, it appears that life skills have a cross-cultural relevance, further research is required to examine the content of life skills more closely. At this level the content varies across cultures. So whilst basic life skills areas, like decision making and communication skills, are relevant across cultures, the content of activities to teach these skills depends upon the culture and local needs.

For example, while decision making skills in Europe and the USA strengthen the individual's autonomy, in South Asia, the family, rather than the individual, is in many cases the "unit" for decision making. Whereas in mainstream culture in Europe and North America, a young woman generally selects her own life partner, in South Asia it is usually the family which arranges when and to whom the young woman will be married. Decision making skills, in an authoritarian structure, for the young South Asian girl, involves understanding where the locus of decision making power lies in the family, and also requires the ability to negotiate appropriately for her own needs to be met.

For agencies actively promoting life skills programmes, the concepts need to be adapted through the lens of each culture with great sensitivity. The Convention on the Rights of the Child can be used as a yardstick against which to check the importance of life skills for young people. Assertiveness in girls, for example, may contradict behavioural norms in some cultures, yet life skills programmes may seek to challenge such norms when girls' rights are at stake. The most effective way to ensure a sound, culturally-appropriate development or adaptation of life skills approaches is to involve the learners themselves in identifying the most important life skills for their own culture and environment, in their own language.

Few corners of the world remain untouched by the globalisation of information and entertainment. For most people 'culture' is no longer experienced as a self-contained, single code for values and behaviour. Alternative value systems and conflicting behavioural expectations now put enormous pressures on people, particularly youth. Global youth culture, as characterised by satellite music channels, may be in direct confrontation with traditional values. Young people see assertiveness, for example, modelled on TV, and yet at home they may be expected to be acquiescent to adults. Within one society, a wide gulf may also have appeared between the "culture" of the elite and that of the wider population. With societies in a state of rapid transition, life skills interventions need maximum flexibility to be relevant and appropriate. Specific work needs to be done to encourage more open communication between generations, to promote greater understanding.

Gender issues are also intricately related to cultural practices. In many societies, life skills, as defined in this chapter, will be encouraged and accepted more readily in boys than in girls. Special consideration must be given to girls and women, to establish their life skill needs as distinct from those of males. A gender perspective also forms a vital part of any life skills programme, to enable learners to think critically about gender inequality and stereotypes for male and female behaviour. This can help people to recognise gender roles as social constructs, open to change, rather than as fixed and immutable.

Constant vigilance, flexibility and openness are required by those implementing life skills programmes to try to ensure the cultural appropriateness and relevance of the programme content over time. The best way to achieve this is through involving participants – young people, their parents, adult learners and community leaders – in the design, implementation and ongoing evaluation of the programmes. In small, community-based projects this can be accomplished through workshops, interviews and informal discussion. In large or national programmes, participant involvement can still be successfully maintained through a sustained programme of research, including focus group discussions, to provide continuous feedback to the planners and managers.

Research related to programme development and implementation

Research related to life skills programmes is discussed towards the end of this chapter. In practice, when considering life skills programme development and implementation, research should be among the first issues to be explored.

When decisions are to be made about life skills education, questions about the proven effectiveness and value of this approach will certainly be asked. Advocates for the life skills approach should therefore be armed with some facts and figures based on research on life skills programme effectiveness carried out elsewhere. Fortunately, there are numerous studies to draw upon. Research studies of life skills programmes include reports of a positive contribution to: substance abuse prevention (Botvin *et al*, 1980, 1984); suicide prevention (LaFromboise, 1994); violence prevention (Gainer *et al.*, 1993); and the prevention of the spread of HIV/AIDS (McLean, 1994). Life skills education approaches are also associated with mental health promotion outcomes (Ennett *et al.*, 1994; Elias *et al*, 1991), and improved school performance (Navarrette, 1987; Parsons *et al*, 1988).

Positive outcomes of research studies have undoubtedly served as an argument for further development and investment in this domain. However, when applying the concept to a new setting or culture, the first step is to determine whether the life skills approach is appropriate, and if so, what type of life skills programme is required? What are the needs and what resources exist to satisfy these needs? An important component of any needs assessment is to investigate the perceived needs of the eventual users of the life skills programme. Users in the life skills context refers to a wide group of people who are likely to be involved in its implementation, reception, and support.

If it is decided that a life skills approach is the right one, further research could investigate what the content of the programme should be and what methods and strategies are most appropriate for implementation. Formative research into these issues could guide the development of programme materials and training modules. However, even when these are developed, a period of trial testing of the training and programme materials is required to assess their appropriateness and potential effectiveness.

With feedback from a pilot test period, training modules and programme materials can be revised. This process helps to ensure the contribution of the eventual users of the life skills programme in determining some of the basic content and methods, as well as the mode of implementation and ongoing evaluation.

Evaluation of the programme and training by its users should also be built into the design of life skills education materials and training manuals. In particular, "processing questions" can be used to gain user feedback at the end of each life skills lesson or training workshop. Such questions include: Did you enjoy the session? What did you find most and least useful about the contents? Are there particular activities which were not understood? And so on.

It is important to investigate issues related to the implementation and reception of a life skills programme before considering an evaluation of the programme outcomes. However, it is the evaluation of the programme outcomes which is going to answer one of the most important research questions: does the programme work? Does it achieve what it set out to do and what other effects does it have? These are essential questions to address. No intervention can escape the need, at some point, to evaluate its outcomes. Unfortunately, however, if this question is addressed too late, many years after an intervention has been implemented, there is likely to be little scope for revision of the programme content. Furthermore, any claims made about the programme outcomes, which are not later verified in research, are likely to lead to the intervention being discontinued and considered a failure. Early evaluation, on the other hand, allows scope for re-evaluation of the claims made about expected long-term programme outcomes. It also helps to identify other programme outcomes which could be used to promote the intervention.

For example, life skills programmes have sometimes been developed and implemented in schools, based on a single stated objective, e.g. substance abuse prevention or violence prevention. However, perhaps more interesting to the education sector, and more persuasive in gaining longer term support for the programme, are the potential effects of the life skills programme on factors related to school performance, such as school attendance, academic performance and student-teacher relationships.

Evaluation is clearly a central component of any life skills intervention. Built into the whole process of life skills programme development, implementation and maintenance, research can gauge the appropriateness and effectiveness of a programme in the longer term. It is therefore an important part of any sustainable strategy for life skills education.

The research process summarised here is described in more detail in the context of life skills education in schools in the WHO document Life Skills Education: Planning for Research (WHO/MSA 1995). Wider issues of programme evaluation are examined in the final chapter of this book.

Communicating life skills concepts through other channels

Life skills concepts can also be promoted through other channels, raising awareness of the need for and value of these skills. The work in the field of "education through entertainment", discussed in the previous chapter, has some lively examples of how life skills can be demonstrated through popular, entertaining films and radio series, songs, newspaper cartoon strips and other media. The power of this approach is to reach out to people by reflecting their own experiences through stories in, for example, "edutainment" soap operas. These stories can show empathy and insight into the stresses and problems of ordinary people's lives, but also, through the stories, can demonstrate people using life skills.

UNICEF's Meena and Sara Communication Initiatives, in South Asia and Eastern and Southern Africa, respectively, both attempt to harness the power of the entertainment media to promote life skills for girls (see Box 11). Both initiatives have developed a range of materials which seek to give girls a positive role model to counteract pervasive gender inequality. The animated film series, radio series and comic books, which form the core of these two initiatives, present stories in which the heroine is seen to communicate her needs and to surmount barriers to her goals by acquiring life skills. The communication materials are accompanied by facilitators' guidelines. These illustrate how the Meena and Sara stories can be used by any programme as "trigger" material to initiate discussion about gender issues and life skills. The users' guides suggest activities to relate this learning to the group's own lives.

Street Kids International, with the National Film Board of Canada, has also produced two animated videos, *Karate Kids* and *Goldtooth*. These have been developed for children living on the streets and explore how they can develop life skills for making healthy, positive choices to avoid risky situations. The first film sets this in the context of HIV/AIDS; the second considers substance abuse. The films, and accompanying print materials, aim to build up the street children's self-esteem. For example, they actually acknowledge

11 Communication initiatives for the girl child

UNICEF's Meena Communication Initiative in South Asia and Sara Communication Initiative in Eastern and Southern Africa both seek to promote the status of girls and develop their life skills. Educating through entertaining adventure, drama and comedy, the two projects revolve around the stories of two girls, Meena and Sara. Their stories are related through a range of media, including animated film, radio, comic and story books, songs, puppets, drama and posters. The audiences identify with the girls as they struggle with discrimination, gradually gaining life skills to negotiate for their rights and fulfil their aspirations. (Aghi, 1995)

In one episode, Meena, the South Asian heroine, plays a simple game – exchanging roles with her brother for a day – to give her family a more objective and critical insight into the way girls are discriminated against in terms of workload and food distribution.

In one of the African stories, Sara uses critical and creative thinking to play on her uncle's political ambitions and so convince him that keeping her in secondary school will be to his own advantage.

Both these characters represent a dynamic role model for girls and an appealing communication symbol for girls' rights. While the stories deal with the different issues faced by girls, the underlying theme is the development of life skills in children and young people. In the Sara Initiative, which deals with adolescents, this includes the questions surrounding the formation of relationships with the opposite sex. The intiatives confront the fact that the practice of life skills is often denied to girls because of their social and cultural conditioning. They bring gender concerns into the heart of life skills programming.

Both the initiatives are grounded in an extensive process of formative research, to ensure that the representation of the girls' lives and their demonstration of life skills is credible and acceptable. For example, detailed research has been necessary to establish the nature and degree to which girls' assertiveness and critical thinking skills can be enhanced before provoking a backlash of resistance in societies where girls are expected to be submissive.

The communication materials are reinforced by educational modules guiding facilitators on managing group discussion, reflection and action. The audience observe the use of life skills in the story, and then process the concepts and internalise and practise the skills through facilitated discussion and activities. The second stage is based on the principles of active learning, which take the learners through a process of enquiry, in which they reflect on the issue (e.g. Sara being pressurised to undergo female genital mutilation and how she resolves the problem) through the lens of their own experience. This aims to stimulate people to re-evaluate their ways of thinking, feeling and behaving and to develop confidence that change is possible. The Sara Initiative has developed a life skills manual to address a broad range of youth health and development issues.

While being popularised through the mass media, these materials are also being used as a resource for life skills, health and gender education in formal and non-formal schooling, youth programmes, as well as community group settings. They provide a tangible, relevant and entertaining way to communicate about life skills.

UNICEF: 1996

Illustrations from UNICEF's Sara (left) and Meena (below) Communication Initiatives

the children's coping skills in using drugs as their way of dealing with the street's harsh existence, but then offer alternative ways of coping. "To influence the behaviour of these young people, both in and out-of-school, we need to reach them with empathy, and show them other ways to fulfil these real and urgent needs through their own choices, in relationship with friends and mentors." (Lowry, 1994: 6) The Street Kids International materials are also based on an extensive process of formative research.

As well as producing their own targeted materials, agencies interested in promoting life skills can act as a resource and catalyst for the entertainment industry, advising on the development of programmes. Such collaboration is illustrated in the South African soap opera, *Soul City*, (see Chapter 3, Box 16), which has popularised a wide range of health and social issues. The scenarios provide lively and credible examples of life skills, and indeed, the problems arising when people lack them.

The mass media is often accused of having an anti-social impact, through images of violence and exploitation. Collaboration between social development agencies and the mass media offers an opportunity to counter these criticisms by promoting "pro-social" images and role models.

The great benefit of the "edutainment" approach is its appeal to young audiences. It reaches them through their own media, engaging their interest. In Uganda, cartoons on life skills, including Sara cartoon strips, appear regularly in the teenage newspaper, *Straight Talk*, which is widely distributed in the country. The cartoons depict simple situations where the cartoon characters use their life skills, or show that they need to learn life skills.

These initiatives have an important role in promoting life skills through the mass media. The materials are also a valuable resource for life skills education, acting as a 'trigger' for stimulating discussion.

Summary of lessons learned

Experience of life skills programmes around the world has provided a number of key lessons learned, summarised here:

- Life skills need to be learnt in an integrated, holistic manner, since real-life problems require a range of psychosocial skills. Life skills programmes should be developed to address the "whole person" within his or her environment.
- Life skills education is a long term process and requires follow-up activities to ensure that learners continue, over time, to apply their life skills in different contexts and have a chance to reflect on their experiences.
- Learners, their families and communities, need to be involved in

identifying risky behaviours and the related life skills which are significant to them, to ensure the relevance of the programme and its cultural appropriateness.

- In programme planning, implementation, monitoring and managing, all efforts should be made to promote community ownership of the programme for long-term sustainability.
- Learners require opportunities for practice of skills and positive reinforcement. Consultation and parallel life skills training with other family members, parents, peers and the community can aim to make the environment more supportive.
- Early interventions with children of primary school age enable them to acquire life skills before they may become involved in risk-taking behaviours.
- Both qualitative and quantitative research are an essential part of the whole process of life skills programme development, implementation and maintenance.
- The participatory, active learning approach required for life skills education makes new demands on the abilities of educators. Teacher/facilitator training and follow-up support need to be given priority.
- When designing risk reduction programmes, on AIDS, substance abuse, etc., the life skills required to address the issue should form the central focus. These life skills will then define the learning objectives, the content, materials and educational methods, as well as the behavioural outcomes to be evaluated.
- Work with the media, to promote positive life skills modelling, helps to provide other sources of motivation and examples for the acquisition and practice of life skills, especially for young people.
- Life skills programmes should be underpinned by a human rights stance, giving special consideration to the promotion of the Rights of the Child, and the prevention of gender, racial and other forms of discrimination.
- While strengthening the capabilities of individuals, life skills programme developers should also recognise the importance of wider environmental factors which can constrain people's behaviour and limit their choices. Agencies need to collaborate, working simultaneously at a structural level to promote a more positive environment.

The next chapter discusses the "enabling environment": how an environment can be made more supportive and conducive to behavioural change. This provides the complement to our vision of life skills: an education which empowers individuals and groups to act upon their environment for the promotion and protection of personal and social health and well-being.

References

Aghi, M. and Carnegie, R. (1995) *Formative research process in the Meena Communication Initiative*. Kathmandu: UNICEF Regional Office for South Asia.

Bailey, D., Hawes, H., Bonati, G. (1992) *Child-to-child: A resource book*. London: Child-to-Child Trust.

Bandura, A. (1977) "Self-efficacy: Toward a unifying theory of behaviour change". *Psychological Review*, 84, 191-215

Botvin, G.J., Eng, A. and Williams, C.L. (1980) "Preventing the onset of cigarette smoking through life skills training". *Preventive Medicine*, 11, 199-211.

Botvin, G.J., Baker, E., Botvin, E.M., Filazzola, A.D. and Millman, R.B. (1984) "Alcohol abuse prevention through the development of personal and social competence: A pilot study". *Journal of Studies on Alcohol*, 45, 550-552.

Campbell, G. (ed.) (1987) *Health education,youth and community*. Sussex: Falmer Press.

Chisuo, L. (1995) *Report on an evaluation of the implementation of Grade 7 AIDS action programme book "Let's talk" in schools in Zimbabwe*. Harare: UNICEF.

Elias, M.J.; Gara, M.A.; Schuyler, T.F.; Branden-Muller,L.R.; Sayette, M.A. (1991)"The promotion of social competence: Longitudinal study of a preventive school-based program". *American Journal of Orthopsychiatry*, 61 (3), 409-417.

Ennett, S.T.; Tobler, N.S.; Ringwalt, C.L.; Flewelling, R.L. (1994) "How effective is drug abuse resistance education? A meta-analysis of Project DARE outcome evaluations". *American Journal of Public Health*, 84, (9), 1394-1401.

Freire, P. (1973) *Pedagogy of the oppressed*. London: Penguin.

Gainer, P.S.; Webster, D.W.; Champion, H.R. (1993) "A youth violence prevention program". *Archives of Surgery*, 128(3), 303-308.

Hamburg, B. (1990) *Life skills training: Preventive interventions for young adolescents. Report of the life skills training working group*. Washington, D.C.: Carnegie Council on Adolescent Development.

LaFromboise, T.D. and Howard-Pitney, B. (1994) *The Zuni life skills development curriculum: a collaborative approach to curriculum development.* American Indian Alaskan Native Mental Health Research Monograph Series. 4, 98-121.

Lloyd, J. (1994) *Skills for the Primary School Child: National Evaluation of Dissemination and Practice.* London: Department for Education/Salford: TACADE.

Lowry, C. (1994) *Preventive education for drugabuse demand reduction amonghigh risk groups: Outreach to street children.* Toronto: Street Kids International.

McLean, D.A. (1994) "A Model for HIV risk reduction and prevention among African-American college students". *Journal of American College Health*, 42 (5)220-3.

Moon, A. (1992) "Child production programmes in schools. *Pastoral Care in Education*, Vol. 10 No. 1.

Navarrette, C. (1987) *Interim evaluation of Somos El Futuro Project.* Portland: Interface Consultants.

Parsons, C.; Hunter, D.; Warne, Y. (1988) *Skills for adolescence: An analysis of project material, training and implementation.* Canterbury: Christ Church College, Evaluation Unit.

Pick de Weiss, S.; Aguilar Gil, J.A.; Rodriguez, G.; Vargas Trujillo, E.; and Reyes Pardo, J. (1988) *Planeando tu Vida.* Inst. Mexicano de Investigacion de Familia y Poblacion, A.C.

Pick de Weiss, S.; Diaz-Loving, R.; Andrade-Palos, P.; and David, H. (1990) "Effect of sex education on the sexual and contraceptive practices of female teenagers in Mexico City". *Journal of Psychology and Human Sexuality*, 3 (2), 71-93.

Pick de Weiss, S.; Atkin, L.C.; Gribble, J.; and Andrade-Palos, P. (1991) "Sex, contraception and pregnancy among adolescents in Mexico City". *Studies in Family Planning,* 22 (2), 74-82.

Quest International, Lions Clubs International and TACADE (1986) *Skills for adolescence: Activities and assignments.* Salford: TACADE.

Somerset, A. (1988) *Child-to-child: A survey.* London: Child-to-Child Trust.

TACADE (The Advisory Council of Alcohol and Drug Education) (1990) *Skills for the primary school child.* Salford: TACADE.

UNICEF Harare (1994) *Report of study tour of school AIDS education programme in Zimbabwe.* Harare: UNICEF.

UNICEF Kampala (1997) *Life skills for young Ugandans: Primary teachers' training manual.* Kampala: UNICEF.

UNICEF New York (1996) *Drawing insight: Communicating development through animation.* Penang: Southbound.

Wallerstein, N. and Bernstein, E. (1988) "Empowerment education: Freire's ideas adapted to health educatarch agendas". Paper presented to the Meeting of the Association for Women in Development, Washington, D.C.

Wilson, D. (1994) *Gwero City Council peer education programme: Survey of coverage and reported impact.* Harare: Department of Psychology, University of Zimbabwe.

WHO/MNH (August 1992) *Skills for Life Newsletter*: No.1.

WHO/MNH (1994). *Life skills education in schools.* "Parts 1 & 2. Introduction and guidelines to facilitate the development and implementation of life skills programmes". Geneva: Division of Mental Health, World Health Organization. WHO/MNH/PSF/93.7A.Rev.1

WHO/MSA (1995). *Life skills education: planning for research.* Geneva: Division of Mental Health and Prevention of Substance Abuse, World Health Organization. (Draft).

WHO/UNICEF (1994). *The development and dissemination of life skills education: An overview.* Geneva: Division of Mental Health, World Health Organization/New York: Health Promotion Unit, UNICEF. MNH/PSF/94.7

Women, who are members of the Bangladeshi Rural Advancement Committee in the village of Aglakanda, Mymensingh, meet to count money to repay their loans and deposit their savings against future loans from a microcredit programme aimed at supporting women's small business initiatives in Bangladesh.

5

Making change possible

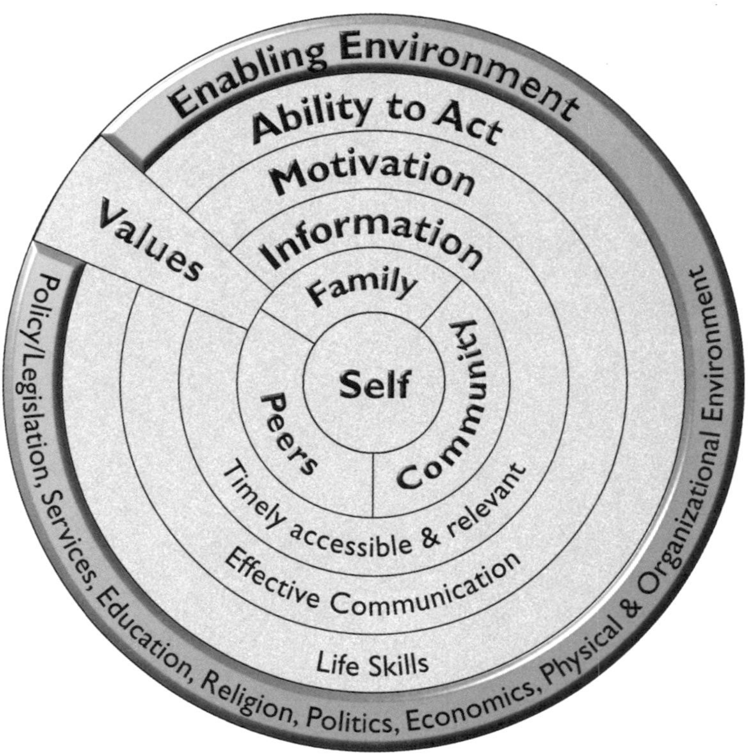
Enabling Environment
Ability to Act
Motivation
Information
Values
Family
Self
Community
Peers
Timely accessible & relevant
Effective Communication
Life Skills
Policy/Legislation, Services, Education, Religion, Politics, Economics, Physical & Organizational Environment

FIVE

Making change possible: Creating an enabling environment

Rachel Carnegie, Neill McKee,
Bruce Dick, Pamela Reitemeier,
Esther Weiss, Chin Saik Yoon

PART I: SETTING THE CONTEXT

Introduction

What do we learn if we trace back the stories of the many adolescent girls who have babies that they don't want; the young people of both sexes who contract STIs, including HIV/AIDS, or become addicted to drugs; the women who die each year in childbirth; the people who fall sick from tobacco-related diseases or are injured in occupational accidents; the infants who suffer from malnutrition? We would discover that even if they or their parents or guardians had the right knowledge to prevent these problems from arising, even if they were highly motivated and had developed the necessary life skills, they would still face a range of barriers to attaining good health.

In many development programmes, much more effort is currently put into "getting the messages across" than into making sure that the behaviours promoted are actually possible, given the constraining factors in the environment in which people operate. For example, young people may be motivated to try to make use of available health services for contraception or for the treatment of STIs. Even if they have the skills to negotiate through the disapproval or sanctions of family and friends, at best they may then have to deal with health workers who are brusque, judgmental and demonstrate little respect for confidentiality; at worst they may be denied access to health services because of policies that restrict young people's use of such services unless accompanied by their parents.

So, even with knowledge, motivation and skills, people can often still face difficulties in adopting new behaviours, particularly if they lack the power to change the circumstances in their lives which block the path they are seeking to follow. To support these actions, they need a more "enabling environment".

While Chapter 4 discussed the way in which enhanced life skills can enable an individual to take greater control over the decisions affecting their health and well being, this chapter considers factors in the wider environment which are beyond people's immediate control but still influence and constrain their behavioural choices.

The first part of the chapter gives an overview of the need for an enabling environment. The second part examines how different factors in the environment affect or determine people's behaviour and reviews various interventions which have sought to make the environment more supportive. These environmental factors include:

- Policy and legislation
- Service provision
- Education system
- Cultural factors
- Religion
- Socio-political factors
- Socio-economic factors
- Physical environment
- Organisational environment

The chapter concludes with a summary of key lessons learnt, identifying opportunities for action.

Why an enabling environment?

All too often, people wanting to make changes in their lives face the resistance of their family, peers and community. Health services are often inadequate for their needs or insensitive to their situation. The education system often fails them. They may also face religious, cultural, economic, or social pressures – or a lack of structural and legislative support – that constrain their freedom to choose healthy and safe options.

All too often, programmes designed to improve people's lives have focused on the "vulnerable individual", exhorting them to change their lifestyles. Such programmes not infrequently ignore the wider environment and the forces which push people into doing things that undermine their health, such as having unwanted or unsafe sex, using drugs, being subjected to female genital mutilation (FGM) or using breast-milk substitutes.

At the same time, health promotion programmes can gain far greater impact by building on existing cultural, social and other factors which support safe and healthy choices, for example, in discouraging the use of tobacco or alcohol.

When programming for behaviour development and change we therefore need to think in much broader terms, beyond the individual whose behaviour we are concerned about. Programmes that aim to decrease the number of people who smoke, the number of people injured in car accidents, the number of children who remain without immunisation, the number of teenage girls becoming pregnant, have to do much more than develop individuals' knowledge, motivation and skills to be effective. They have to focus on creating a supportive and enabling environment for these individuals. Such programmes need to build on those aspects of the environment which are supportive to positive behaviours and minimise or change those which are negative or resistant.

For example, women's ability to breast-feed their children has required a range of supportive actions, including developing, implementing and monitoring codes of marketing among the manufacturers of breast-milk substitutes; promoting maternity entitlements; creating environments where breast-feeding is encouraged and supported, at home, in the community and at work; and ensuring support for mothers within the health services.

The need for a more comprehensive approach has recently been discussed by Sweat and Denison in the context of HIV/AIDS programmes:

> The typical theoretical approach to AIDS prevention is based largely on individual psychology. Prevention programs frequently attempt to motivate people to reduce their risk behaviour, or maintain low-risk behaviour, through persuasion. Education, information, counselling, HIV testing and other services are provided to influence individual psychological processes that appear likely to produce changes in behaviour . . . while it is important to target the individual in attempting to prevent AIDS, a more comprehensive approach, including interventions on the structural and environmental level, may allow the effectiveness of prevention programs to expand beyond that realised from only individualistic approaches.
>
> (Sweat and Denison, 1995: S 251-257)

Conventional strategies which focus on the individual, therefore, need to be underpinned by more broad-based programming, which research and address the wide range of determinants in the individual's environment. Such "enabling" strategies intend to remove barriers or constraints to positive action or, conversely, to erect barriers or constraints to risk-taking and harmful behaviour. A combination of approaches is therefore necessary to promote the individual's capacity for action within a supportive environment. Box 1 makes the important distinction between the different levels of intervention, as represented in this book's model, which combine to motivate people, to equip them with the skills to change their behaviour and to create an environment which enables such change to occur.

The examples in Box 1 illustrate the value of addressing the environment at a structural level, for example, through strengthening of service provision or through advocacy for policy change. They also emphasise the importance of building upon the capacity of individuals themselves to effect change in their circumstances, demonstrating the dynamic relationship between people and their environment. The environment is seen to determine personal behaviour, but at the same time individuals and groups can be empowered to act upon their environment, for example, through the formation of lobbying groups or through collective bargaining to improve the safety of working conditions. Reinforcing the concept of critical thinking skills (as discussed in Chapter 4), this chapter also explores the learning process by which people become objectively aware of the limiting factors in their environment and defines strategies for collectively tackling these factors and gaining more control over their environment.

If there is one underlying current throughout this book, it is the premise that increased participation of client communities in programme development and implementation can considerably enhance programme effectiveness. It is essential to listen to the people for whom interventions are being developed. This seems an obvious principle, but it is all too often left out of the planning

Examples of multi-level strategies for HIV/AIDS programmes

Client group	Motivating strategies	Life skills promoting strategies	Enabling strategies
Youth	Motivational films, stories on safe sex	Life skills education on assertiveness and negotiation for safe sex	Provision of condoms by health services
Sex Workers	Peer drama troupes demonstrating how to persuade clients to use condoms	Support for collective bargaining to improve safety of working conditions	Health checks and services for sex workers; regulation of brothel operations
Injecting Drug Users	Peer outreach work	Development of support groups	Syringe and needle exchange schemes

Author, adapted from Gordon, 1996:7

process. Involving clients in design, planning, implementation and evaluation must be central to determining a programme's scope and priorities. We often underestimate clients' capacities for identifying barriers to development, even those underlying causes which seem so far from their immediate, day-to-day experience. Community members, better than anyone else, understand the obstacles which make it difficult or even impossible for them to do what is best for their own or their children's health and development. Theirs should be the first, not the last, voice to be heard. They need to be helped and supported to identify ways to turn their frustration into positive societal change.

While broad categories for environmental factors can be defined, the constellation of factors which surrounds each individual or community will be unique in the way that it affects their capacity for behavioural change. Some environmental factors may be relatively easy to impact upon for positive change. In more extreme situations, such as war, civil conflict or emergencies, which are inherently unsafe and unhealthy environments, the room for manoeuvre is severely curtailed.

Service-provision might be considered as one factor which is tackled most frequently, and with greatest vigour, by various organisations. As a result, we have seen many positive changes occurring in this rapidly evolving field. When we look at the more difficult factors to influence, such as economic, political, or cultural factors, there is the danger of feeling that we can do little to influence such fundamental issues. This chapter offers some examples of practical action which development programmes have been able to take.

There is a great need to advocate for more comprehensive approaches, since a critical area of change is in the perceptions and attitudes of development professionals, themselves, and in the support they receive within their organisations. In the current aid climate, organisations are recognising the need to streamline their structures, focus their energies and develop core skills. Through building partnerships with other organisations, it is still possible to establish comprehensive programmes. Rather than one organisation trying to move on all fronts, it may be more efficient to form coalitions, where different organisations tackle different strategic issues, which together create a more enabling environment.

Analysing the environment

There are two major dimensions of the environment to consider, that overlap and are interrelated. The first refers to the "immediate environment" of parents and family, friends and community members, where interpersonal communication is the major influence on behaviour. Then there are those factors in the "wider environment", such as culture and religion, health and education systems, news and entertainment media, which both influence and are influenced by pervading social values.

The Behaviour Development and Change Model (see below) reflects these two influences. The wider environmental factors are placed on the outer circle, encompassing all, while the immediate environment of family, peers and community are placed at the heart of the model. The preceding chapters have all discussed in some form the issue of people's personal relationships: Chapter 1 looked at different behavioural models which explain the interaction between individuals and the people in their immediate environment; Chapter 3 showed how such community networks can be used to reach and motivate individuals; Chapter 4 illustrated the life skills needed to deal constructively and assertively in family, peer and community relationships.This chapter, therefore, focuses in more detail on those aspects of the wider environment which influence and constrain behaviour choices. These include: policy and legislation; service provision; education systems; cultural factors; religion; socio-political factors; socioeconomic factors; and the physical environment. While each factor is discussed separately, in programming terms they need

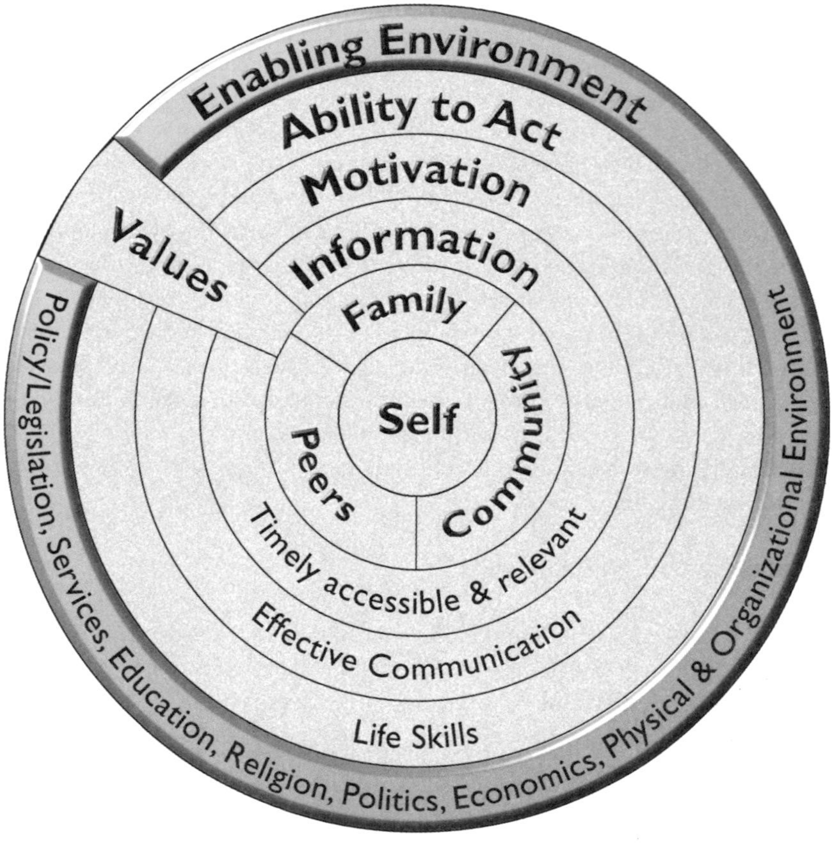

to be addressed in an integrated way, reflecting the manner in which they relate to a specific issue.

In analysing each factor, a general overview is followed by examples of specific interventions. These serve both to inspire us that change is possible and to remind us of the complexities involved. When designing a programme, selecting which factors need to be addressed differs according to client needs and perspectives, as well as programme goals. The list presented here is by no means exhaustive. Nor are the factors independent – in fact most of them are interrelated and inextricable linked. The various examples indicate how a programme overtly tackling one area, may also impact on others. For example, credit programmes for women, addressing their economic needs, inevitably affect gender relations in shifting the power balance between men and women.

The discussion of the range of factors centres on the environments of people for whom programmes are designed. However, the section on the organisational environment, placed after the eight other factors, takes an inward look at the environment of development programmers themselves (i.e. of the government department, development agency or NGO). Programmers also operate in a working environment which can either support or inhibit innovation. Without such support, it is difficult for them to initiate change in their working practices, especially in large organisations. We are all aware of constraining and supportive factors in our own organisations. This section emphasises how an enabling environment at our own work-place is the starting point in our quest for better practice.

Part II: Key factors in the environment

Policy and legislation

Introduction

In many countries the plethora of parallel projects by governments, NGOs and other agencies may fail to achieve their potential impact at the macro level if they are not delivered within a consistent policy environment, which achieves synergy through coordinated action. The efforts of individual programmes can ultimately only be sustained and expanded when underpinned by supportive policy and legislation. Such legislation must also be held by the political will to enforce its provisions. Development organisations have a crucial role to play through advocacy in strengthening this political commitment.

Global starting points

The importance of providing individuals with a safe, supportive and enabling environment is well-recognised in the following global declarations and conventions:

- Universal Declaration of Human Rights
- Convention on the Rights of the Child
- Convention on the Elimination of All Forms of Discrimination against Women

Similar principles have also been promoted through global initiatives, including:

- World Conference on Education for All (Jomtien, 1990)
- National Action Plans following the World Summit for Children (1991)
- International Conference on Population and Development (Cairo, 1994)
- Fourth World Conference on Women (Beijing, 1995)
- Habitat II (Istanbul, 1996)

The support that children, young people, women and men need, in order to behave in health promoting ways, has been defined as a basic human right. Governments and civil societies therefore have an obligation to see that the words of these internationally-adopted conventions and resolutions are turned into action and upheld by law. These conventions and conferences make key contributions to creating a supportive environment at global advocacy levels. However, at national level it is important to recognise that there is often a gap between what is legislated and what is actually enforced. Nearly all countries are signatories to the Convention on the Rights of the Child (CRC) but nevertheless children around the world continue to have their basic rights ignored and undermined. Similarly, despite many signatories to the Convention on the Elimination of All Forms of Discrimination against Women (CEDAW), discrimination and inequities based on gender continue to abound.

The reality is that such broad-based Conventions have only been adopted at a theoretical level in many societies. Many governments have ratified them through international advocacy and pressure, not through a belief that they can or must enact their provisions immediately. There has been much criticism of such "jumping on the bandwagon" in order not to be seen as a bad guy on the international scene. However, there is another side to this issue. If a country ratifies an international convention through international pressure, it can, thereafter, be held accountable, and the power of advocacy for the enactment of the convention's provisions may increase. In other words, if international and national lobbyists can succeed in getting governments to pass important social laws and social policies, they can then use such legislation for leverage, even if it will actually take years for all the provisions to be implemented.

"Education for all"

Leverage and momentum has been gained as a result of the declaration of universal primary education made by many governments since the World Conference on Education for All in Jomtien, Thailand, in 1990. A number of countries declared primary education as "free for all", and passed legislation for this, long before they were ready to receive the flood of new pupils. They judged that the only way to make an accelerated leap forward was to put pressure on the system all at once. Few people in those countries believed that it would be possible to accommodate all children at once, but the declaration put pressure on the system to find solutions.

Of course, if parents send their children to schools with rundown facilities, where teachers lack support, training and motivation, they may pull them out immediately, thereby frustrating the goal of universal education. On the other hand, the legislation may give parents the voice and the authority they previously lacked to demand change at the local level. If the right leadership and organisational conditions are engendered, they might band together with other parents in building or rebuilding a school facility or in demanding better standards of teaching. In other words, such policy change can spark change at the local level. Programmers can help this process by ensuring local people are aware of relevant national policy and legislation and are supported in finding a voice and role to play in making these policies a reality for their community.

The policy has also facilitated the growth of the non-formal education sector to meet the needs of those students not reached by the formal sector. However, the challenge in many regions is still daunting. In some countries, such as Uganda, the declaration of "Education for All" was met with such an overwhelming response, that the education system has had to take a step back and plan for a more systematic phasing in of universal primary education.

Health policy

There are many more examples of social policy and legislation for specific health concerns. Following advocacy by local breast-feeding coalitions, supported by international agencies, many countries have enacted policy and legislation over the past 15 years to ban inappropriate advertising of breast-milk substitutes. With complementary initiatives in the health services and in communication, these policies have created a supportive environment for mothers. It is only today, in the face of evidence that about 15 percent of HIV-positive mothers transmit infection to their babies through breast-milk, that this strong policy and legislative framework is beginning to crack, in spite of evidence that the environmental hygiene risks to the child fed on milk powder are usually higher. However, this example does highlight the need to be responsive in advocacy and communication work to the changing environment.

Another example of health policy development with the accompanying legal framework is the programme for universal salt iodization. People suffer from goitres, cretinism and mental retardation in many developing countries because of the lack of iodine in their diets. Beginning in the early 1980s, a movement began to iodize all salt destined for human consumption by the year 2000. Once again, advocacy with appropriate government ministries and departments by UNICEF, WHO and other agencies, led to the passage of the proper policy and legislation, followed by the development of guidelines for salt producers and importers.

The development of policy and laws did not lead to changes overnight, however. It has taken a decade or more to sensitise government regulators, salt producers and importers; to install the equipment to iodize salt; to develop and implement communication campaigns in countries where there are many sources of salt (including cross-border smuggling), or where there were taboos and beliefs against iodization. This work would have been made much more difficult without the policy and legal framework to back it up.

Another, and perhaps more difficult issue, lies in the area of sanitation. To many people, sanitation and hygiene practices are seen as a private affair. However, legislation has been enacted to prevent people's sanitary habits from affecting the health of others. Public Health Acts only came into practice with industrialisation and urbanisation in the North. They have yet to be fully enacted and enforced in the South.

In the area of environmental hygiene, a debate has often been heard concerning the role of legislation. Some say it is possible to legislate behaviour change, that is, to enforce bye-laws which will force people to use latrines or for those preparing food for public consumption to maintain certain standards of cleanliness. However, experience has shown that legislation alone cannot bring about sustained change in this area. It is very difficult for people to change their most private and personal behaviour. The destruction of unsanitary facilities by authorities often only prolongs the problem, or diverts it in another direction. Motivating people through force, alone, on matters of personal and environmental hygiene, will seldom have lasting effects.

By contrast, legislation and its effective enforcement have been a crucial component of road safety programmes. With meaningful sanctions imposed, drivers in many societies now generally comply with speed limits and permitted levels of alcohol consumption, as well as the compulsory use of seat-belts.

Bottom-up policy change

The example of the anti-smoking legislation provides another interesting case. In the North, many lobby groups are at work to promote policy and legislation which will inhibit the freedom of people to smoke in public and decrease the growth of the smoking habit, especially amongst young people. To a large extent, especially in North America, this lobby has been successful. Their advocacy has increased limits on public places where smoking is permitted. The change in attitudes and legislation on smoking is an example of policy change being initiated from the bottom up. It has been the work of anti-smoking campaigners which has won the dramatic change in government policy and public behaviour in many industrialised countries.

In advertising, tobacco manufacturers have been forced by governments to provide counter-marketing messages on their own products, stating that they are harmful to health. In some countries they have been prohibited from advertising on television and radio, the most popular channels for targeting youth. However, tobacco manufacturers continue to find ways to promote their products, for example through sports sponsorship, although some governments are also attempting to crack down on this too.

With the increasing restrictions in the North, however, tobacco manufacturers are turning more of their attention and resources to the South, where there are still very few restrictions on advertising and where the population is becoming increasingly youthful and open to influence. The international health lobby has not yet gathered enough energy and resources to advocate for policy and legislation that will help to counter the rapid increase of smoking in the South and, as it stands, this will be one of the major causes of death and disability in the developing world in the years to come. Policy and legislation are urgently needed to help develop the enabling environment under which anti-smoking communication campaigns and counselling services can flourish. However, a number of developing countries have tagged their economies to tobacco production, making it doubly hard for them to change. This issue relates to the later discussion on the global economic environment.

Barriers to implementation

Many of the above cases do not tell the whole story. Policy and legislative change is very difficult to engender on many social issues, especially those which run counter to traditional practices and beliefs. For instance, governments around the world have ratified CEDAW, the Convention on the Elimination of all forms of Discrimination Against Women, yet continue to allow many forms of discrimination to persist. However, the convention does provide a position for leverage by agencies and social groups concerned with women's rights. A later section on cultural factors explores these gender issues in more detail.

Conclusion

There are many examples of effective development of policy and legislation in the creation of an enabling environment for change. In fact, in many instances, getting new policies passed has been relatively easy. More difficult has been effectively implementing their provisions. As such, policy and the development of national laws can usually only provide a framework for change, except in relatively clear examples, easily enforced by the authorities, such as the enactment and enforcement of car seat belt legislation.

We may want to force change through legislation but it is often the cultural values, as well as the socio-political and socio-economic forces which inhibit change in any society, or, conversely, provide an opportunity for change. And so we now turn our attention to these other arenas.

Service provision

Introduction

No matter what we do to give people clear and accurate information, to motivate them to change existing practices or to adopt an innovation, and to assist them in developing the skills needed for positive change, our efforts will be largely in vain unless there is a commensurate improvement in the quality of services made available to support such behaviours. Such services include health and education provision, safe water supply, sanitation facilities and waste disposal, and agricultural extension services. These services need to be affordable and accessible, and of a standard to meet the needs of the client community. As the illustration of the "Education for All" policy showed, service delivery factors must be tackled in conjunction with policy and legislative change.

Delivering appropriate, accessible and affordable services is an essential element of creating an enabling environment for behaviour development and change. Some of the best lessons learnt have been derived from the programme areas of sexual and reproductive health and the delivery of youth-friendly services.

Sexual and reproductive health

Too often service provision has concentrated on numbers reached as opposed to the quality of service offered. This is evident in the case of family planning programmes in developing countries which have, historically, focused on quantitative goals, especially increasing contraceptive use, in order to reduce fertility rates. Today, there is an evident shift in focus from the numbers of individuals reached to qualitative measurements of service provision (Finger, 1993:10).

The need for qualitative improvement is very apparent in the field of sexual and reproductive health where there is often a great deal of resistance to using available services. Throughout the developing world, relatively few people with STIs utilise the formal sector for health care. Communities often regard formal health services as inadequate and difficult to access, providing services of poor quality, with long delays for attention and with a lack of privacy, confidentiality and sensitivity in dealing with patients with STIs. Women may want to be examined by a female doctor (and, in some countries, are obliged to do so by regulations). However, female doctors may not be available, particularly in rural areas.

A 1991 study in Chile reported that the most important element of service provision for women clients was "being treated like a human being". The cleanliness at the facility, adequate time spent with a staff person and encouragement to learn about their own health were some of the main criteria listed by clients (Vera, 1993:11).

Several new initiatives to improve the quality of family planning and sexual and reproductive health programmes focus on clients' needs and encourage staff members to work together in identifying problems and solving them themselves. A case study from a family planning clinic in Kenya showed how the staff team used a quality improvement method adapted from business techniques, called Total Quality Management, to review and reorganise the way they offer services. They visualised the service delivery processes using tools such as graphs and flow charts, so that as a team, they could evaluate their progress (Blaney, 1993:14).

In 1990, the Population Council set out a six-point framework for assessing the quality of care in family planning services (see Box 2).

2 Framework for the quality of care

1. ***Choice of contraceptive methods*** which includes the number and types of choices available for various groups;

2. ***Information given to clients*** which includes appropriate choice of methods, how to use the method and possible side effects;

3. ***Technical competence*** such as maintaining aseptic conditions, observing protocols and competent staff;

4. ***Interpersonal relations*** which refers to how the client perceives interaction with providers;

5. ***Mechanisms to cover continuity*** such as reminder cards and home visits;

6. ***Appropriate constellation of services,*** given that clients need convenient and acceptable services, this may mean integrating family planning with other reproductive health services such as maternal and child health or postpartum services.

Bruce, 1990:12

Central to quality improvement in service provision is the participation of clients in identifying needs and the team work of the staff in providing solutions.

Youth-friendly services

A growing area of concern throughout the world is that of youth health and development. In addition to a greater emphasis on developing young people's life skills to make safe and healthy behavioural choices, there is a parallel push to make services more "youth-friendly" – more accessible and relevant to young people's needs.

People between the ages of 10 and 19 currently constitute 20 percent of the world's population and the United Nations estimates that their numbers will grow by another 20 percent over the next 15 years (United Nations, 1994). In other words, the world's population is growing younger and younger. Ironically, little attention has been paid to this age bracket until recently. While international agencies, donors, governments and NGOs have spent a great deal of attention and resources in providing services to the adult population and to children, adolescents were not clearly segmented or targeted for special attention. It was assumed that they were being adequately reached through other service provision programmes.

However, it is now evident that young people have special needs which require special approaches. They are more vulnerable, in many ways, to health and development threats such as HIV/AIDS and STIs, unwanted pregnancies, sexual abuse, substance abuse, violence and suicide. People under 25 constitute about half of all HIV infections and up to 60 percent of new infections in developing countries occur in the 15-24 age bracket, with females outnumbering males two to one (Weiss *et al*, 1996: 3).

Attempts to reach young people with services, including counselling and supplies, through channels designed for adults often fail because of the "unfriendly" or "judgmental" attitude of the service providers. Unless such providers are willing to change their attitudes and their way of interacting with adolescents, the young people will simply avoid further contact and remain at risk. A recent study in Zambia noted: "Young people fear nurses and consider them to be unfriendly and lacking in any confidentiality. Secrecy and confidentiality appear to be major factors for young people, who tend to seek treatment with private clinics and traditional healers, away from the public space of the clinic environment." (Webb, 1997)

There are now a number of programmes designed to address this gap through youth-friendly clinics. Typically, they are run by NGOs or municipal governments. Several models are evolving, located in youth centres and health centres, or, increasingly, through outreach programmes in the community and work-place. There is a recognition of the essential importance of youth participation in the planning, implementation and monitoring of activities. Young people and health staff work together to design messages and materials to popularise the services. There is also a growing reliance on peer education for providing information and condom supplies, particularly when contacting difficult-to-reach populations, such as street children, young mothers out-of-school, and sex workers. Peer educators act as a bridge between young people and the health service providers.

Evidence from a number of countries indicates that outreach programmes using peer promoters are less costly and more effective than fixed centres in both HIV/AIDS and reproductive health programmes. Furthermore, young people prefer peer counsellors and educators to adults, and peer educators appear to be more effective in this role (Senderowitz, 1997).

There are a number of successful case studies in the area of youth sexual and reproductive health. Examples, such as the Jamaica Women's Centre, illustrate the potential for providing fresh educational and vocational opportunities to pregnant or parenting young women, while helping them to avoid further pregnancies. This project in Jamaica has now expanded to seven main centres and 13 rural outreach centres. Recently, additional activities designed to delay first pregnancy have been added, including academic sessions and family planning counselling out of school hours.

The evaluation of this project has indicated excellent results. Between 55 percent and 73 percent of recent graduates from the centres had returned to school, compared to only 15 percent in the control group. Only 8 to 15 percent of graduates, compared to 39 percent of the control group, had repeated pregnancies (McNeil *et al*, 1990).

In the past decade, there have been rich lessons learned in delivering adolescent-friendly services. Some of these are detailed in Box 3.

3 ***Lessons learned in running youth-friendly services***

- **Strategic approach** – design activities which are practically, financially and politically feasible. Start with research and findings of others. Start with a solid plan but remain flexible.
- **Target audience identification** – the prime target group according to demographic data – such as age, marital status, whether sexually-active, gender, residence, in or out-of-school – should be selected to correspond to the overall strategic objectives (e.g. linked to HIV prevalence rates).
- **Needs assessment** – to be conducted with precise target groups.
- **Youth involvement** – not only for needs assessment and determining programme strategies, but to foster "ownership" of the programme's goals. Peer education has proved particularly effective.
- **Community involvement** — starting with the planning stage to help explain objectives and win support for the programme, thereby reducing the risk of opposition once the programme begins. The "community" here may include policy makers and religious leaders who may need special attention and involvement.
- **Parental involvement** – from the beginning to reduce the risk of opposition and to involve them in playing an active and supportive role.
- **Evaluation and monitoring** – for designing the programme (formative), for adjusting the programme (process or monitoring), and for measuring impact (summative or impact). Staff and peer leaders should play a part in the evaluation. Base line information will be needed for impact evaluations. Service statistics are essential for monitoring progress. Feedback opportunities for staff and clients are essential.

Senderowitz, 1997.

Conclusion

The lessons learnt from these two areas of health service delivery can also be applied to other sectors with other client groups. The increasing push by donors towards user-fees and privatization of social services has, in some ways, increased the user-friendliness of those services. People will not access services which they feel do not fulfil their needs, which are not efficient and friendly, especially if they have to reach into their pocket to pay for them and if they have choice of service points to make.

However, with the effects of structural adjustment programmes, the challenge to many countries is to maintain social services for the poorest of the poor – those most hit by such policies. Many governments are struggling for ways of simply maintaining the most basic of services. The development of a strategic alliance between donors, governments, NGOs, the private sector and the clients themselves in the delivery of services provides some hope for the future.

Education systems

Introduction: Do schools empower or oppress?

Although education is part of service provision, it merits a separate discussion, given its formative role in determining people's behavioural patterns.

For those who have been to school, their educational experience is probably the most significant determinant of the way in which they receive, process and use information. Many examples exist, as described in Chapter 4, of educational initiatives which promote the development of life skills, including the capacity for critical thinking, decision making and problem solving. In this light, such education systems can be seen to develop the capacity of people to work proactively within and upon their environment for constructive change. The key to this transformation lies in the quality of the educational process. The way in which the learner experiences the learning process can either encourage or inhibit positive behavioural development and change. However, while globally many education systems are working actively to improve the quality of teaching, it remains a fact that the majority of educational environments serve only to promote passivity in learners.

A bleak but influential view of this educational approach was taken by Paulo Freire who characterised it as a "pedagogy of oppression" (Freire, 1973). He sensed that such forms of education can keep people locked in a closed world in a "culture of silence". In this context, education becomes a series of facts passed on from the "knowledgeable" teacher to the "ignorant" student through rote learning. This follows what Freire called the "banking concept" of education, whereby teachers believe their role is to "fill" their students with knowledge. Education suffers from "narration sickness". "Narration leads the students to memorise mechanically the narrated content. Worse still, it turns them into containers, into receptacles to be filled by the teacher." (Freire, 1973: 45) Despite recognition of this "sickness" and widespread attempts to regenerate the education system, the prevailing approach still represents the very antithesis to our vision of the empowerment of individuals for positive behavioural development:

> The dominant model of education in the world today is one of information transfer in which the teacher possesses the knowledge which he or she then passes on by a variety of means, modern or otherwise, to the learner."
>
> (Macdonald, 1993:140-141)

Where the education system itself is rigid and autocratic, from the style of management at the top, down to delivery in the classroom, it may appear resistant to change. The way society is organised can be reflected and reinforced by the way people are educated: either enforcing acquiescence within a hierarchy or, conversely, encouraging a democratic openness and questioning. However, education systems can be mobilized to challenge social norms and become a catalyst in changing the way people think and behave. For instance, educational initiatives in the North promoting citizenship education aim to help young people gain a sense of community responsibility, challenging pervasive individualism. Educational reform is possible, albeit slow and incremental.

Many sectoral programmes, particularly in health, water and sanitation, and agriculture, seek to use school systems as a key channel for disseminating their messages. However, such information will likely remain unused unless the learning process encourages enquiry and innovation. Outreach will also be limited unless more students are retained in the school system. Two key issues therefore govern the potential of the education system to contribute to creating an enabling environment. The first relates to the continuing quest for improving quality in teaching; the second to increasing access to and retention in schools.

Issues of quality in education

The 1990 World Conference on Education for All helped to mobilize international political will to view education in terms of the quality of delivery, not just the quantity of students enrolled. It was recognised that education must address the basic needs of the majority of students who will not graduate beyond primary school. The quality of teaching must be improved to ensure that children enjoy and benefit from the process of learning. Education has to become a joyful rather than an alienating experience for children. This builds an essential foundation for life, whereby knowledge is seen as accessible to individuals and regarded as both a useful tool and an enduring pleasure. For this transformation to be effected, teachers need to feel more valued and to have better pre-service training and in-service support.

Quality also relates to the relevance of the curriculum. Relevance can be assessed in relation to **context** and **needs** (Hawes, 1990). As argued in this chapter as a whole, education strategies cannot be designed in isolation from the environment in which people learn. Nor can a curriculum be designed without reference to the needs of the learners. We need to ask "whose needs" are being met by the curriculum. Education must be perceived by children and their parents as encompassing skills required in their own lives. In essence, learning must be child-centred, related to their own lives and environment, so that they can contribute their own experiences to an active process of learning, rather than becoming passive recipients of (possibly irrelevant) information. Through this active process, education helps individuals to understand the environment in which they exist, but also to analyse the part which they have to play in challenging and perhaps changing the constraining factors in that environment.

Within one country, even within one community, the context and educational needs of different groups of children and adults will vary greatly. Consider the child who is a domestic servant; the child who lives on the street; the girl who has a heavy burden of domestic chores; the adolescent boy who never went to school; the child of a farmer who may farm himself; the child of a doctor who may become a doctor herself. Each has different learning needs and different opportunities for study. Thus the conclusions of the Jomtien conference called for flexible, complementary but varied approaches within a unified national policy for basic education. The formal education system can be complemented by non-formal programmes which can have more flexibility to meet the needs of specific, perhaps disadvantaged, groups of learners.

Models of success in addressing these questions of quality need to be promoted. These initiatives often centre on upgrading teachers' skills and enhancing their status and self-confidence. A model of a flexible, cost-effective approach is the Escuela Nueva programme in Colombia. "This successful programme, bringing education to rural areas since 1975, allows children to be absent in peak agricultural periods; promotes practical problem-solving rather than learning by rote; and reduces costs by allowing one teacher to cover five grades in small rural schools with the help of elected student leaders." (UNICEF, 1997)

Another such model is found in Bangladesh, where the Bangladesh Rural Advancement Committee (BRAC) and a wide range of other NGOs offer non-formal education to children and adults from various disadvantaged groups in both urban and rural settings. In some cases the non-formal programme offers a basic education tailored to the specific needs of its learners, such as numeracy, literacy and legal awareness for working children. In other programmes, children are given the opportunity to study in a more flexible learning environment and thereby to "catch-up" and re-enter the formal system.

Access and retention

The Convention on the Rights of the Child insists that primary education must be universal. Yet today it is estimated that 140 million children between 6 and 11 years do not attend school. This represents 23 percent of primary school aged children in the South. It is also estimated that an equal number of children drop out of school early. Moreover, two-thirds of those children out of school are girls. (UNICEF, 1997: 48-52)

Initiatives in the formal and non-formal sector are bringing schools physically closer to children, through small, multi-grade classes or single class non-formal schools. Efforts, such as the recruitment of more female teachers for primary schools, have also had a demonstrable impact on closing the gender gap in enrolment of girls. Gender sensitivity, both in the learning materials and in teacher attitudes, is also central to the retention of girls in school. In many non-formal contexts, the teachers are recruited from the local community to increase their sensitivity to the learners' situation. Increasingly, schools are also recognising the importance of involving parents, particularly mothers, in the life of the school, to promote the attendance of girls.

At the heart of the issue is the financial cost of education, both to families and to the nation. Even where primary education is ostensibly free, families may face a daunting range of costs for uniforms, books, transport and "extra-tuition", in addition to the perceived lost opportunity costs of the child's labour. Primary education must be made free to all children. But such commitment, backed by investment in infrastructure and in qualitative improvement, requires vast resources to be mobilized by aid donors internationally and by national governments themselves. There is evidence that a higher priority is now being given to the funding of basic education, but this must be seen in the light of overall declining aid budgets, structural adjustment programmes and the overwhelming debt burden carried by developing countries.

Conclusion

The education system provides the most crucial point of interface between individuals and their environment. A positive educational experience can prepare people to participate in creating a more supportive environment, in redefining the terms on which they live. For example, disadvantaged groups, who have learnt about the rights to equality before the law, can work individually or collectively to challenge social practice and to lobby for changes in policy and legislation. In terms of programming for an "enabling environment", investment in education becomes the central priority, for education opens the way for people themselves to influence their environment and widen their options for action.

Cultural factors

Introduction

In development programmes the role of culture is often ignored, for example, in analyses of social change which take a purely economic and political perspective. In other instances, where the influence of culture is acknowledged, it is still considered to be either sacrosanct (in representing a "unique" traditional culture) or immutable, and certainly not within the domain of the development programmer. However, as this book's model suggests, cultural values form the overriding determinant of behaviour, which cuts across all other factors. People's behaviour is guided by their personal values, governed by the pervading cultural values of their social group.

A holistic approach to creating a supportive environment recognises the complexity and interrelationship of the various factors determining behaviour, of which culture plays a very significant and influential part. In this section we will review examples of how programmers, in partnership with their client communities, have been enabled to step back objectively and identify ways of working positively with cultural forces.

The first question to be asked is: What do we mean by culture? A useful definition is offered by the South Commission, a group of distinguished world leaders and development experts:

> Culture (can be) viewed as a sum total of values, beliefs, attitudes, customs and patterns of behaviour in a given society . . . .
>
> (South Commission, 1990)

For our discussion, we can adopt a working definition of "culture" as a set of values and practices shared by a group. The domain of such a culture is therefore determined by the number of people or communities who identify with and subscribe to its shared set of values and practices. This results in layers of cultures and subcultures within a single society.

Culture as dynamic not fixed

It is then equally important to stress that most people do not experience culture as a single, homogenous force. With societies in constant transition, culture becomes a dynamic element, shifting between the tensions of "traditional" and "modern" values, between "indigenous" and "global" values. As has been discussed in the previous chapter, young people, in particular, may experience plural cultures. Their parents' values may be in direct conflict with those of their peers.

It is therefore important that we do not make generalised assumptions about the cultural influences on people's behaviour. We need to look more closely at the culture or subculture with which the specific group most closely identifies. This may be affected by age, sex and socioeconomic class and other variables. Only by working through participatory processes can we establish how each individual or group experiences cultural pressures. By considering a particular behaviour, people can identify what in their cultural environment is:

- supportive and can be built on;
- neutral and can be lived with;
- harmful and needs to be overcome or circumvented.

To enable people to analyse their culture in this way gives them a significant sense of objective distance, and hence a measure of control, over those perceived cultural obstacles in their lives. They can also come to recognise those cultural forces which would be supportive to the changes they wish to make.

The agreed set of values and practices, which constitute a culture, is, therefore, not static, but depends upon the consensus of the group. Over time people collectively can and do change their cultures. Programmes which seek to address cultural issues need to analyse the forces at work and tap into this evolutionary process. As the South Commission observed:

> It is only by the affirmation and enrichment of cultural identities through mass participation that development can be given strong roots and made a sustained process.
>
> (South Commission, 1990)

People's participation in affirming positive and challenging less positive cultural forces is therefore central to the development process. From a planning perspective, however, this evolution is gradual and incremental and occurs over many programme cycles. There is no quick fix solution. This long-term process must be reflected in the evaluation design.

The theory and practice around gender and development provide a number of useful tools for addressing the broader cultural environment. Gender is one of the key and recurring dimensions of culture which impact on all aspects of programming and will provide a concrete focus for our discussion.

Culture and gender

Behavioural norms based on gender stereotypes are embedded in all cultures. Gender-based discrimination, evidenced in a range of harmful attitudes and practices, is prevalent in most societies. Many programmes seek to bring gender issues into the mainstream of development work and some also address the most damaging practices, such as female genital mutilation (see Box 4) and violence against girls and women. The Beijing World Conference on Women, in its Declaration and Platform for Action, observed:

> Girls are often treated as inferior and are socialised to put themselves last, thus undermining their self-esteem. Discrimination and neglect in childhood can initiate a lifelong downward spiral of deprivation and exclusion from the social mainstream.
>
> (United Nations, 1996: 145-146)

Both the cultural practices to which girls are subjected and the socialisation process which confines them to their gender roles, serve to perpetuate these discriminatory attitudes, which are also reflected in girls' and women's self image.

As with other environmental factors, far-reaching impact will depend on identifying and working with allies within the society. The building of alliances will be successful if it works on many levels: governments and international agencies, NGOs and human rights groups, the media, and community-level activists. Women's advocacy has put gender-based violence on the international human rights agenda. To deal with the many forms of

4 *Female genital mutilation*

Female genital mutilation (FGM) provides a powerful example where programmes are trying to tackle one of the most culturally charged issues of today. For many years, development programmers have been hesitant in entering this cultural minefield. Early attempts by some governments aimed to limit the health risks, through a medicalisation of the procedures (having the operation conducted by medics in sterile conditions). However, this could be interpreted as giving a "green light" to communities. (Dorkenoo, 1995: 10) Women's groups, working within their own cultures, have advocated for a direct challenge to the culture of FGM. In 1982, WHO issued a policy statement saying that under no circumstances should FGM be performed by a medical practitioner. FGM was increasingly being recognised as a source of major psychological trauma, not solely of physical risk. There is now growing international awareness and legislation by governments, accompanied by advocacy from political leaders. For example, the late head of state of Burkina Faso, Thomas Sankara, made a statement which linked FGM to the inferior status of women in society:

> It shows an attempt to confer an inferior status on women by branding them with this mark which diminishes them and is a constant reminder to them that they are only women, inferior to men, that they do not even have any rights over their own bodies or fulfilment either bodily or personal.
>
> (Sankara quoted in Dorkenoo, 1995:54-55)

However, legislation and political support has to be met by a radical shift in the cultural valuing of FGM within communities.

violence against women and girls, action will also need to be taken in a number of different spheres – in legislation and its enforcement, in service provision, in education for legal awareness, in access to legal aid and protection, and in the media.

It is evident that issues such as violence against women can also be tackled indirectly by working to meet women's other gender needs, thereby challenging their subordinate position in society. Greater equity can be achieved and the worst manifestations of gender discrimination confronted, if women are enabled to achieve greater economic self-reliance. This is discussed in greater detail in the section on economic factors.

In terms of gender planning, there is a wide body of experience and literature now which provides concepts and tools for use in analysing gender roles and needs. One such model distinguishes between women's practical and strategic needs:

> Programmers need to approach such sensitive cultural issues, first and foremost, as listeners: We must always work from the assumption that human behaviours and cultural values, however senseless or destructive they may look to us from our particular personal and cultural standpoints, have meaning and fulfil a function for those who practise them. People will change their behaviour only when they themselves perceive the new practices proposed as meaningful and functional as the old ones.
>
> (WHO, 1994)

UNICEF's Sara Communication Initiative for the adolescent girl in Eastern and Southern Africa (see Chapter 4), has researched attitudes and produced materials on FGM. Through focus group discussions, communities aired their views on the issue and identified any positive elements related to the practice. Many believed that, as a rite of passage, the ceremonies as a whole gave a sense of cultural identity to young people and provided a form of family life education to young girls. People were aware of the negative impact on the girls' and women's health, yet girls highlighted the anxiety caused by resisting the practice individually, since an uncircumcised girl may be mocked and considered potentially unmarriageable within her community.

The debate in the focus groups centred on whether it was possible to reject the negative while retaining the positive elements of this rite of passage. People also considered who would be the most likely and effective initiators of change within the community as a whole. The Sara film and books reflect these research findings, and seek to stimulate debate on FGM at community level and also advocate for greater support at policy level.

Authors

> Practical gender needs are the needs women identify in their socially accepted roles in society. These needs do not challenge, although they arise out of, gender divisions of labour and women's subordinate position in society. They are a response to immediate perceived necessity . . . They are practical in nature and often concern inadequacies in living conditions such as water provision, health care and employment.
>
> Strategic gender needs are the needs women identify because of their subordinate position in society. They vary according to particular contexts, related to gender divisions of labour, power and control, and may include such issues as legal rights, domestic violence, equal wages, and women's control over their bodies. Meeting their strategic gender needs assists women to achieve greater equality and change existing roles, thereby challenging women's subordinate position.
>
> (Moser, 1993: 230-231)

This model illustrates the interface between culture and other environmental factors – service provision, legislation, political and economic rights – in the way they collectively impact on gender concerns. Such analytical tools can help both programmers and the communities they work with to gain an objective view of the cultural values and practices in their environment. In strategic terms, they are then better equipped to analyse where the supportive and constraining elements lie. The range of interventions on gender and development indicate that it is possible to take on cultural factors and to mark, over time, perceptible shifts in values and practices.

Culture and mass media

The Beijing report rightly identifies the mass media as being a major contributing factor to perpetuating discriminatory attitudes towards women:

> The continued projection of negative and degrading images of women in media communications – electronic, print, visual and audio – must be changed. Print and electronic media in most countries do not provide a balanced picture of women's diverse lives and contributions to society in a changing world. In addition, violent and degrading or pornographic media products are also negatively affecting women and their participation in society. Programming that reinforces women's traditional roles can be equally limiting.
>
> (United Nations, 1996: 133)

The media has a large and growing influence on the formation of values and attitudes, particularly among children and youth. In countries recently reached by satellite television, exposure to the values of the so-called global culture, through soap opera, music and advertising, is having a dramatic and rapid impact on local culture. In India, it has been noted that the demands for dowry payments have increased in recent years due to rising consumerism, which in large part has been stimulated by exposure to the global media.

The media is certainly a potent agent for changing attitudes, but the impact of the media need not necessarily be negative. The mass media has a central part to play in advocacy and in shaping public opinion and government policy, an influence which can be used constructively. It is possible to work in partnership with the media in identifying topics and helping to shape the values portrayed. The South African soap opera, *Soul City* (see Chapter 3), is an example of just such a partnership. Once again we find that the development of this programme is based on extensive formative research, to tease out the various threads of social and cultural influences which shape people's behaviour. These programmes gain greater impact when reinforced by life skills education to enable people to view media images and advertising with a critical distance.

Conclusion

As with the other factors in this section, the discussion of culture and behavioural change merits a whole book in itself. However, the review of gender programmes offers some general lessons which can be applied more broadly to other aspects of culture. It emphasises the value of a programmer's role as a listener, learning about people's culture through formative research. This insight allows initiatives to tap into the evolutionary process of culture, building on the value and behavioural shifts that communities believe are desirable and possible. Such work can be reinforced by establishing alliances with other agents in society, particularly harnessing the power of the mass media.

However, as culture exists as a set of values and practices shared by a group, change cannot be imposed from without, but will evolve within communities through a participatory process, in which people are enabled to become more objectively conscious and to consider possible transformations.

This finally brings us to the ethical issues which a programmer needs to consider when dealing with cultural issues. Community participants need to be fully conscious that efforts to reform their culture may lead to social disruption. It is they, not the programmer, who carry the risk in challenging their cultural norms. As with the example of FGM, interventions concerned with culture are more appropriate in addressing the community as a whole, on all its levels, rather than isolated, and possibly vulnerable, groups within the community.

Finally it is worth remembering that programmers too, from whatever society, may subscribe to an "international development" culture, their own shared set of values, which could also benefit from a regular, critical scrutiny. In its worst manifestation, this could be portrayed as a sense of cultural superiority, implicit in same policy statements, "particularly when programmes involve 'educating' a 'target population'" (Allen, 1992: 338). Our guard against this is to adopt a listening stance and approach our work with communities as a process of mutual learning.

Religion

Introduction

The discussion of religion clearly has an overlap with our previous review of cultural factors. However, organised religion has such a pervasive and powerful influence on the way people of all cultures live that it merits separate consideration. Like culture, religion is a complex area for programmers to address and is all too often sidestepped.

> Because the subject is ultra-sensitive and emotionally charged, development planners treat religion as a non-subject. At meetings and conferences this subject is virtually taboo in discussions about development. But religion, be it Christianity, Hinduism, Islam, or Buddhism, is an all-pervasive force, whether consciously realized or subconsciously assimilated, in the lives of people everywhere; and as such, it should be considered. Its implications for the success or failure of development projects should be discussed.
>
> (Carroll, 1983: 1)

Religion has controlled and directed human behaviour for millenniums past. It has almost universally, at some point in history, been used as the mainspring of social control and human law. Even with the increasing secularisation of many cultures, religion still often guides the most private aspects of people's lives.

Religion and society

In some cases, religion is associated with the idea of control of the masses. The precepts of original religious texts, many of which contain emancipating concepts, may sometimes appear to be interpreted in a more oppressive light. However, there are progressive and fundamentalist tensions in most religions. As their internal debate demonstrates, religious interpretation is not necessarily static - although the right to interpretation is in itself a central issue. There are examples where religion has worked to reinforce the status quo, but, equally, examples where religion has been a catalyst for radical change. In some contexts, religion has become the language of political dissent and social transformation, as with liberation theology in Latin America and elsewhere.

Liberation theologists took the precepts of the Second Vatican Council in 1965, which gave the Church a clear role to play by asserting that development should go beyond economic equations to embrace a wider view of social and spiritual transformation. Its document, *Gaudium et Spes* (The Church in the Modern World) (Second Vatican Council: 1965:4) created a vision of development as "a painstaking search for a better material world" but also as "a parallel spiritual advancement":

> (The human being) ought therefore to have ready access to all that is necessary for living a genuinely human life: for example, food, clothing, housing, the right freely to choose his state of life and set up a family, the right to education, work, to his good name, to respect, to proper knowledge, the right to act according to the dictates of conscience and to safeguard his privacy, and rightful freedom even in matters of religion."
>
> (Second Vatican Council, 1965:26)

The debate over the Church's role in promoting such a society ranged from traditional concepts of charity – in 'feeding the hungry and clothing the naked' – to more radical versions of transformation for social justice. Liberation theology became more than religious debate, it became an ideology for social change. With the apparent demise of Marxist ideology, liberation theology is now commonly held to be of less relevance, although the principles still inspire the work of many priests working with the world's poorest communities. (Claver, 1995:1-19) In other situations, such as in Myanmar, Buddhist monks are seen to be taking a leading role in campaigning for the respect of human rights.

Finding areas for collaboration

The point for programmers is to find ways of working constructively and in trust with religious forces. It is necessary to identify and support those positive forces within the religious structures. Religious leadership can be, and has been seen to be, responsive to changes in cultural and social attitudes, as illustrated by the ordination of women into the priesthood of some Christian churches.

A case in point is the issue of female genital mutilation and religious interpretation. Religion is often given as the reason for the custom, especially Islam, since most communities which practise FGM are Muslim. These communities may genuinely believe that the custom is demanded by their faith. However, the *Qur'an* itself does not refer to FGM, and the majority of the Muslim world do not follow the practice. In many initiatives on FGM, religious leaders and scholars have now actually become key advocates for change. This illustrates how, far from being an obstacle, religion can become a positive force for transformation. Religious leaders help to interpret and explain the reference made to female circumcision in the Hadith, providing a clear lead to their communities to stop the practice, while basing their teaching on authentic holy texts. They quote how the human body has been created in perfect form and that humans should not alter it. In behavioural change initiatives, where religious belief or tradition is seen to bear influence, the religious hierarchy needs to be involved from the start in discussions on policy and strategy. Local religious leaders also need an opportunity to discuss these issues with scholars. (UNICEF, 1999)

The advent of AIDS and the role of condoms, as a form of protection from HIV, as well as a contraception, has provided a particular challenge to many religious teachings. Religious groups worldwide have wrestled with conflicting moral ethics on this issue. This highly-charged debate has been characterised, in many cases, by a recognition of the genuine moral dilemma and a desire for some flexibility in the face of the devastating threat of AIDS.

Interesting examples also exist where religious leaders have joined the social alliance for promoting child survival issues. Concerns such as immunisation and oral rehydration are generally uncontentious. The value of this collaboration is to offer the authority and coverage of the religious establishment to reach the people. Successful examples of such work include UNICEF's partnership with Muslim leaders in Bangladesh and Egypt. In Bangladesh, local Imams attended training on child survival issues and became an important information source within their communities.

In another example, collaboration with religious leaders and community elders in Uganda sought to reduce the spread of HIV/AIDS by limiting the risk elements of the custom of widow inheritance, whilst incorporating other positive aspects of this traditional practice.

At the individual level, religious belief and association with religious institutions can clearly influence behavioural choices. For example, a review on over 200 research studies in the United States analysed the multiple antecedents of adolescent sexual risk-taking behaviours. The results showed that the level of an adolescent's religiosity or attachment to a religious institution were protective factors, in many studies impacting to delay the initiation of sex or to decrease the number of sexual partners. (Kirby, 1999: 7)

As with our discussion of culture, working with religious forces requires an open-mindedness to listen to people's own perspective on their religious values and customs. In this most sensitive of areas, change can only be initiated from within - within the religious structures and within the individual conscience. As programmers we can work with those elements which are supportive, while encouraging reflection on those which are not. In the final analysis, the central tenets of most religions promote compassion, humanity and a concern for the wellbeing of the poor and vulnerable. It is on this common ground that the seeds of collaboration can take root.

Socio-political factors

Introduction

Bringing about true change to a socio-political system, without outright revolution, is a long term process. In large part, the recent political changes around the world, which have seen one-party states replaced by multiparty democracies, have not been as a result of a grassroots cry for change. The transition has come about because of the end of the Cold War with the collapse of the Soviet Union. Many one-party states in the developing world thereby lost the sustaining support of their Soviet allies. No longer are there two major models to choose from or to play against each other. The free enterprise model has won, for the time being at least. And with that system has come increasing pressure from the IMF, World Bank and other donors for multiparty elections and "good governance" on Western terms.

The term "good governance" includes the principles of popular participation in governance, ensuring full representation of and accountability to the electorate. Good governance also involves respect for the rule of law and for human rights. It allows for the growth of civil society, through organised activity by and representation of groups such as religious bodies, NGOs, trade unions, and traditional councils, which are neither part of government nor profit-making organisations.

While the evidence is mixed on the link between democracy and economic development, the broader concept of good governance is now, in the new development orthodoxy, commonly linked to issues of poverty alleviation. This premise suggests that for shared economic prosperity, a society needs a level of stability and confidence to encourage investment and a degree of pluralism and participation to fulfil the potential of its population.

Within the new socio-political environment, social change may, arguably, be more feasible. Political reform has, however, come at a price to some. For example, the people of the former Soviet Union may welcome their new found political freedom, but the poor and vulnerable may regret the passing of the socialist security net.

While there is relatively little that the development programmer – especially ones working outside of their own country – can or should do directly to influence the political environment at the macro level, they need to recognise that the political context will dominate the scope and direction of their work. The same applies for the client communities involved in development programmes. In the most extreme scenarios, political unrest or revolution can partially or wholly disrupt development programmes. In areas of conflict, communities may be internally displaced or forced out of the country as refugees. Development programmes are interrupted and emergency programmes begin.

Development organisations will often attempt to influence the socio-political climate, at a range of levels. Apart from direct project activities, many agencies have given long-standing support to socio-political movements – such as land reform or the abolition of child labour – which may not be about quantifiable objectives, but rather are concerned with advocacy to create a climate of opinion for governments to take political action. At a different level, support is often given to promote local government and to give local people more say in the development process. In some cases, local NGOs have put up political candidates from landless groups for local district elections. In areas of conflict, such as Rwanda and Burundi, agencies are trying to address the turbulent socio-political environment by introducing peace education and conflict resolution processes into communities traumatised by ethnic violence.

In more stable political environments, programmers may find different parties on the political spectrum more or less receptive to their work's goals and vision. This may determine whether such an initiative remains a pilot project or is taken up as national policy. It is important to be conscious of the current direction of political thought and social policy and to work strategically within the political realities. At the same time, however, organisations should aim to maintain a clear and predetermined human rights policy, so that ethical concerns are not sacrificed to political expediency. Such human rights policies need to be developed, negotiated and internalised by the organisation as a whole, and applied to local circumstances in consultation with their client communities.

The 1980s and 1990s have seen the mushrooming of democratic systems across the globe. For development organisations it will not automatically be easier to promote progressive policy and legislation under these new multiparty systems. In fact, it may become more difficult since more voices have to be heard on every issue. The environment may now allow more policy debate, but democratic processes obviously take more time. The hope is that such processes will foster true social transformation instead of superficial change.

However, the international pressure for political reform has not brought about change and reform in all social fields. With the end of the Cold War and the near collapse of many economies, governments in developing countries may have become more vulnerable and less able to stand up to policy pressure from the international community. The delivery of primary health care services, for instance, has been restricted, largely because of the adverse affects of structural adjustment policies, as we will discuss in the next section. Such decisions have real and often devastating impact on those most distant from the corridors of political power.

Widening access to political power

Despite political transformation, access to power often still remains restricted. In some cases the same dominant clique is still in control under a new political system. Until there is broader access to political power – for the poor, for women, for different ethnic groups – the views of the vast majority of the population will not be adequately represented in government nor their needs appropriately translated into policy. The political changes that have come about throughout Eastern Europe, Central Asia and the South in the last decade have not resulted in more political power for women. Many people believe that until sufficient women walk the corridors of power, whether this be in political, economic or other centres of influence, then radical changes to benefit poor women will remain vague, paper promises. The situation of Latin America and the Caribbean is mirrored worldwide:

> The absence of women in boardrooms, ministries, legislative chambers, and other centres of decision-making in most Latin American and Caribbean nations inevitably translates into a lack of policy attention to the needs of women and girls. The results in country after country are indifference to the multiple barriers that block women's access to decision-making, leadership and career opportunities, and the failure of political and legal systems to address outright and subtle discrimination against women.
>
> International Centre for Research on Women
> (ICWR, 1997)

Programmers can support political moves to widen access to leadership roles, by promoting discussion amongst policy makers, but also by offering training and forums for wider debate. For example, ICWR has helped to establish a network of women leaders from throughout North and South America and the Caribbean. This aims to promote women in leadership positions, eliminate legal and other barriers to women's participation, and hold governments accountable for commitments made at the Beijing Conference. Not least, development agencies should actively demonstrate that they have broken their own "glass ceiling", allowing opportunities for promotion to all staff.

There have been a number of initiatives, such as the Salzburg Seminar Special Session on Global Women's Leadership held in August 1997, to share and promote "lessons from success and best practices". Participants looked at successful examples from business, politics, non-profit and multilateral organisations that have promoted women's rise to leadership, to draw from these patterns of success and potentially replicable models. The objective of the Seminar was to help establish new guideposts for women's leadership roles to meet the challenges of a fast-changing world.

This initiative came from growing recognition that, although women have made some remarkable gains in the last two decades, female leaders are still quite rare in the world, especially in business and elected office. The last decade has seen increasing numbers of women in the upper echelons of corporations, but in the United States, for example, this is still limited to five percent of top management and only about two or three percent of chief executive officers. Ironically, two-thirds of the living women heads-of-state, current or former, come from developing or transition countries, where economic and political participation rates of women are among the lowest. However, it must be acknowledged that some of these women are the wives or daughters of former male leaders.

As stated by the International Centre for Research on Women:

> Globally, if women are to bear the disproportionate burden of poverty, illiteracy, dislocation, violence, poor nutrition and health, then women should have access to those benefits of society that will permit them a voice in developing policies and finding solutions to these global problems . . . . the equal involvement of women in leadership positions is a global economic, political and social necessity.
>
> (Merrick, 1997: 1)

Affirmative action is already being taken by many governments and non-government agencies and by the private sector to ensure that excluded groups, including women, ethnic minorities and deprived social classes (such as the lower castes in Indian society), are given access to political position and leadership roles. This action needs to be combined with opportunities for training in management and leadership. Such training actually begins in the earliest years, at home, and in primary school, where all students (not just bright boys) need to be given chances to be leaders amongst their peers. Anti-discrimination policy therefore needs to be combined with a transformation in the education and socialisation process of young people.

Conclusion

In summary, the socio-political system is the macro-context of the enabling environment. It will determine how and when positive change can come about. It will determine if and when the results of successful pilot projects can be replicated or become national policy. It will determine who has a voice in the system and who will therefore benefit from policy and legislative change. Without adequate and positive change in the socio-political system, the poor will remain poor and the voiceless will remain without a voice. Innovations may be allowed for publicity purposes, but vested interests will ensure that they remain contained and do not spread.

Socio-economic factors

Introduction: Poverty and the global economy

When development professionals using participatory methods work closely with client communities to assess their needs, economic survival is usually the key priority for people. In fact, in general discussions on development issues, "poverty" usually comes up as the root problem, no matter what the subject. Poverty is multifaceted. It can be defined from the perspective of income levels, but it also relates to a whole range of deprivations people face. "Although income focuses on an important dimension of poverty, it gives only a partial picture of the many ways human lives can be blighted." (UNDP, 1997:16) Poverty is a symptom of a series of underlying problems in a society.

The socio-economic environment is, perhaps, as we have seen, the most difficult to change. It is also the aspect of the enabling environment which is usually mentioned as the key to sustainable development. Yet, except for a few examples, there have been scarce answers on how to bring about change in this sphere.

Before confidence in their markets collapsed in late 1997, the "tiger economies", the rapidly expanding economies of several East Asian countries, were often cited as an illustration of how nations can achieve phenomenal rates of growth to pull themselves out of poverty and become key players in the global economy. However, this vision is far from the reality of many less developed countries, and especially those of Sub-Saharan Africa. In these countries failed development policies combined with levels of debt repayment to the rich countries cripple any attempts at economic expansion. These countries are caught in the "debt trap": they cannot develop because a major proportion of their national income is lost in servicing debt interest; they cannot pay off their debts because they are unable to develop their economies. Countries in the North share a responsibility in this in having issued numerous loans somewhat irresponsibly in the first place. Although some efforts are being made to support specific countries which are regarded by the donor community as having the potential for reform, these initiatives are too limited and too late for the millions of vulnerable people who have been affected by cuts in social service provision.

According to Professor Adebayo Adedeji, former Executive Secretary of the UN Economic Commission for Africa:

> So severe has been the exacerbating burden of debt on the ordinary people in the debt-distressed countries that its destructive impact is comparable only to that of war, the only difference being that it is children rather than soldiers that are dying and instead of millions of wounded, there are millions of unemployed. The warlike impact of debt is tearing down schools and hospitals and rending the fabric of societies.
>
> (Adedeji, 1996:1)

In the late 1990s, a movement began called Jubilee 2000 which envisaged the debt of developing countries being cancelled in one splendid, once-only gesture to mark the millenium. Campaigns were launched in a number of countries, lobbying key decision makers in governments and international financial institutions (Jubilee 2000 Internet website). Signatures continue to be collected for a Global 2000 Petition, perhaps the world's largest ever petition, for submission to the world's economic decision makers and powers. Even if this initiative does not meet its full objectives within its original time frame, it is a powerful symbol of the world's people challenging the global economic order and bodes well for changes in the future. However, today the poorest of the poor remain victims to political mismanagement and the fallout from structural adjustment policies required by the World Bank, the International Monetary Fund and other donors.

In recent years the World Bank has attempted to ameliorate some of the gravest suffering resulting from structural adjustment policies, through support to social safety nets, including food for work programmes and employment creation schemes for the poorest. It has also developed techniques for participatory poverty assessment, already conducted in a number of African countries. This process is used to understand the nature of poverty from poor people's perspectives, establishing their own sense of needs, vulnerability and seasonal deprivation. With these insights the aim is to design policies which least adversely affect poor people or at least provide a safety net. At best, however, these approaches can only provide minimal relief from structural adjustment policies.

Over the last few years, for the first time, there has been a reduction in levels of international aid commitments, which is having a drastic impact on those most vulnerable. For example, the US government has cut back dramatically on its financing of family planning programmes, in 1996 down by 35 percent from its 1995 levels (Mehra, 1996:16). The international community should encourage donors to recall the promises made at the Cairo Conference on Population.

> The Cairo Conference called for a roughly fourfold increase in total annual financial commitments to $17 billion by the end of the decade. This quantum leap reflects the projected doubling of the number of women, men and adolescents in need of services . . . . If $17 billion a year sounds like a lot of money for global population programmes, keep in mind that the world spends $40 billion annually to play golf!
>
> (Mehra, 1996:16)

The United Nations Development Fund's Human Development Report in 1997 outlines six priorities for action to eradicate poverty:

(1) Everywhere the starting point is to empower women and men – and to ensure their participation in decisions that affect their lives and enable them to build their strengths and assets.

(2) Gender equality is essential for empowering women – and for eradicating poverty.

(3) Sustained poverty reduction requires pro-poor growth (economic growth which benefits the poor) in all countries – and faster growth in the 100 or so developing and transitional countries where growth has been failing. Pro-poor growth policies include restoring full employment and avoiding "ruthless" growth that leads to increasing income inequality.

(4) Globalization (of trade and foreign investment) offers great opportunities – but only if it is managed more carefully and with more concern for global equity.

(5) The state must provide an enabling environment for broad-based political support and alliances for pro-poor policies and markets. In every area of policy the state must advance the interests of poor people.

(6) Special international support is needed for special situations – to reduce the poorest countries' debt faster, to increase their share of aid and to open agricultural markets for their export. (UNDP, 1997: 6-10)

Opportunities for pro-poor growth are affected by factors at different levels. The international trading and investment climate has a major effect on opportunities for labour creation. While individual agencies are probably powerless at this level, organisations working together have been able to raise public awareness and influence international agreements – such as the Multilateral Agreement on Investment and the Multi-Fibre Agreement – which can make a great difference to employment opportunities and conditions for poor people.

The policies of national governments also support and regulate different types of economic activity. Advocacy and lobbying by development agencies can contribute to how and where jobs are created and how much benefit the poor receive. For example, the development and regulation of the garment manufacturing industry in Bangladesh has created new employment opportunities for women. UNICEF, ILO and other agencies have also been able to work with the government and manufacturers in regulating issues of child labour in the garment industry, which in the long term will have considerable impact on adult employment opportunities.

In describing policies which promote pro-poor growth, the Human Development Report highlights the needs of the rural poor, who form three-quarters of the world's poorest people. For these people key priorities include: "creating an enabling environment for small-scale agriculture, micro-enterprises and the informal sector, (including access to credit and other financial services); fostering technological progress; and reversing environmental decline in marginal areas." (UNDP, 1997:8) This is combined with the provision of basic education and health care for all, an investment which has been demonstrated to provide among the most powerful forces for economic growth. Here again, we see the linkages between the different factors in the environment, and how they impact upon the health and development of the poorest communities.

Many development agencies concentrate on projects to promote income earning opportunities outside formal employment. Perhaps the most cited positive experience is the Grameen Bank of Bangladesh which has provided credit facilities for hundreds of thousands of Bangladeshi women through a disciplined, group-borrowing scheme. Women have been targeted because, it was widely recognised, if they were given economic power, they would be able to pull their families out of poverty. The Grameen Bank has raised the status, well-being and safety of women in their communities by allowing them to borrow for approved income generating schemes, such as the purchase of livestock or the production of materials for resale. The discipline and peer pressure instilled in the borrowing group has ensured over 90 percent payback of loans and a similar success rate in sustained income generation. The philosophy and mechanisms of the Grameen Bank have been replicated or adapted by many other organisations in Bangladesh and around the world, including in the United States, where disadvantaged groups now have access to credit along similar conditions. An alternative approach some agencies have adopted is to facilitate saving schemes among the poor.

Some development professionals would say that when programmes fail to address this pressing need of income generation, but focus instead on predetermined programme goals (e.g. in reproductive health, or use of sanitary latrines, etc.), then the programme may falter. This is a debatable point, as we shall see. Not all development agencies are set up to deal professionally with income generation and there are more failures than there are successes.

In 1994, the International Centre for Research on Women undertook a series of four case studies of field-based credit schemes run by U.S. NGOs for rural women. The findings illustrated that some NGOs were not professionally or technically equipped to operate these initiatives. In some cases, women were not offered training, new technology, or support, such as agricultural extension services, to enable them to make profitable use of their credit. "The case studies showed that projects designed to build on women's ongoing economic activities and to take account of women's skills and experience, were likely to be more effective and sustainable." (Mehra, 1996:2) The report concluded that "it may not be appropriate for NGOs to establish micro-finance operations themselves. Neither is it necessary because, in many countries, it is possible to tap into more specialized institutions that provide micro-financial services." (Mehra, 1996:3) Field based programmes working in other sectors do, however, have an important role to play in providing the complementary training and technical services.

In sexual and reproductive health programmes, there is also clear evidence that the determinants of risk behaviours, for example in sex work or in the "sugar-daddy" syndrome, are often directly related to economic need. Sexual and reproductive health programmes need to consider the economic factors influencing risk behaviours. In the case of sex workers, effective strategies appear to have involved collective action at local level. This includes establishing credit schemes to increase the income of sex workers giving them more financial confidence to reject clients who refuse condoms. For example, in India, sex workers have formed a legally-recognised cooperative society which conducts income-generation activities to supplement their existing income, demands legal rights for its members and undertakes social marketing of condoms. (Gordon, 1996:15)

Income generation schemes for disadvantaged women in the South have not remained fixed on traditional activities for women. Professor Muhammad Yunus, Managing Director of the Grameen Bank in Bangladesh, is a lateral thinker who sees, for example, the arrival of new information-communication technologies as opening new avenues of micro-enterprise development, even for the poorest of the poor. A recent scheme sees rural Bangladesh leap-hopping several decades of technological development. Cellular telephones are proposed as an income-generating activity for rural women.

> She will become the mobile phone booth in the village . . . Imagine every village in Bangladesh with a cellular telephone floating around – or dozens of them . . . The nature of communications would be different. The nature of democracy would be different. Also the terms of business would be different. At present, poor people make a long journey to the market, and then have to take whatever price they can get. Instead, people could choose to go to the market only when the price was right. That gives you control over the market because you have information.
>
> (Yunus, 1996:2)

Conclusion

It is evident from the above that projects which generate income for the poor have a unique potential for empowerment in the new information age, the context in which this book was set in Chapter 2. The socio-economic environment is, in large part, the macro-environment in which development programmes are set. As has been demonstrated by the above analysis, it is possible to engender an enabling micro-socio-economic environment for disadvantaged groups and some programmes have taken such activities to scale.

However, not all development programmes can or should try to address poverty or income generation head on. Failure leads to people's further frustration and lack of motivation to act or to gain new skills. Rather, it is important that when "poverty" or "income generation" comes up through participatory action research at the grass roots or consultation with field staff and programmers, that such factors are taken into account in a programme's design and that the programme does not offer solutions which are unrealistic in the socioeconomic context.

Additionally, if programmes are not designed to address the socio-economic environment, it is important to ask what other agencies are dealing with such factors in the same locality. It should be possible to work cooperatively, and in a coordinated manner with others who may be addressing income generation, for instance. Their inputs should be considered and accounted for in the design of a new programme, especially if the same community is involved. Likewise, if no programme is addressing evident income generation needs in the region, the onus is on the programmers to seek partners who have expertise and a successful track record in this area, therefore engendering an enabling socio-economic environment within which their own interventions can be sustained.

Physical environment

Introduction

Programmers have a long tradition of factoring the physical environment into their work. This, most familiar of all environments, refers to the land, weather, and access to resources such as water, fuel, and other material inputs, which are indispensable in our home and work-place. Disruptions to the physical environment often wreak havoc in people's life. Typhoons, tidal waves, earthquakes, volcanic eruptions, floods, droughts, plant and animal diseases have all wiped out decades of successful development work in many communities in the past. These major upsets in the physical environment are usually beyond the control of programmers.

The environmental lobby has argued that while development programmes cannot control forces of nature, they can weaken the environment considerably and inflict permanent damage if they do not take into account the long term cumulative impact on the environment of their work. The most infamous examples of this is the extensive application of insecticides on farms which has been known to kill both humans and wildlife who consume either poisoned farm products or toxic water running off the land. Equally infamous are the many dams in the developing world which were constructed to tap opportunities offered by the deliberate management of water resources but ended up causing many more major problems than they solved.

However, cases such as the dam projects in the Namada Valley in India show that lobbying can be effective in highlighting the threat of environmental damage from such large-scale initiatives. Intense international pressure, combined with widespread national lobbying by, and in support of, the people to be displaced by the scheme, have detered donors and continue to challenge the planners.

Poverty and the environment

The international aid community now also invests far greater resources in studying the relationship between environmental programmes and poverty alleviation. The Flood Action Plan in Bangladesh, supported by the World Bank, proposed to build structures to control the flood waters passing through the country's rivers, to prevent frequent, sometimes devastating flooding. The government favoured this programme as promoting national economic development. The intention was to provide protection from flood waters, but also to increase agricultural production. However, after a series of feasibility studies, the project was drastically altered, as it became apparent that many communities would be potentially worse off. There were concerns about the risks of a massive buildup of pressure on the embankments, and of disruption to the natural drainage system, with water bursting the banks and getting trapped on the far side. Moreover, the plan would interfere with traditional agriculture and fishing practices, whereby farmers benefit from the soil nutrients and fish carried in the annual flood water. Fish is the main source of protein for Bangladesh's rural poor. Established fisheries, as envisaged by the Flood Action Plan, would require investment beyond the reach of the poor. (Adnan, 1994)

The concerns of health and other behavioural change programmes probably focus more on the micro aspects of the physical environment. New behaviours which require the input of material resources hold out better chances of being effectively promoted if these resources are available to the people. Some of the more obvious limitations of the physical environment may not be so evident to programmers who are "foreign" to a project site. The experience learnt from the promotion of oral rehydration therapy (ORT) in Nepal is relevant here. Among the steps prescribed by one of the ORT teams to mothers was the use of boiled water in the mixing of the rehydration salts. Follow-up studies revealed that mothers seldom boiled the water even though they were mixing the salts to the correct volume of water and feeding it to their children in the prescribed way. When asked, the mothers told the programmers that fuelwood was in such short supply that it was carefully rationed to cook only the main meals of the day. Fuel was so scarce that using the small quantities they had for boiling water was perceived as an extravagant practice they could not afford to adopt.

Agricultural extension programmes are replete with other examples of practices being promoted in the past, which could not be supported by the resources available on the land: high yielding crop varieties which require more water and nutrients than the land and local weather could provide; bulky farm produce grown in isolated rural communities with no convenient transport facilities to send the produce to market; and the introduction of farm animals, which consumed more grass and forage than the land could supply during cyclical extended dry seasons.

The proper management of soil has been a tough campaign for many agriculture extension programmes. It should be of critical interest to farming communities who live off the land, yet programmers in many parts of the developing world have found it difficult to convince farmers to adopt improved strategies for managing the fertility of the land they till. The chief obstacle is often traced to the ownership of the land. The poorer farmers are often tenants of the land they work. Their occupancy of the land is tenuous, and they are ever mindful that they can be evicted from their farms at any time. Such farmers are, therefore, driven to exploit the land to its full while they still have access to it. The conservation of its fertility understandably rests at the bottom of a tenant farmer's priorities. Therefore, campaigns aimed at promoting improved management of such land will only succeed if the rural poor see the implementation of policies giving them greater security of land tenure.

Protecting the environment

There is now universal concern over the state of the global environment and the effect that global warming and other environmental phenomena will have on human survival and development. The ascendancy of environmental concerns has resulted in the popular promotion of sustainable development approaches in all regions of the planet: both developing and developed. Fundamental to this activism is advocacy for reduced consumption of the earth's resources. However, this global campaign comes at a time when governments all over have adopted trade as their main instrument for in-country development and external relations. Trade, except perhaps for the services sector, means increased consumption. This runs counter to arguments for sustainability through the conservation of finite resources. This campaign will test, to the extreme, the skills of programmers in advocating for supportive legislation and public policy.

The drive for environmental protection will severely test programmers in one other way. The concept has been found to be abstract and rather remote for most communities not exposed to the ravages of a degradated environment. The issue of a quickly-depleting ozone layer, the imminent exhaustion of carbon fuel reserves, and the disastrous consequences of decimated bio-diversity, are all too far removed from the experiences of most people to mobilize them to stop driving cars or cutting down forests, or to make other drastic changes in how they lead their lives. The ability to facilitate people's connection of local action to global impact, and their taking a stake in the well-being of the planet, rests at the core of this communication challenge for environmentalists – as all development practitioners must become.

Organisational environment

Introduction

The organisational setting is the last feature of the enabling environment to be analysed because of a change of focus. That is, the organisation of both the programmer and the clientele must be examined and addressed. Too often we have tried to empower people at the grass roots without empowering the field staff who work with them, or indeed the programmers who organise the field staff. An enabling environment needs to be set up from the top level at the centre of an organisation, right down to the field level. Every member of the organisation should have a clear mission and the power to carry it out, without excessive supervision. Too often we attempt to promote the participation of client communities without making our own institutions more participatory.

All too frequently, however, we see that organisations are poorly aligned: there is a gap between how they tell others to behave through their programmes, and how they manage themselves. Johnson and Cooperrider define alignment as being a truly fundamental characteristic of what they call global social change organisations: "Alignment is the extent to which employees understand, value, and are intrinsically motivated to achieve the mission or cause of their organisation." (Johnson & Cooperrider, 1991:233) Organisations have to confront their own internal need for "behaviour change" in their management processes to become a truly **enabling organisation.**

Creating an enabling organisation

Two strategies here are key: one focusing on an organisation's internal operations, the other on its external relationships.

Internal alignment around the concept of the learning organisation

The concept of a learning organisation is not new, and certainly not easy to espouse or sustain. Senge breaks the learning organisation into five components which he calls core disciplines:

Personal mastery: This refers to the relationship between individual staff and the organisation as a whole. This discipline helps us to examine the nature of that relationship and of the commitment which binds individual staff to the organisation.

Mental models: Each of us carries different assumptions or mental models that are deeply ingrained and influence how we understand the world and how we act. We need to become conscious and objectively critical of our own assumptions and be open to others' views.

Shared vision: Rather than espousing any one individual's vision, an organisation needs to develop a shared vision. This involves working through participatory processes to create a shared mission for the future, which fosters genuine commitment and ownership, rather than merely compliance amongst the organisation's staff. This vision will need to be revisited and revised over time.

Team learning: Shifting the organisation's orientation away from individual learning towards team learning represents another challenge. Team learning begins with the practice of dialogue, "allowing the group to discover insights not attainable individually." Team learning is particularly important when we are involved with programmes focusing on behaviour change, which demand intense levels of cooperation.

Systems thinking: Organisations are system-bound by a complex set of interrelated activities. Identifying these interconnections, especially the part we play in them, will eventually allow us to identify and change patterns at a much deeper level. (Senge, 1990:7-10)

Cultivating the disciplines of learning in an organisation is an ongoing quest. "Flexibility, adaptiveness and, most important, the capacity to learn and change are being seen as the key to effective capacity development." (Aga Khan Foundation, 1996 :9) The input-output approach to programming that has guided project design in organisations for decades is being reassessed as it is recognised that the process is, in reality, much more fluid.

Advocates for strengthening social change organisations seem to agree that institutional capacity-building is:

- a long-term and gradual process
- a systematic and continuous process
- a process where it is not always possible to demonstrate a one-to-one relationship between institutional capacity-building and results on the ground
- a process requiring ongoing opportunities for reflection and learning, regular facilitation and consultation, informal dialogues, field visits, exposure to alternative models and methods
- a strong commitment by organisational leaders

(Tandon, 1997:8-9).

In this context, concepts about organisational leadership and team work shift away from independence towards a much stronger sense of inter-dependence. This represents a huge shift and challenge, for both larger organisations, that tend to have rather ossified bureaucratic systems in place, as well as for smaller organisations, that are often struggling to survive.

External alignment with other organisations through partnership building

In terms of its external orientation to its environment, the enabling organisation is one that is flexible and adaptable and able to enter into a wide variety of collaborative arrangements with other organisations engaged in promoting social change. These alliances allow the messages for changing behaviour to be reinforced and multiplied across numerous sectors and populations, spreading the impact much more widely. For many, this represents an enormous shift away from the days of the "Lone Ranger" organisation, which sought to operate on its own terms in a designated programme site.

Partnerships, particularly between international, national and local-level organisations, make sense for a number of reasons. They tend to be more cost-effective in the long run. They can allow each partner to contribute from their own area of expertise, within a comprehensive overall framework. Through work with local NGOs, the partner agencies can become more sensitive to the local conditions. The collaboration can contribute significantly to organisational learning.

These partnerships can take on numerous forms, which are more or less empowering for the different agencies involved. For instance, the range of relationships between an international agency and a national NGO may vary from a contracting arrangement, whereby an NGO is simply paid to provide defined services by an international agency, to a more empowering model where the two agencies seek mutual consultation over each other's policies and practices (Leach, 1994). In other cases, a partnership may refer to a loose form of alliance in which two or more agencies share similar goals, for example, in the abolition of child labour, and therefore seek to cooperate on developing advocacy and programme strategies.

Numerous permutations of such inter-organisational partnerships exist between government and non-governmental organisations, between government and the private sector, between bilateral or multilateral donor agencies and various types of national organisations. A development organisation needs to be clear about the exact nature of its relationship with its partners, both in formal project agreements but also in day-to-day interactions. The form of relationship is the key to creating an enabling environment for learning in both organisations. The mode of working relations also provides critical insight into an organisation's understanding of, and commitment to, principles of empowerment and participation.

Lessons for wider application: Promoting the enabling organisation

Determining some of the key characteristics of the enabling organisation is one thing, but what kinds of approaches can be used to help develop such an environment? These processes must be simple, dynamic, creative and fully participatory. They may well represent a radical challenge to the more usual kind of formal, hierarchical styles of management and planning. Described below are four examples of widely-used processes which can be used by an organisation, both internally and externally, with its programme partners.

Visualisation in Participatory Programmes (VIPP)

VIPP is a collection of participatory methods, combining visualisation and interactive learning. It uses cards of different shapes and colours, on which participants express their ideas. Through the process, they are able to synthesise the thoughts of the group through collectively building up a display of mobile cards on boards. In writing ideas on cards, everyone - however reserved – joins in achieving a consensus. By visualising the proceedings, repetition and circularity in argument are reduced. Using a wide variety of games and exercises, participants share different perspectives and new, creative ideas are generated. VIPP emphasises ongoing evaluation and participants' involvement in problem identification, assessment, analysis and action. It is used in a range of contexts, including programme planning, training, team building, research synthesis, and programme evaluation (UNICEF Bangladesh, 1993). Box 5 illustrates how VIPP was used in Zambia.

Search Conferences

Search conferences enable groups to articulate and plan for a shared vision for the future of an organisation. Such conferences work on the basis of four guiding principles: (1) picking the right "business opportunity" or issue that unites the group; (2) getting the whole organisation into one room; (3) focusing on the future; and (4) promoting self-managed learning and planning. Search conferences usually span across three days, may include over a hundred people, and seek to draw upon a broad spectrum of viewpoints represented in the room. They end with a call for public action commitments for participants to declare their intentions for next steps. Participants may emerge from the conference having themselves gone through the transformative experience of developing a collective guiding image of the future. (Weisbord, 1995)

5 *Using VIPP: the case of Zambia*

Since its introduction through UNICEF in early 1994, VIPP made great strides in Zambia, building upon the foundations of participatory training that already existed in the country. VIPP methodologies have been used for strengthening teams, project planning, strategy development, managing meetings, generating information, and training trainers. Over 300 facilitators at various levels in government, NGOs, and international development agencies have been trained in the use of VIPP, and several partner organisations have espoused the methods for their own programmes.

VIPP has been used with numerous different types of groups and organisations to develop strategies on a range of issues, including: promoting girls' retention in school, improving youth access to media about HIV/AIDS, problem-solving with street children in urban areas, community-based planning, and capacity-building for health reforms in Zambia. VIPP has also been used within UNICEF's Zambia country office to strengthen its own internal management and planning, and for staff team-building.

VIPP methods are particularly appropriate to raise difficult issues. For example, an adolescent involved with HIV/AIDS education for youth in Zambia uses a VIPP card to anonymously ask: "How can I be sure that my partner is wearing a condom?" Police officers and Lusaka street children have frankly exchanged their perceptions of each other, and at the same time defined common ground. Youths have collaborated with senior health providers to better define their needs in reproductive health service provision. Staff members have been able to raise their fear about speaking up in front of their manager in a manner that allows for constructive exploration of this issue in the work-place.

A preliminary evaluation of VIPP's application in Zambia conducted in 1996 indicated that VIPP is most effective for mid-level decision-makers who are often better at talking about the need for participation than at practising it in their own working environments.

Whitney et al, 1998

Appreciative Inquiry

This is a constructive approach to organisational development and change, with a very practical orientation that selectively seeks to locate, highlight and illuminate what are the positive, life-giving forces of an organisation's existence.

This contrasts with the typical problem orientation which seeks to identify problems, analyse them, and come up with solutions. By deliberately highlighting the vital, constructive forces within an organisation, this approach assumes that it will inspire and motivate participants to work with these positive elements. Appreciative inquiry is a process of conducting interviews to discover themes that characterise the organisation, developing a vision about the future, and determining actions to guide the organisation into the future. (Hammond, 1996; Cooperrider, 1995)

Participatory Rural Appraisal (PRA)

PRA is the label which has been attached to a growing family of "relaxed" methods which enable local people, rural and urban, to make their own analysis of their lives and environment and to share information amongst themselves. The approaches enable local communities to plan action for themselves and to monitor and evaluate their activities. PRA has evolved and drawn on many sources, including participatory action research (PAR), applied social anthropology, field research on farming systems and rapid rural appraisal (RRA).

Although PRA and RRA are very different, they share similar methods and some basic principles, including: learning from and with people, directly, on site and face-to-face; learning collectively and progressively; aiming to offset biases (e.g. caused by participants' gender or class, by courtesy, by seasonal differences); reversing roles, to understand and appreciate local people's knowledge and to use their criteria and categories; using triangulation (i.e. using different methods, sources and disciplines, and a range of informants in a range of places, to crosscheck findings). (Institute of Development Studies, Sussex, 1996)

Conclusion

An enabling environment for shared learning, innovation and staff cooperation is, therefore, central to the development of an organisation. In essence, for programmers to promote participation and empowerment with their client communities, we need to operate within an empowering organisation which, itself, uses participatory processes and is in constant quest for better practice. It means we, ourselves, must take responsibility and are accountable for promoting a learning environment at multiple levels. In these pages, we have offered some tools which can help us to create an enabling organisation.

Part III: Summary of lessons learned on creating an enabling environment

• Development practitioners need to be conscious of the full range of environmental constraints and influences on behaviour. All aspects of the enabling environment are important for initiating and sustaining behaviour development and change.

• The range of positive examples in this chapter show that environmental factors can be successfully addressed. There is a dynamic relationship between people and their environment: the environment can determine individual and group behaviour, but at the same time, people, individually and collectively, can influence their environment.

• The task of analysing the environment becomes less daunting if we use the Model for Behavioural Development and Change, which places the client at the centre. The different factors in the environment can then be viewed from the client's perspective, in order to identify the relevant areas of concern.

• The process of creating a supportive environment is, therefore, centred on participation (genuine rather than token) of the client communities involved. Planning and monitoring of programme activities must be grounded in local people's own perceptions of their environment. This may require developing critical thinking skills (or "conscientisation", as Friere termed it) to enable people to become more conscious and objective in analysing their circumstances.

• Through participatory processes, local people can identify and analyse which elements in their environment are:

- supportive and can be built on;
- neutral and can be lived with;
- negative and need to be addressed or circumvented.

• It is important not to over-generalise the characteristics of the environment since the constellation of factors which surrounds each community, and influences their behaviour, will be unique. Research will reveal that, even within communities, different interest groups – male and female, young and old, rich and poor, etc. – may experience different factors of their environment, and indeed different elements within each factor, as variably supportive, neutral or hostile.

• Given the unique nature of each group's environment, programmers working at a national or even regional level, need to allow flexibility and indeed encourage local adaptation to meet local needs. Especially in terms of mass communication or education programmes, the materials and approaches require sufficient openness and sensitivity to be modified for each specific context.

• It is necessary to build alliances with other agencies in the government, non-government and private sectors, since no one programme can seek to work on all fronts at once. Each agency can focus on its own area of expertise, working alongside other organisations to develop a more comprehensive approach to creating a supportive environment. Collectively, this allows networks of agencies to deal with the range of environmental factors at different levels – global, national and local.

• Working through participatory processes to create a more enabling environment, and discerning the impact of these changes on people's behaviour, requires significant investment in terms of resources and time. Programmers will need to advocate within their organisations to gain appropriate funding, and a realistic time frame beyond the usual three to five year planning cycle.

• The repeated emphasis on the essential value of research raises two important issues: first is the need for advocacy to gain more funding for research; second is the need to ensure closer support and collaboration between researchers, programmers and client communities, so that such research is well publicised and acknowledged by those who can make best use of it. Research obviously has a key part to play in advocating for a broader approach to programming.

• A strategic approach to planning, which encompasses what is doable, not everything that is desirable, is necessary in programming for an enabling environment. Programme plans should fall within the limits of an organisation's technical expertise and financial resources, should be practically and politically feasible, and should not raise unreal expectations in clients. Solid plans can be developed in consultation with the client communities, but they should, at the same time, remain flexible and responsive to changing needs and to findings through monitoring.

• Finally, programmers need to collaborate on developing appropriate indicators to detect changes in environmental factors which have impacted positively (or negatively) on people's behaviour. Working at the broadest level of the environment presents a challenge to establish indicators of concrete, attributable impact. This challenge for evaluation is taken up in the next and final chapter of this book.

References

Adedeji, A. (1996) "Debt" (leaflet). Washington D.C.: World Development Movement.

Adnan, S. (1994) *People's participation and the flood action plan*. Dhaka: Oxfam.

Aga Khan Foundation (1996) "Muddles, challenges and opportunities: The current states of capacity development". Background paper prepared for Aga Khan Foundation, Canada.

Allen T. and Thomas, A. (eds) (1992) *Poverty and development in the 1990s*. Oxford: Oxford University Press.

Blaney, C.L. (1993, August) "Quality aims for clients often relies on staff". *Network in Family Health International*, Vol 14, No 1.

Bruce, J. (1990) "Fundamental elements in the quality of care: A simple framework, in studies". *Family Planning*, 21 (2).

Carroll, T.F. (1983) *Women,religion and development in the Third World*. Oxford: Oxford University Press.

Claver, F. (1995) *Liberation theology and development activism*. Tokyo: Sophia University.

Cooperrider, D. and Associates (1995) *Appreciative inquiry: An approach to organisational analysis and learning*. Cleveland: GEM Initiative, Case Western Reserve University, Weatherhead School of Management.

Dorkenoo , E. (1995) *Cuttingthe rose: Female genital mutilation: The practice and its prevention*. London: Minority Rights Publications.

Finger, W.R. (1993, August) "Choice, access, information are among clients' rights". *Network in Family Health International*, Vol 14, No 1.

Freire, P. (1973) *Pedagogy of the oppressed*. London: Penguin.

Gordon, P. and Sleightholme, C. (1996) *Review of "best practice" for targeted interventions*. London: International Family Health, HIV/AIDS/STD Resource Centre.

Hammond, S.A. (1996) *The thin book of appreciative inquiry.* Plano: Kodiak Consulting.

Hawes, H. and Stephens, D. (1990) *Questions of quality: Primary education and development.* Harlow: Longman.

Institute of Development Studies (1996) *The institutionalisation of participatory approaches: PRA topic pack.* Institute of Development Studies, Sussex University.

International Centre for Research on Women (ICRW) (1997, June) "Upcoming events: Women's leadership in the Americas and the Salzburg Seminar on Women's Leadership". Internet website: http:/www.icrw.org

Johnson, P.C. and Cooperrider, D.L. (1991) "Finding a path with heart: Global social change organisations and their challenge for the field of organisational development". Research in Organisational Change and Development, Vol. 5: 223-284.

"Jubilee 2000" Internet website: <www.oneworld.org/jubilee2000>

Kirby, D. (1999) "The multiple antecedents of adolescent sexual risk-taking behaviour, pregnancy and childbearing, and their implications for research and programmes." (Draft, yet to be published)

Leach, M. (1994) *Models of inter-organisational collaboration in development.* Boston: Institute for Development Research.

MacDonald, J. (1993) *Primary health care: Medicine in its place.* London: Earthscan Publications.

McNeil, P., Shillingford, A., Raffray, M., Gribble, J.N., Russell-Brown, P., Townsend, J.W. (1990). *The effect of continuing education on teenage childbearing: The Jamaica Women's Centre.* Washington D.C.: Jamaica Women's Centre and the Population Council.

Mehra, R., Buvinic, M., Johnson-Welch, C., Paolisso, M., Weiss, E., Whelan, D. (1996) *Taking women into account: Lessons learned from NGO project experiences.* Washington D.C.: ICRW and Interaction (American Council for Voluntary International Action).

Merrick, J. (1997) Executive Summary, ICRW and Salzburg Seminar: *Special session on global women's leadership: Lessons from success and best practices*. Washington D.C.: International Centre for Research on Women.

Moser, C.O.N. (1993) *Gender planning and development: Theory, practice and training*. London: Routledge.

Second Vatican Council (1965) *Gaudiam et Spes* (The Church in the Modern World). Rome: The Vatican.

Senderowitz, J. (1997, April) "Reproductive Health Outreach Programmes for Young Adults (draft #4) For Focus on Young Adults", Seattle: Pathfinder International.

Senge, P.M. (1990) *The fifth discipline*. New York: Doubleday/Currency.

South Commission (1990) *The challenge to The South: The report of The South Commission*, Oxford: Oxford University Press.

Sweat, M.D. and Denison, J. (1995) "Reducing HIV incidence in developing countries with structural and environmental interventions" in *AIDS 1995*, 9 (Supp. A): S251-S257.

Tandon, R. (1997) *Capacity building in civil society*. New Delhi: Society for Participatory Research in Asia.

Tawil, O., Verster, A. and O'Reilly, K.R. (1995) "Can We Modify the Environment and Minimise the Risk?" in *AIDS 1995*, 9 (12):1299-1306.

United Nations (1994) *The age and sex distribution of the world's population: 1994 revision*. New York: Department for Economic and Social Information and Policy Analysis. ST/ESA/SER.A 144.

United Nations (1996) *Beijing World Conference on Women: Declaration and Platform for Action*. New York: United Nations.

UNDP (United Nations Development Programme) (1997) *Human development report*. New York: Oxford University Press.

UNICEF (United Nations Children's Fund) (1997) *State of the world's children*. Oxford: Oxford University Press.

UNICEF Bangladesh (1993) VIPP: *Visualisation in Participatory Programmes: A manual for facilitators and trainers involved in participatory group events.* Dhaka: UNICEF.

UNICEF ESARO (2000) *Some things can change: A resource book for youth and community action on female genital mutilation.* Nairobi: Sara Communication Initiative, UNICEF East and Southern Africa Regional Office.

Vera, H. (1993) "The client's view of high-quality care in Santiago, Chile". *Studies in Family Planning*, 24(1).

Webb, D. (1997) *Adolescence, sex and fear: Reproductive health services and young people in Zambia.* Kinshasa: UNICEF.

Weisbord, M. and Janoff, S. (1995) *Future Search: An action guide.* San Francisco: Berret-Koehler Publishers.

Weiss, E., Whelan, D., Gupta, G.R. (1996) *Vulnerability and opportunity: Adolescents and HIV/AIDS in the developing world: Findings from the Women and AIDS Research Programme.* Washington D.C.: International Centre for Research on Women.

Whitney, B. and Wyss, E. (1998) *A process evaluation of VIPP in Zambia.* Nairobi: UNICEF East and Southern Africa Regional Office.

WHO (World Health Organisation) (1994) "Female genital mutilation: Statement of the WHO Director-General to WHO's Global Commission on Women's Health, 12 April 1994" quoted in *Female genital mutilation: information kit.* Geneva: Family and Reproductive Health, WHO. (WHO/FRH/WHD/96.26.)

Yunus, M. interviewed by Peter Stalker (1996) Bangladesh: *Visions and hopes.* Dhaka: UNICEF.

UNICEF/HQ96-0573/Nicole Toutounji

A woman health worker updates a set of medical records while her colleague holds an infant, at a health care centre in the village of Kefrim, near Damascus, the capital of Syria.

6

Behaviour and beyond

Enabling Environment
Ability to Act
Motivation
Information
Values
Family
Community
Self
Peers
Timely accessible & relevant
Effective Communication
Life Skills
Policy/Legislation, Services, Education, Religion, Politics, Economics, Physical & Organizational Environment

SIX

Behaviour and beyond: An evaluation perspective

Erma Manoncourt and Douglas Webb

Introduction

The changing focus of many social programmes (from individual behaviour change to community empowerment, sustainability, etc.) combined with a proliferation of emergency programmes, and a conservative financial climate, has fostered an increased interest in **evaluation**. Simultaneously, there continues to be a growing awareness of the importance of **participatory evaluation processes** – involving multiple stakeholders in design, implementation and needs assessment, as well as concerns related to expanding ("going to scale") successful programmes to national implementation (Stoeker, 1992 &1993, Goodman *et al*, 1994, Narayan, 1993). These trends, in turn, have highlighted the need for programmers (and communicators in particular), to be conversant with evaluation methods, or at least sufficiently knowledgeable about them to communicate effectively with internal and external evaluators.

Although this chapter's focus is on evaluation, it is important to remember that it is a significant dimension of broader programme planning processes and hence must be considered at the very beginning of a programme's design and development. In terms of programme planning, evaluation results can be used to consider different strategies for the next phase of a communication supported programme or to develop a new programme. For example, if the programme's original objective was to teach mothers the benefits of breast-feeding and increase this practice, and an evaluation shows that this has been achieved by a critical mass of mothers, staff can make plans to sustain the practice and move on to something new.

Evaluation results are also used to improve a programme. These changes would be similar to those made or considered during early impact and follow-up monitoring studies.

There are many different audiences (or stakeholders) for whom, and purposes for which, evaluations are undertaken. These considerations suggest different evaluation designs and implementation approaches – each with advantages and limitations. In planning an evaluation, one must not only take into account its purpose, strategies and potential trade-offs (e.g. feasibility, given limited resources, time, etc.), but also the following conceptual and technical issues.

Conceptual design issues (see Box 1) must be addressed in the planning phase of an evaluation and require that expectations, and the general parameters of the evaluation, are clearly defined by all concerned. This minimises misunderstanding and confusion at the evaluation's end.

1

Conceptual design issues and choices

EVALUATION ISSUE	POSSIBLE CHOICES
Primary stakeholder/ interest group	Programme staff, govt. policy makers, donors, NGOs, allies, participants, community at large
Purpose/focus	Context, process, impact, outcome
Evaluator type	Internal (programme staff, evaluation/ audit unit), External (expert consultants, stakeholders)
Political considerations	Stakeholders, context (e.g. organisation's policy, country situation)

Deciding on the type of evaluation needed

Although a formal programme evaluation could include all four types of evaluation described below, this is usually not feasible. The type of evaluation conducted is often dependent on the availability of time and other resources (financial, personnel, etc.) needed. Webb (1997) reminds the reader that it is useful to know what information can be gathered in relation to the amount of resources allocated. For example, the more funds which are available, the greater the degree of behavioural change "measurement" possible, and the higher possibility of attributing the reported (or observed) change to a programme or specific intervention. The various conceptual and technical design issues that are discussed in this chapter are also considerations that influence one's decision about evaluation type.

Context evaluation: What is its purpose and what type of question does it try to answer?

The context of an intervention refers to the naturally occurring events, influences and changes that occur in the environment (e.g. social, physical), or programme setting (structure, organisational procedures, etc.), that may contribute to, or impede, programme success and outcomes (Israel, 1995, p. 368).

The key purpose of this type of evaluation is determining and documenting which of the above factors is, or has been, most influential in the "real life" of a programme. This is particularly true in the case of emergency programmes where programme staff have even less control over events and situations that may affect programme success and failure. Data collected in this type of evaluation range from documenting the expressed needs of beneficiary groups (stakeholders) to identifying political, social, economic, cultural and geographic factors that influence programme activities. For example, stakeholders may indicate a desire for employment opportunities while new donor funding increase local government's capacity to subsidise economically depressed areas.

Practice application

Example 1: Diarrhoeal Disease Control (CDD) Programme
Context question(s): How has a shift in emphasis to a child rights approach to programming affected the CDD communication strategy? What is the impact of current inflation having on the cost of ORS packets and is it a factor in mothers' ability to purchase them at a nominal cost? How does local production of ORS packets change its availability and accessibility and consequently, how does it affect mothers' use rates? To what extent does health workers' job satisfaction influence their counselling with mothers?

Example 2: AIDS Prevention among Young People in a Camp for Displaced
Context question(s): What effect did signing the Convention on the Rights of the Child by the Government have on young people's access to AIDS education and condoms in camps where there is a high rate of HIV infection? How will the outbreak of renewed fighting and the recent influx of displaced persons in the country affect sexual behaviour among adolescents in areas to

which they have migrated? What government policies are in place to support this action?

Process evaluation: What is its purpose and what type of question does it try to answer?

Evidence from the field shows that programmes are rarely implemented as planned. The primary purpose of process evaluation is to provide feedback on the extent and quality of programme interventions, stakeholders (e.g. participants, staff) experiences and reactions to programme activities, staff performance and competence, quality assurance of programme inputs (e.g. operations, plausibility and specificity of programme objectives, funds, personnel, space, etc.). Complementary to the other types of evaluation discussed later in this chapter, it also useful in identifying a programme's strengths and weaknesses by:

- describing variations in intervention processes between programme strategies and assessing operating procedures;
- highlighting unintended consequences which may result from programme activities and;
- clarifying how, why and among which segments of the target populations desired changes were, or were not, achieved.

The value-added of process evaluation is its role in determining how programme impact and outcomes have been achieved and in helping staff to interpret subsequent impact or outcome results in the light of known deviations from the intended programme. With this in mind, Israel and her colleagues have emphasised three areas that need more attention in future process evaluation efforts (Israel, 1995, p.374-5):

- Coverage – To what extent does the programme reach the intended beneficiaries and to what extent were the participants exposed to programme activities?
- Using theory – Assuming that programme interventions have been theory informed, what linkages have been drawn between intervention activities and important factors that influence the outcomes of interest?
- Staff and stakeholder interactions – What is the level and quality of the interpersonal relationships between programme staff and participants, and how does this relationship affect the building of capacity and competence among programme participants?

Needless to say, the findings from this type of evaluation are most useful when collected and analysed in conjunction with outcome data.

Practice application

Example 1: Diarrhoeal Disease Control (CDD) Programme
Process question(s): How often are health education sessions, devoted to CDD, held at the health centre, or in the villages? What Oral Rehydration Therapy (ORT) messages are developed and how often are they disseminated through different communication channels – radio, television, traditional? How do mothers feel about the quality of counselling provided by local health workers?

Example 2: AIDS Prevention Programme in a Camp for Displaaced
Process question(s): What types of condoms have been distributed in the camps and how often? To what extent are local young people involved in planning and/or implementing AIDS prevention activities? What is the nature of the relationship or interactions between project staff and displaced persons being served by the programme? Which logistics were in place so that condom distribution was available at the right time? What are the young people's perceptions and feelings about the programme and staff? What could have been done differently to obtain the condoms on time?

Impact and outcome evaluations: What are their purposes and what type of questions do they try to answer?

Programmes designed from a behavioural perspective make a clear distinction between impact and outcome evaluation. Although sometimes the terms are reversed in meaning, impact evaluation attempts to study short- or medium-term effects of a programme; while the outcome evaluation puts an emphasis on its long-term effects. In practice, both are guided by the desire to assess to what extent programme goals and objectives have been achieved and to determine "what works". Green *et al* (1991, p. 229) summarise this distinction in the Box 2 on the next page.

Conducting impact and outcome evaluations enable development programmes to continue, redirect, or intensify their efforts, if they have not met their objectives. They also provide staff with justification for choosing new objectives (in order to sustain the improvements), or moving in new directions (taking advantage of a window of opportunity). They can demonstrate the success of a programme, the credibility of its approach, and the professional competence of those involved. In addition, findings can be used to redesign future activities, strategies, materials and messages.

Impact and outcome evaluations use many of the same designs and methods, but they provide answers to different questions as will be discussed below. However, they share a common interest in determining answers two key questions: "Was there a change?" and "Was that change caused by the intervention?" When conceptualised as an objectives-based evaluation, they also attempt to answer the question "were the programme goals and objectives met?" In each instance, these evaluations are undertaken as a means of statistically demonstrating that changes are unlikely to have occurred randomly and suggesting a cause and effect relationship between the intervention and specific outcomes.

Impact evaluation

2 ***Levels of evaluation***

EVALUATION CHARACTERISTICS	IMPACT EVALUATION		OUTCOME EVALUATION	
Focus	Predisposing, enabling, Reinforcing factors	Protective & harmful behaviours or environment	Health	Social Benefit
Target of Change	Knowledge, Attitudes, Skills, Resources, Social Support, Policy	Behaviour - timing frequency, population distribution & Environment Quality	Mortality Morbidity Disability Risk Factors	Quality of Life Poverty Education

Green et al, 1986, 1991

As shown above, this type of evaluation is used to assess a programme's effectiveness in achieving desired changes in knowledge, attitudes and behaviours of a target group. Thus, it focuses upon the immediate effects of a programme and/or various components. It assesses the behaviour and environmental factors that are felt to influence health and social outcomes.

Usually, in the case of communication and education activities, impact evaluations focus on the behaviour changes defined in the objectives. Impact evaluation data also helps determine if, and to what extent, the target audience is assimilating the expected knowledge and attitude changes and their level of initial adoption of behaviour; (for example, using ORS, purchasing iodised salt or practising safe sex).

Outcome evaluation

Outcome evaluation is research designed to account for programme accomplishments, and long-term effectiveness, for example in health status changes achieved by the target audience. Its primary areas of interest are health status and qualify of life indicators – reduction in mortality, morbidity, hunger, poverty, unemployment, homelessness, etc. Data will demonstrate the level of impact the communication intervention had on the programme goals in terms of health status indicators, as well as epidemiological statistics; (for example, decline in the incidence of malaria, or reduction in infant and/or maternal mortality).

Practice application

Example 1: Diarrhoeal Disease Control (CDD) Programme
Programme objective: Decrease by 50 percent infant mortality due to diarrhoeal disease causes

Outcome question(s): What is the incidence and prevalence of diarrhoeal disease in a specified community? What is the current infant mortality rate by cause?

Impact question(s): How many mothers know the signs of dehydration? How many families have potable water available to them? What percent of mothers wash their hands before preparing family meals, especially food for their children? What percent of mothers know how to administer ORT appropriately?

Example 2: Nutrition Programme in an Emergency Situation
Programme Objective: Reduce malnutrition by 50 percent among children less than five years old

Outcome question(s): What is the prevalence of malnutrition among children less than 5 years? How many deaths can be attributed to malnutrition?

Impact question(s): How many mothers know the signs of marasmus or kwashiorkor? What percent of mothers provide nutritionally balanced meals with locally available produce? How many mothers are breast-feeding their children during their first six months?

Process question(s): What foodstuffs have been distributed in the camps and their frequency? Who actually is receiving the food and how much? To what extent are local community groups involved in planning and/or aiding in the food distribution?

Monitoring: What is its relationship to evaluation?

A discussion on evaluation is incomplete without some mention of monitoring, which is a type of programmatic self-evaluation or assessment of work, in progress. As a complement to programme evaluation, monitoring is an important process that allows staff to document and track intervention processes and activities during the implementation phase of a programme. As a result, its findings are useful in answering such questions as: What is happening? How? and how well? A variety of monitoring methods exist, but some of the most common include the following:

(1) Periodic reviews of programme documents (i.e. registers, work-plans etc.) and regular audits of materials at representative distribution points;

(2) Listening to broadcasts to ensure that messages are aired at the contracted hours;

(3) Spot-checks to see if target groups remember seeing/hearing different interventions (i.e. messages and media) to which they may have been exposed; These checks often occur at:

(a) public places (market places, sports arenas, bus terminals, street corners, cinema halls, etc.)

(b) designated gathering places of specific target groups (schools for children, health centres for mothers, youth clubs, etc.)

(4) Central location intercepts to ask for the perception of tag lines or programmes slogans;

(5) Regular field trips to demonstration sites to check on availability of products or supplies; and

(6) Observations at service delivery points, points of sales, counselling or training sessions, small group discussions, etc.

Ongoing monitoring of behaviours need not exhaust programme resources if it is planned carefully. For example, while on regular site visits, supervisors may check to be sure that activities for Polio Eradication National Immunisation Days are being implemented as planned – i.e. regular meetings with appropriate partners, mobilising community workers, etc. In practice, the frequency of monitoring activities will depend on programme resources, where problems are anticipated, and when staff can reasonably make programme changes in response to the findings.

Lessons learnt in conducting programme evaluations

Determining if a programme makes a difference in behaviour change

What is the relationship between behaviour theory and programme evaluation? The former explains or predicts what can happen behaviourally and is useful in identifying critical factors or determinants that are influential and can be the target of specific interventions. Impact evaluation is useful in determining factors to which the observed or expected behaviour can be attributed and whether the findings are a result of the intervention. The desire to prove that behaviour change is a direct result of a specific programme or intervention is a challenge to evaluators. It is problematic for two reasons. First, behaviour change is a continuous process that is subject to a variety of external influences.

Secondly, the ability to identify direct causal relationships between programme activities and observed or reported behaviour change poses a methodological challenge. For example, in terms of large-scale media campaigns, it is impossible to attribute, with certainty, behavioural change to a specific communication. Why? People who are inclined to change their behaviour are also more likely to respond positively to communication messages on different information channels. Given a programme's inability to control all communication messages that may be directly or indirectly related to a desired behaviour, it is possible that change occurs, but in response to messages external to programme input.

Attributing changes in a target audience to a particular programme and/or its interventions requires evidence. The strength of this proof depends on the evaluation designs selected and data collection methods used. An evaluation design is the research framework used by an evaluator and has as its purpose: "to reduce the possibility of errors in the interpretation of the results by maximising the reliability and validity of information collected during the evaluation process" (Green *et al*, 1991, p. 236).

Generally speaking, impact and outcome evaluations are based on comparisons. Programme accomplishments (i.e. changes in target group behaviour) are often compared to:

- other similar programmes or groups who were not beneficiaries of the original interventions;
- established standards, such as national or international goals;
- the accomplishment, itself, over a specified period of time, or before and after specific interventions.

Evaluation design

Ideally, a programme's interventions should be based on the findings of baseline information. However, field realities are such that it is not unusual that projects are initiated without baseline information being collected. As reflected in the discussion below, this situation should not prevent an evaluation from being conducted.

The selection of an evaluation research design is an important task in planning either an impact or outcome evaluation. Its selection can depend on the type of evaluation results needed. The Academy for Educational Development (1995) advocates the following criteria in choosing an evaluation design:

- If the purpose is to show results from the process point of view, then the most appropriate design is **descriptive**, which includes a summary of patterns, trends and observations. This is common to process evaluation;
- If the purpose is to show impact over time, then the most appropriate evaluation design will be the **time series**;
- If the purpose is show behaviour or health status change at a given point of time, then the **comparative design**, also know as **before/after**, will be best suited for this purpose.

Secondly, the presence or absence of baseline data, which is usually quantitative in nature, also should determine the type of evaluation design chosen. As a basis for programme planning and evaluation, the data, which are related to specific indicators, act as a comparison when assessing progress at a later stage in the programme cycle. A brief description of the most common impact and outcome evaluation designs used in development programmes are described below (Windsor *et al*, 1984, p.135-138):

After only design X Ob_1

From a technical viewpoint, this is the simplest, but weakest of the evaluation designs that can be used to assess behaviour change. It is conducted without baseline data and studies behaviour in a single group compared to some other standard. However, it is not uncommon to find programmes that only want to document target population behaviours (**Ob_1**), and assess the effects after an intervention (**X**) has taken place. Data on key programme indicators (i.e. behaviour, attitudes or knowledge, health status, etc.) are collected; but findings must be compared to some external standard to increase their utility. These standards can be: (a) **scientific**, based on theory or state-of-the-art research;

(b) **normative**, such as national or international goals; and (c) **historical**, such as past national trends/patterns or precedents in particular country, etc.

Before/after design Ob_1 X Ob_2

In this design, baseline information on key indicators such as knowledge, attitudes, practices, or behaviour are collected prior ($\mathbf{Ob_1}$) to the intervention (**X**). At a predetermined time period afterwards ($\mathbf{Ob_2}$), a repeat study is conducted, and these same indicators are reassessed to note changes or variations. This is probably the most common evaluation design used in the field, but is less powerful in its ability to ascertain whether changes in the target population are actually due to programme interventions. Although baseline data should be collected before the start of a programme or intervention, it can be collected during programme implementation. Its primary flaw is that it does not take into account other contextual factors such as environment, policy changes, etc. that may have impacted on the objects of interest in the evaluation.

Before/after with comparison group design $\underline{Ob_1}$ $\underline{X}$ $\underline{Ob_2}$
Ob_3 X Ob_4

Similar to the previous design, this involves a before/after comparison in the programme area of interest. It enlarges the analysis to include a comparison or control group in some attempt to take into account external and other contextual factors over what may impact on participant behaviour. In addition to baseline information collected on the target group, data are also collected during the same time period on the same indicators in another comparable community or population ($\mathbf{Ob_3}$ **and** $\mathbf{Ob_4}$).

The comparison group has similar target population characteristics (i.e. age, sex) to the intervention group, but does not benefit from programme services or activities. At the termination of the programme, both groups are then observed and changes in behaviour are noted and studied for differences and similarities. Inherent in this design is the premise that if the comparison group was selected appropriately, any contextual factor that was operating during the programme period would have affected both groups equally and, therefore, changes found can be confidently attributed to the programme and not to external factors.

Time series design Ob_1 X Ob_2 Ob_3 .... Ob_N

This evaluation design is a research approach that tracks behaviour, over time, usually comparing pre- and post- intervention. Information is collected through the use of time series charts and on a defined, periodic basis in which data over time for a given clinic, group or individual are charted. For example, numbers of weekly prenatal clinic visits over similar two-month periods (matched for seasons and schedules) can be charted before and after the implementation of a maternal mortality awareness campaign. One of the major advantages of the time-series design is that it permits programme staff to distinguish results of the interventions from changes that would have occurred in the absence of the programme but due to external factors.

In terms of their effectiveness in attributing causality in behavioural change intervention, the various evaluation designs are compared and summarised in Box 3 below:

3 *Evaluation type by level of attribution and resources required*

Time series	Provides strongest evidence that reported changes are due to the intervention and not external factors.	Considerable and technically demanding. Exceeds scope of most development programmes.
Before/ after with comparison group design	Provides good evidence that reported changes can be correlated to the intervention. PRA can determine perceived influences of other interventions.	Technically demanding with small evaluation team.
Before/after design	Provides some evidence that reported changes may have occurred and are possibly the result of programme intervention.	Technically moderate and demanding.
After only	Provides qualitative evidence for both behavioural change and the influence of the intervention.	Technically basic – more reliance on qualitative information and use of secondary data (collected by others).

Assuring programme quality

Similar to monitoring, process evaluation has a role in enriching the results of impact or outcome evaluations. Findings can be used to explain what has worked in a programme and how the intervention may have been effective.

Data collection techniques used in process evaluations should include: observations by staff and beneficiaries; interviews; and the review, analysis, and interpretation of records and documents. All documentation, including programme plans, monitoring forms, memos, and activity reports that will provide evidence to determine whether programmed activities were, in fact, carried out according to plan and to programme decisions, should be considered. Interviewing stakeholders who have close contact and knowledge about the programme can provide insight into how staff and community feel about a programme and make suggestions about improvements and possible modifications.

Observation

This data collection method is common to process evaluation. It is best used with an observation guide and can be applied to process evaluation in several different ways and for different purposes. Observations can be made of:

- individual or groups when they are performing behaviours of interest over a period of time
- events or activities such as important staff meetings and/or meetings with local NGO/agency partners and government counterparts that affect policy decisions.

In some instances, **participant observation** is sometimes used, wherein a staff member or evaluator temporarily joins the target population as a means of experiencing the programme from the community's perspective and viewpoint.

Individual Interviews

Using open-ended questions, these interviews are in-depth in nature and constructed in such a way that the information gathered provides insight into what is happening during implementation. Interview guides are designed to generate and stimulate ideas and thoughts as well as gather information from interviewees that shed light on the entire process – e.g. activities, timing, frequency, etc. – and identify differences or gaps between what was planned and what has actually been implemented. Interviewees, often referred to as "key informants" are carefully selected, based on their familiarity with the programme and/or context within which it operates.

Designing the evaluation protocol

After considering the conceptual aspects of the evaluation and deciding on an evaluation design, the next step is developing the evaluation protocol. It is a plan that describes from whom and how participants will be determined (i.e. sampling strategy). Besides reflecting the evaluation design, it specifies the timeframe of the research, data collection methods, analytical framework and needed resources. The questions highlighted in Box 4 can be used to weigh possible protocol options and decide on a plan that is optimal, given field realities (Israel, 1995, p. 371; Patton, 1987):

4 *Evaluation considerations*

Issues	Choices
1. What are the units of analysis?	Individuals, groups, social networks, organisations, programmes ....
2. What will be the sampling strategy?	Random, stratified, cluster, quota ...
3. What types of data collected? From whom? How?	Quantitative, qualitative, mixed surveys, interviews, observations, case studies, focus groups, PAR techniques ....
4. What type of evaluation designs or comparisons, if any, will be made?	Before-after, comparison group, time series, historical or normative comparisons ....
5. How will data be analysed?	Statistical analysis, content analysis, combinations
6. How will validity of and confidence in the findings be determined?	Multiple data sources, collection methods and investigators;
7. How will data findings and evaluation results be shared with others?	Internal reports & publications: (programme, donor, audit reports; media publications; presentations etc.);
8. What is the time frame of the evaluation (e.g. sequencing, phasing)?	Midterm, annually, end of intervention period, fixed versus open times, rapid data collection, long-term ....
9. How will logistics and administrative practicalities be handled?	Gaining entry to setting, access to people, training;
10. How will ethical issues and confidentiality be handled?	Informed consent, Organisational Code of Ethics (if available), protection of human subjects ....
11. What type of resources will be needed? How many/much?	Personnel, supplies, data collection, costs for coding & analysis, reporting & publishing, evaluation budget ....

Adapted from Israel et al (1995, p. 371)

Choosing monitoring and evaluation (M&E) indicators

Selecting indicators is an important aspect of any evaluation protocol and process. They are used to measure the progress towards achieving objectives and thus also serve an important role in programme planning and design. In relation to human behaviour, there are many different indicators that can reflect different stages of the behavioural change process. Deciding which indicators are appropriate can be done in different ways, and it depends on the nature of the programme objectives, the activities undertaken and the information already available.

As indicated in Box 5, there are five types of indicators that can be developed. Baseline indicators generally reflect levels of knowledge, attitudes, and behaviours of target populations or levels of social/health problems prior to an intervention. They serve as the foundation for future measurements and comparisons at a later period in a programme cycle. Process indicators focus on the implementation phase of a programme – specifically the operational components, interactions and relationships established as part of programme activities. As the name implies, they are used to document programme processes. Output indicators are specified to denote the level and quantity of programme activities undertaken. Impact indicators address levels of knowledge, attitudes, practices and immediate behaviours. Outcome indicators are measurement criteria for changes that occur, related to health status, economic status, or social well-being.

Where possible, indicators that are already in use, for example baseline information, demographic and health survey data, or other relevant research studies, should be used. Continued use of the same indicators shows trends in behaviours over time. Ideally, indicators should be decided upon before the start of an intervention.

Whereas objectives state desired behavioural changes in target populations as outcomes and impacts, indicators specify what aspects of particular behaviours should be measured. However, the specification of indicators should logically flow from the objectives and activities, and should be measurable, factual, valid (i.e. accurately represent the behaviours), verifiable and sensitive. Above all, indicators should be chosen with the methods of how to measure them and available resources in mind. For example, some sample indicators for different types of development programmes are shown in Box 6.

There are certain "core" indicators that are relevant across many different programmes, and some are suggested in the box mentioned previously. It is vital that the indicators are agreed upon between the key actors before the evaluation, and ideally even before the intervention is initiated. Consultation can occur with programme participants, counterpart staff, local NGOs,

5 Programme cycle and type of evaluation indicators

Programme Stage/ Activity	Type of indicator	Thematic examples
Pre-intervention stage: Participatory exploratory research Existing data review	Baseline	Existing attitudes and self-reported behaviours Service utilisation data Teenage pregnancy rates
Implementation stage: Training, Community participation, Service delivery/ provision, Information distribution, Media campaign	Process	Characteristics of programme participants Quality of communication between programme staff Method of decision-making
	Output	Number of communication materials produced; Number materials distributed, by type; Number of meetings held with NGO partners; Number of health services, by type; Percentage of programme activity outsourced.
Post-implementation stage:	Impact (Immediate effects)	Percentage changes in short -term knowledge and attitudes; Percentage of target audience who developed skills
Post-implementation stage: Medium term	Impact (Intermediate effects)	Self- reported adoption of positive behaviours Increased service utilisation
Programme terminated: Long-term, sustained	Outcome	Maintained positive self reported behaviours Prevented onset of risky self-reported behaviours Morbidity/mortality rates Vaccination coverage Teenage pregnancy rate Changed social/peer norms

6 *Sample indicators by programme focus*

Indicator type	Programme focus	Sample indicators
Process/output	Child protection	Quality of youth participation forums # youth NGOs formed # and gender breakdown of adolescents trained as peer educators
	Girls education	Quality of informational materials distributed # parent-teacher conferences held
	Safe motherhood	Participant perceptions of health education sessions held % of communication materials that are pretested among the target population
	Water and sanitation	Duration & content of community meetings % VHC trained in simple hygiene education methods
Impact (Immediate/ intermediate effect on behaviour)	Child protection	% families and community groups who speak out against exploitative child labour % working children who also attend schools
	Girls education	% families who are sending their girl children to primary school during harvest season % girl children who complete their primary school education
	Safe motherhood	# of villages or communities that have organised themselves to ensure transportation for women with obstetrical emergencies % of husbands who say they would take wife to hospital if danger sign(s) appeared
	Water and sanitation	% families that clean and maintain household latrines % communities that protect and maintain communal water source
Outcome (Long term results)	Child protection	% working children who are in exploitative/ hazardous occupations
	Girls education	school dropout rate for girl children
	Safe motherhood	maternal mortality rate
	Water and sanitation	incidence of water-borne diseases

representatives of target groups and community leaders. Small-scale focus group discussions and interviews can provide an opportunity to discuss what is being measured through the agreement on what changes people think are significant.

Many programmes in the past have chosen indicators with no specified means of measurement. They then become useless. Percentages should be used where possible, as aggregate numbers can be misleading and difficult to compare. For example, the proportion (percentage) of outpatients presenting with symptoms of a sexually transmitted infections (STIs) at a health clinic is a more useful indicator than an absolute number of reported cases. It should be remembered that in sexual health the indicators used are almost always "proxy"; they are indirect measurements of sexual behaviour but they are always prone to some degree of error. In addition, indicators should be disaggregated by sex and age, wherever possible.

Suggested core indicators for sexual health programmes

There is a wide range of field programmes that address issues of sexual health and behaviour change. These are specific indicators that have been shown to be (a) good predictors of sex-related behaviours and (b) valid (but generally a proxy) representatives of behaviours themselves. For example, in one study it was found that men who knew that the latency period for HIV was longer than five years were more than twice as likely to report condom use than those who did not. Similarly, a study amongst youth in Namibia found that those who believed that their sexually active friends use condoms were more likely to report condom use themselves. A complete list of behaviour change indicators related to sexual behaviour is provided in Box 7. As shown, only programme indicators that are behaviour-related and most appropriate to either an impact or outcome evaluation are discussed.

Pointers for choosing M&E indicators

It is important to remember that there is no simple formula for choosing indicators. However, Bertrand and Kincaid (1996, pp. 148-150) suggest some basic steps that can demystify and guide the selection of behavioural indicators:

(1) Identify a limited number of indicators that are consistent with programme objective(s) by clarifying the results desired (over short-term or medium term), specifying the major intervention activities and defining the main purpose of the evaluation (e.g. mid-course correction or results documentation/tracking).

(2) Identify the types of data needed for each indicator by specifying

7 *Sample impact and outcome indicators for behaviour development and change in the context of sexual health programmes, using PRECEDE/PROCEED framework*

Programme objective: Reduce HIV infection

Impact – Immediate effects (Knowledge, attitudes, perceptions of social norms)

% stating that once a relationship has started, they have sex with anyone else;
% believing that sexually active peers are using condoms;
% correctly stating that the incubation period of HIV is greater than 5 years;
% correctly stating what can result from STDs;
% correctly stating that there is an increased risk of getting HIV if you have another STD;
% of target population that know how to prevent STD/HIV;
% of target group that know of at least one source of information and/or services for sexual and reproductive health;
% of target group who know of at least one contraceptive method;
% believing that AIDS is a local health problem;
% of adolescents who desire pregnancy;
% of adolescents who intend to use protection at first/next intercourse;
% believing that they are personally at risk of HIV infection.

Impact – Intermediate effect on self-reported behaviours

Age at first intercourse;
% ever had sexual intercourse;
% reporting that they have changed their behaviour;
Number of sexual partners: lifetime/last 12 months/last 4 weeks;
% of sexually active who ever used a condom;
% of sexually active who have used a condom in the past 12 months;
% of condom users who report consistent use;
% of sexually active who used a condom at first/most recent intercourse;
% of males who have ever had sex with a prostitute;
% of girls who ever had sex with an older man;
% ever had an STI;
% of previously sexually active who now abstain from sexual intercourse;
% reporting that the most recent intercourse was the first sexual contact with that partner;
% continuing sexual activity after the appearance of a genital ulcer;
% of those who have suffered from STI, who sought treatment in the formal health care sector.

Outcome (Long term results)

STI and HIV prevalence in a defined target population;
STI/HIV related cause-specific mortality rate among teens
Proportion of adolescent pregnancies that are wanted;
Teenage pregnancy rate.

Sources: Catania, et al., 1996; Global Programme on AIDS , 1994; Dallabetta and Hassig, 1995; Stewart and Eckert, 1995; McCombie et al, 1992; Barton, 1997; Malamba et al, 1994; UNICEF Namibia, 1996.

data source(s) and determining if data already exists or new data must be collected.

(3) Categorise indicators according to their importance to the programme and ease of data collection and measurement.

The following grid (see Box 8) can be a useful tool in guiding indicator selection:

8 ***Illustrative table for classifying indicators***

	DATA COLLECTION		
	Easy (Routine data)	***Feasible but requires effort*** (New data)	***Difficult*** (New data, obstacles)
IMPORTANCE: ***High***	High priority A	Worth collecting if possible B	Worth collecting, if possible C
Low	Worth collecting only if D	Worth collecting only if E	Low priority F

Bertrand and Kincaid, (1966) pp.148-150

From a pragmatic viewpoint, it reflects that high priority should be given to indicators that are based on routinely collected data and have high importance to the programme (Cell A). In contrast, lower priority would be given to indicators that require data that are difficult to collect. Some reasons for this difficulty include: a lack of technically qualified staff, the amount of stigma associated with the type of information needed (e.g. sexual abuse, abortion) or if a study population is located in a politically unstable situation or inaccessible geographical area. This, coupled with a low importance rating, would indicate that indicators in Cell F be given lowest priority.

(4) After selection, group indicators by data source and determine the number of different linkages required and separate data collection activities needed. These groupings can include, but are not limited to, service statistics, programme or administration records, observations, surveys, etc. Based on this analysis, one can then determine the staff resources, logistics, time and budget that will be needed to obtain necessary information to monitor the indicators.

Common problems with core indicators

Several studies have sought to question the aspect of the "usefulness" of indicators through analysis of the methodology employed to measure it, and how representative the indicator is of risk behaviours themselves (to determine its "validity"). For example, in studies on sexual behaviour, some problems regarding validity have emerged which are worth being aware of:

(1) Many people report behaviours in themselves (such as premarital sex) which they deem "unacceptable" in others. Accepted social norms or mores regarding sexual behaviour are thus not consistently adhered to in practice.

(2) Men tend to over-report frequency of sexual activity compared to females, even in married couples (Schopper *et al*, 1993).

(3) People tend to over-report condom use. For example, a study in Blantyre, Malawi, amongst female STI patients, actually found that the incidence of STI was highest in women reporting sex with "consistent" condom use (Taha *et al*, 1995).

In discussing the barriers that often face health education programmes in developing countries, Hubley (1986) stresses the importance of, but difficulty in, identifying relevant indicators as part of the evaluation process. Past experience has also shown that different stakeholders will find different indicators of greatest significance. In fact, it has been found that the relative importance of different indicators will vary over time, even within the same community or programme (Narayan, 1993).

Choice of evaluation methods: Combining qualitative and quantitative data

Data collection methods used in evaluation are varied and can be both quantitative and qualitative in nature. The most commonly used data collection methods in development work are quantitative in nature. They are useful in identifying the magnitude of a particular behaviour or problem of interest in a given population. The results are often presented and summarised according to different socio-demographic characteristics, such as by age, sex, geographic location, ethnicity, etc.

In comparison, qualitative evaluation data provide in-depth information and increase one's understanding of values, beliefs, attitudes held by a specific population as well as their practices that may inhibit or accelerate the change or acceptance of new or different behaviours. Qualitative methods are most often used in process evaluation and formative research but are increasingly undertaken during impact, or summative programme evaluations. Excellent manuals already exist in the areas of formative and qualitative research, including the pretesting of materials. The interested reader is encouraged to read references found in the bibliography of this chapter.

Given the nature of behavioural change and programming, there is increasing emphasis being placed on the use of multiple methods in programme evaluation. Steckler *et al* (1992, p.8) describe four ways that qualitative and quantitative methods can be used in a complementary manner and integrated into evaluations of programme strategies:

- qualitative methods are used to develop quantitative measures
- qualitative methods are used to help explain quantitative or statistical findings
- quantitative methods are used to help explain qualitative results
- qualitative and quantitative methods are used together to explain findings for the purpose of cross-validation and triangulation.

A summary of some the common evaluation methods used in development work are listed below.

Knowledge, attitude, practice, behaviour (KAPB) surveys

KAPB Surveys are a research technique for obtaining information when that information needs to be used to describe a large population group. A written, standardised questionnaire (generally composed of close-ended questions) makes it possible to collect information about a large number of factors in a relatively short period of time. Since surveys do not allow for much in-depth probing, they can be of limited use in researching deeply-held attitudes and self-reported behaviours.

Focus group discussions (FGDs)

This is probably the most frequently used, and abused, method of formative research. This method, adopted from market research, involves a guided, in-depth discussion with a group of homogeneous, potential adopters of an idea, a service, a message or set of messages, or a product. A set of questions is followed but the order and depth of questioning may vary according to the interest of the group. Probing on particular matters is required to develop a full understanding of what people are feeling and believing. The greatest problem in the use of FGDs in developing countries is gathering a homogeneous group of people who do not know each other and therefore will not be influenced by the responses of others in the group. Very often, focus groups are conducted with members from the same village or community and responses are biased by relationships – there are always opinion leaders and their followers.

In-depth interviews

The in-depth interview is the most common alternative to focus groups when pretesting of materials or messages is needed. It is an especially appropriate method to elicit responses to partially-completed products, new materials or novel ideas and exploring deeply-held beliefs and attitudes.

This method is usually conducted with one person, or a couple of closely related people, depending on the subject. Instead of completing a questionnaire, as in quantitative survey research, the evaluator has a set of guiding questions to stimulate the discussion. Similar to focus groups, follow up or probing questions are used to elicit in-depth opinions and feelings on a particular subject. A decision must be made on the degree of structure given to the process of interviewing since its length allows for asking the same question in several different ways. Answers are either written down or taped on audiocassette. It is essential to get permission to do either and to make the interviewee feel comfortable through an introductory conversation.

Intercept interviews

The purpose of the intercept interview is to gain immediate insight into the reasons for interviewees' decisions or their feelings toward a particular service, product, programme or event. It is designed to catch people who have made a decision, such as a purchase, or adopted a specific behaviour, or who have just participated in an event. For example, this can also be an exit interview of mothers leaving a prenatal consultation.

Individuals are stopped at the point where the audience is most likely to be found. These interception points are generally in high traffic areas (clinic waiting rooms, market areas, etc.) thereby permitting an evaluator to contact a large number of people in a short period of time. Although the setting may be informal, the questions are usually fairly structured. In practice, intercept interviews combine behavioural observation techniques with brief, close-ended (or multiple choice) questions developed for focus groups or in-depth interviews.

Observation studies

This is one of the most common data collection methods in development work. In an effort to validate survey data or identify key components in complex behaviours or behavioural interactions, the evaluator blends into the social setting, or process, that is being studied. By using direct observation and gaining the confidence of key informants, evaluators can learn how individuals behave in their daily lives, within the context of their social milieu. For example, an evaluator may observe such actions as: (a) how women behave while gathering water at a well, or (b) how health workers treat clients at an immunisation site. For reference purposes, the list of hygiene-related behaviours discussed in Chapter 1 (Box 8) is a good basis for developing an observation guide for a Hygiene Education Programme.

Although a set of guidelines or checklist generally guides field observation, the evaluator should in no way intervene in what is being observed. In fact, it may take a few days before the evaluator is accepted as a natural part of the environment under study – this depends, of course, on what is being observed. Data can be recorded using three different techniques:

Binary Recording (yes/no) – documents if specific behaviours occur under various conditions. Example: Observe (a) whether a nurse has checked the temperature of the vaccine storage unit on routine immunisation days or (b) if health education materials are easily visible to mothers when they attending counselling sessions.

Frequency recording – counts the number of times a given behaviour occurs within a specified period of time. Example: Observe: (a) the number of vaccinations given on a National Immunisation Day, or (b) the number of questions asked by a health worker during a prenatal consultation.

Duration Recording – measures the length of time that different behaviours occur during a pre-defined observation period. Example: Observe (a) the duration of a single breast-feeding episode, or (b) the amount of waiting time that mothers spend at a local health clinic.

This method may not be applicable to all behaviours or events (for example – sexual behaviour!), and it is strongly recommended that observation methods are used in combination with other methods.

Document and record reviews

There are multiple records that a programme keeps as it is being planned and implemented, such as memoranda, minutes of meetings, letters, implementation plans, epidemiological data, and systematic activity reports. All of these documents constitute the living history of the programme and its implementation.

Usually collected and considered separately, they provide different pieces of information. This process of relating project documents to what was expected should be an ongoing and evolving process throughout any programme. For example, activity reports (monthly, quarterly or other) can be used to track how the implementation was carried out, the type of activities undertaken, as well as, to compare what occurred to what was initially planned.

Analysis of such documents is generally reported as part of a process evaluation exercise or can be an integral source of information during the programme monitoring process.

Participatory rapid assessment (PRA), also known as participatory learning method (PLAM), rapid rural appraisal (RRA)

PRA is an intensive, systematic, but semi-structured learning experience carried out in a community by a multi-disciplinary team, which includes community members (Theis and Grady, 1991). Rapid assessment and participatory learning approaches were formulated as an alternative to and complement to conventional sample surveys.

PRA is a compilation of research methods that are based on the premise that understanding the qualitative dimensions of a situation or problem are equally as important as generating averages and percentages. Within an evaluation context, these research methods are centred on the principle that community members, development workers and evaluators often see and interpret environments and problems in different, but equally important ways. In essence, the primary purpose of PRA methods is to gain an understanding of the complexities of a problem or situation rather than to gather highly accurate statistics on a list of variables. Nonetheless, PRA methods do not exclude quantitative techniques and can be used simultaneously with them.

Having a strong emphasis on community participation, PRA methods are used to study, analyse and assess constraints and opportunities, and make informed and timely decisions regarding development programmes. PRA processes are a way of learning from, and with, community members – they raise awareness, help communities analyse complex issues, and determine potential solutions. As such, the PRA methodology is based on anthropological and ethnographic influences and techniques. First, there is an emphasis on triangulation. In practice, this often occurs in such a way that evaluation teams have mixed participation (by gender, age, insiders/outsiders etc.); information and data are collected from a variety of sources; and a mix of tools and techniques are used. Second, there is a degree of flexibility and informality that allows easy adaptation and modification as field work or data collection proceeds. Third, community members are an integral partner of the evaluation process – their involvement is a critical component in gathering, analysing, and interpreting collected data. Fourth, PRA teams collect only essential data (a function of what type of information is needed, its purpose and accuracy level needed) and involves data analysis as an integral part of the fieldwork. This means that PRA teams constantly review their processes and assess data as a means of identifying/determining new directions or missing areas. Finally, there is a strong effort made to avoid potential bias by incorporating the most disadvantaged (often women and children), and other target groups that are left out of mainstream decision-making.

Rapid assessment and participatory learning approaches can be characterised by their short duration, low to medium cost, preference for semi-structured interventions and group discussions, on-the-spot analysis feature, minimum amount of statistical analysis and high participation. The common tools and techniques used in PRA methodology are: ranking, diagrams, direct observation, mapping, time trends – most of these techniques are visual and do not require literacy among evaluation partners.

Triangulation: Combining qualitative and quantitative methods

The process of collecting data from several sources, using different methods and sometimes different researchers, is called triangulation. It has the advantage of: (a) identifying intervention effects that may have been missed if only one method was used; (b) highlighting lack of agreement across sources; (c) demonstrating a need for further investigation and; (d) enriching the explanation of evaluation findings.

In evaluation, both qualitative and quantitative research methods should be "triangulated"; that is, using more than one method to validate data collected. In this way, different measurements, or observations by different methods of the same phenomenon, will ensure that the evaluator has an accurate view of the situation being studied. Since qualitative methods usually do not involve a large enough sample for claims of reliability and validity, triangulation can help a great deal, both in programme decisions and in persuading decision-makers about the importance of findings.

The challenge of analysing evaluation data

Quantitative data analysis

Quantitative data are analysed using descriptive (e.g. number counts, sum, means, percentsages) and analytical (e.g. multiple regression, chi-square) statistics. In the latter, scientific formulae are used to calculate statistical significance as a means of showing that relationships exist between different factors (i.e. correlation, cause-effect). They are the standards used to confirm that impact and outcome results can be attributed to a specific programme and/or its interventions.

When making programmatic decisions, field personnel tend to emphasise the "practical significance" of quantitative results. Even if a result may not be statistically significant, its magnitude, expressed in percentages and numbers, can be used to decide on intervention strategies and plan implementation activities. For example, a KAPB survey may find that 90 percent of the young girls in one region of the country are circumcised as compared to 75 percent in another region. Given the sheer magnitude of the problem, staff working in a programme to eradicate FGM would be interested in tacking the problem, even if the difference in percentage between regions was not statistically significant.

Examples of computer software that are commonly used are EPIINFO (developed by the Centers for Disease Control in Atlanta, Georgia and WHO) for simple statistical analysis and SPSS for more advanced statistical analysis. Both are available for use on microcomputers.

Qualitative data analysis

Qualitative data are organised in the form of written statements and narratives (transcripts) that reflect actual comments (word by word) made by respondents. Unlike quantitative data analysis, numerical counts are less important than analyses of content and domains of interests and identification of patterns and trends.

Analysis of qualitative evaluation data may be carried out in a number of ways, such as content analysis of recurring themes, concepts and words, or domain analysis of predetermined content areas (often theory-based). In this type of evaluation method, there is usually no attempt to quantify participant responses to questions asked. It must be remembered that unless appropriate numbers and statistical selection techniques are used, results are not statistically valid. Data interpretation requires sorting, coding and rearranging text – these processes are now facilitated through the use of microcomputer software such as: *Ethnograph, Nota Bene, NuDIST.*

Case studies

Besides evaluations, development organisations are increasingly documenting their lessons learned from field experiences in social mobilisation, such as UNICEF's study of childhood immunisation and nutrition in Tanzania "We Will Never Go Back" (UNICEF 1993). Case studies such as this are most useful in describing the contextual factors (i.e. situation analysis) and providing an in-depth analysis of a programme and/or selected behaviour and communication interventions. By combining methods such as interviews with programme staff, community participants and other stakeholders; reviews of programme records and documents; and actual observations of different activities, coupled with small survey data, "best practices" can be identified and further developed into practice guidelines. UNICEF's publication entitled

Social mobilisation at the grassroots: Experience from West Africa (1997) compares three case studies in West Africa to identify different practices and their programming implications.

Participatory evaluation

As mentioned earlier in this chapter, the changing focus of development programmes requires that programmers address not only behaviour change and development, but also consider new strategies that incorporate service delivery, capacity-building and empowerment (UNICEF Multi-Donor Evaluation, 1994). Emphasis on both capacity building and empowerment of local stakeholders (i.e. community groups, NGO partners, government counterparts, etc.) has particular significance for programme evaluation – whether the interest is on behaviour change or communication activities. Participatory Action Research (PAR), also known as participatory evaluation, is an approach that holds much promise and needs more application in the field.

This evaluation method differs from the conventional evaluation paradigm in that it is a participatory process in which local stakeholders are actually involved in the design, data collection and analysis processes of evaluation. Evaluation, then, is not restricted to "external", "objective" evaluators but deliberately incorporates the "insider's view and understanding", given their membership of the evaluation team.

By involving community members in this manner, the language used in the evaluation questions and process are grounded in socio-cultural realities. Participatory evaluation requires a combination of qualitative and quantitative methods to gather information – i.e. social mapping, matrix ratings, critical incident logs, status ranking, informal (semi-structured) interviews, etc. (Goodman and Wandermann, 1994, Narayan, 1993).

As such, the PAR approach is based on the premise of cooperation and co-learning, reflection and action-oriented decision making. The information obtained remains in the community and is used to help improve the programme and address problems of interest. Its secondary goal is to increase a collective, problem-solving capacity as community stakeholders gain experience in evaluating and learn skills that enable them to make better-informed decisions.

Evaluation in the future

As is evident in this discussion, much is happening in the discipline of programme evaluation. Because effective planning and programming is linked to effective evaluation, it is no longer the special domain of specialists, but of all programme staff. This has many implications on the type of attention, resources and commitment that will be needed for programmes in the future.

According to Israel (1995):

(a) Evaluation should place more emphasis on documenting other events or forces (i.e. different contextual factors) besides country programme interventions that might explain the evaluation results/findings as well as unintended consequences or outcomes. Theory-informed and empirically-tested evaluation designs and methods that identify links between impact and health and social outcomes should guide this process.

(b) Similar to outcome and impact evaluations, process evaluations should be conducted systematically and designed to reflect the views of various stakeholders in determining the feasibility, acceptability, efficacy, satisfaction, implementation and barriers of programme and communication interventions.

(c) Efforts should be made in creating collaborative, multi-disciplinary evaluation teams that involve stakeholders in a participatory process and in developing active partnerships between researchers and programme staff as a means of reinforcing the evaluation mechanism.

(d) The unit of analysis in evaluation should be expanded to focus not only on individuals but on families and communities and on multiple types of change – not just behaviour but also community competence or empowerment, psycho-social factors such as social support, motivation etc.; and

(e) Ongoing training in how and when to use different evaluation methods, data collection and analysis techniques should be provided to all field staff, but especially to programmers and communicators.

In conclusion, as development programmes reassess their directions and consider new options for the future, the evaluation process will take on increasing prominence in programme planning and adapting programme interventions to reflect ever-changing situational realities.

References

Academy for Educational Development (1995) *A toolbox for building health communication capacity*. Reprinted by The Basics Project, 1996.

Barton, T. (1997) *Epidemics and behaviours: A review of changes in Ugandan sexual behaviour in the early 1990s*. Geneva: UNAIDS.

Bertrand, J.T. and Kincaid, D.L. (1996) *Evaluating information-education-communication (IEC) programs for family planning and reproductive health*. Carolina Population Centre, University of North Carolina. WG-IEC-03.

Catania, J.A., Moskowitz, J.T., Ruiz, M. *et al.* (1996) "A review of national AIDS related behavioural surveys", *AIDS,* 10 (suppl A): s183-s190.

Dallabetta, G., Hassig, S. (1995) *Indicators for reproductive health program evaluation: final report of the subcommittee on STD/HIV*, Carolina Population Centre, University of North Carolina.

Goodman, R.M. and Wandersman, A. (1994) "FORECAST: A formative approach to evaluating community coalitions and community-based initiatives, *Journal of Community Psychology*, June 1994, special issue.

Green L.W. and Kreuter, M.W. (1991) *Health promotion planning: An educational and environmental approach*. Palo Alto: Mayfield.

Green, L.W. and Lewis, F.M. (1986) *Measurement and evaluation in health education and health promotion.* Palo Alto: Mayfield.

Hubley, J. (1986). "Barriers to health education in developing countries", *Health Education Research*, 1986:1.

Israel, B.A., Cummings, K., Dignan, M., Heaney, C., Simons-Morton, B. And Zimmerman, M. (1995) "Evaluation of health education programs: Current assessment and future directions", *Health Education Quarterly*, Vol 22 (3).

Malamba, S.S., Wagner, H.U., Maude, G. *et al.* (1994) "Risk factors for HIV-1 infection in adults in a rural Ugandan community: a case control study", *AIDS*, 8:243-257.

McCombie, S., Hornik, R. (1992) *Evaluation of a workplace-based peer education program designed to prevent AIDS in Uganda - Final report*. Kampala: AIDSCOM.

Narayan, D. (1993) *Participatory evaluation: Tools for managing change in water and sanitation*, World Bank Technical Paper, No. 207.

Patton, M.G. (1990) *Qualitative evaluation and research methods*. Newbury Park: Sage.

Patton, M.G. (1987) *How to use qualitative methods in evaluation*. Newbury Park: Sage.

Schopper, D., Doussantousse, S., Orav, J. (1993) "Sexual behaviours relevant to HIV transmission in a rural African population: How much can a KAP study tell us?" *Social Science and Medicine* 37(3) 401-412.

Steckler, A., McLeroy, K.R., Goodman, R.M., Bird S.T. and McCormick, L. (1992) "Toward integrating qualitative and quantitative methods: An introduction". *Health Education Quarterly*, Vol 19.

Stewart, L., Eckert, E. (1995) *Indicators for reproductive health program evaluation: final report of the subcommittee on adolescent reproductive health services*. Carolina Population Centre, University of North Carolina.

Stoeker, R. And Bonavich E., eds. (1992 & 1993) "Participatory research: Parts 1 and 2", *American Sociologist*, Vols. 23 & 24.

Taha, T.E.T., Canner, J., Chiphangwi, J.D. *et al.* (1995) "Reported condoms use is not associated with incidence of sexually transmitted diseases in Malawi, *AIDS*, 10: 207-212.

Theis, J. and Grady, H. (1991) *Participatory rapid appraisal for community development*, London: International Institute for Environment and Development/ Save the Children Federation.

UNICEF Namibia (1996) "Youth health and development programme – Survey findings", unpublished report, Windhoek.

UNICEF New York (1994) *Multi-donor evaluation report*.

UNICEF New York (1993) *We will never go back: Social mobilisation in the Child Survival and Development Programme in the United Republic of Tanzania*, Case Study.

UNICEF New York (1997) *Social mobilization at the grassroots: Experience from West Africa.*

Webb, D. (1997) "Guidelines for the evaluation of behavioural development and change in Sexual Health Programmes". Unpublished paper, Nairobi.

Windsor, R.A., Baranowski, T., Clark, N. and Cutter, G. (1984) *Evaluation of health promotion and education programs.* Palo Alto: Mayfield.

About the authors

Mira B. Aghi started the tradition of formative research for communication programme development in India. She has been training researchers in South Asia, Eastern and Southern Africa and South America in qualitative research methodologies for over 20 years. She received her Ph.D. in Psychology from Loyola University, Chicago. Some programmes in which she has been the principal researcher are: STD (Satellite Technology Development, USA), SITE (India), Intervention in the tobacco habits of a rural Indian population, Meena Communication Initiative (South Asia), and Sara Communication Initiative (Eastern and Southern Africa). Her work consists of designing strategies of communication and education for different behavioural changes, including health behaviour. Dr. Aghi also worked as a Senior Programme Officer with Canada's International Development Research Centre from 1989 to 1992. She is presently working with WHO on a global tobacco use prevention intervention, aimed at women.

Rachel Carnegie has worked in the field of education, communication and gender for the last 15 years in South Asia and Africa. From 1985 to 1988 she worked in Bhutan, first as a primary school teacher with Voluntary Service Overseas (UK), and subsequently as a health education Programme Adviser with Save the Children Federation (USA). She then became Programme Officer with the Child-to-Child Trust at the University of London. In 1991, Carnegie moved to Bangladesh, working initially as a health education consultant to a range of NGOs, including BRAC and CARE. From mid-1991 to mid-1994, she was a consultant to UNICEF Bangladesh, responsible for the creative development of the Meena Communication Initiative which promotes the rights of girls in South Asia. Since 1994 she has also acted as a core adviser to the Sara Communication Initiative for the adolescent girl in Africa. Carnegie is currently a consultant on life skills education, health promotion and participatory communication approaches. Recent work has included writing a communication resource book on Female Genital Mutilation and conducting a review of the life skills education initiative in Uganda. Carnegie has a BA from Cambridge University and an MA in Education from Sussex University.

Bruce Dick completed his medical studies at Guy's Hospital, London, in 1971 (MB, BS) and moved from paediatrics to community medicine while working in South Africa from 1973-1980. He completed his Diploma in Community Medicine (DCM) while working at the University of Cape Town and in a rural hospital in Kwazulu, Natal. After a short spell as a community physician in the National Health Service, UK, when he completed further studies to become a Member of the Faculty of Public Health Medicine (MFPHM), he worked for three years as a research fellow in the Evaluation and Planning Centre, London School of Hygiene and Tropical Medicine. In 1985 he moved to the International Federation of Red Cross and Red Crescent Societies, Geneva, where he was Head of the Health Department. As a result of his growing interest in adolescent health and development he joined the World Health Organisation's Adolescent Health Programme in 1992, and since 1993 has been the Senior Adviser, Youth Health, with UNICEF in New York.

Erma W. Manoncourt is presently Deputy Director, Programmes, UNICEF, India. She was formerly, a Senior Advisor in the Gender, Partnerships and Participation Section in UNICEF, New York where she was responsible for global policy development and programming guidance in the area of Programme Communication/Social Mobilisation. This involved providing technical support to UNICEF field offices throughout the world, and ensuring quality assurance of programmes that promote behaviour development/change as well as youth and community participation as key components of sustainable human development. A former university professor, she retains academic affiliation with Tulane University in the United States. Dr. Manoncourt received a Ph.D. in Health Behaviour and Health Education at the University of North Carolina, Chapel Hill in 1986. She also has a Master's degree in Clinical Social Work and an undergraduate degree in Psychology.

Neill McKee is a Canadian who has worked in communication and education for development since 1968. He started his career in Malaysia as a teacher and later programme administrator for the Canadian volunteer agency, CUSO. He worked as a documentary film producer for CUSO and for Canada's International Development Research Centre for 15 years. He completed an MSc in communication theory and research at Florida State University in 1988. McKee joined UNICEF Bangladesh, in 1990, as Chief of Programme Communication and Information Section where he authored *Social mobilization and social marketing in developing communities* (Southbound, 1992). From January 1994 to mid-1999, he was Regional

Communication Officer for UNICEF in Eastern and Southern Africa, based in Nairobi. He is presently Chief of Basic Education, Child Care and Adolescent Development, UNICEF Uganda. Mr. McKee is the originator of the Meena and Sara Communication Initiatives and a co-founder of Visualization in Participatory Programmes (VIPP).

Pamela Reitemeier has worked for UNICEF for 10 years in the UK, Chad and Bangladesh. She worked initially in press and PR in London, before moving to Chad, where her work with local media included an innovative rural radio project in a country with few communication resources. In Bangladesh, she worked in communication programming, which involved high-level advocacy and social mobilization, with a prime focus on health and sanitation. She made extensive use of Visualization in Participatory Programmes (VIPP), to incite broader participation and more effective decision-making at national and local levels. She is currently working in the UK on a pioneering treatment for young children with autism known as Applied Behaviour Analysis (ABA), which was created by Dr. I. Lovaas of the University of California, Los Angeles.

Douglas Webb obtained his Ph.D. from the University of London in 1995, with a thesis examining the social epidemiology of HIV in southern Africa. He worked for UNICEF Zambia for over three years on HIV/AIDS programme design, focusing on orphan research and evaluation issues. He has also done work with UNAIDS Zambia, the National AIDS Programme and a research study for SAFAIDS, programme evaluation for UNICEF Eastern and Southern Africa Regional Office, and most recently has been designing HIV prevention and AIDS impact mitigation programmes for UNICEF in Mozambique. He is currently working as a consultant at Save the Children UK, based in London. He has published widely, including papers on the nature and extent of the impact of AIDS in southern Africa and HIV social epidemiology. He is the author of the book *HIV and AIDS in Africa* published by Pluto Press.

Rhona Birrell Weisen was Technical Officer for the WHO Life Skills Initiative of the Mental Health Promotion and Policy Unit, Department of Mental Health, World Health Organisation (WHO), Geneva. She was editor of the *WHO Skills for Life Newsletter*, and in collaboration with life skills experts in many countries has developed a set of WHO documents to describe and facilitate life skills education development, implementation, training and evaluation".

Esther Wyss has 15 years of experience with numerous international development organizations in Africa, including local indigenous organizations in Burkina Faso and Zambia, church-based organizations in Congo, Ghana, Nigeria, Benin, and Senegal, government organizations in Niger, international private voluntary organizations in Rwanda and Mali, as well as a number of UNICEF offices, primarily in Zambia. She has a Bachelor's degree in political science, a Master's degree in adult education, and is currently completing a Ph.D. in Organizational Behaviour at Case Western Reserve University in Cleveland, Ohio, USA. Esther continues to work with development organizations in her capacity as participatory training consultant. She is committed to developing a deeper understanding of behaviour change through learning-based partnerships between local and international development organizations.

Chin Saik Yoon is the publisher and founder of Southbound. He has participated in about 50 development information and communication activities across Asia over the past 15 years. His work has focused on the application of communication and information processes and technologies to catalyse and support participatory processes. He has also conducted training on participatory communication methods, and carried out policy research on information and communication technologies for national and international agencies. He recently led an editorial team in publishing "live" on the World Wide Web a conference from Ulaanbaatar, Mongolia on the development of the Internet within the Asian region. Chin also organised and facilitated a month-long virtual conference on participatory communication over the Internet which was jointly hosted by six universities and development groups around the world. He is a member of the advisory committee for UNESCO's *World communication and information report, 1999-2000* to which he also contributed the chapter on the impact of the new information and communication technologies on conventional mass media. He is also an active member of Pan Asia Networking and assists in the development of its content and services. Chin is the Co-Chair (Research and Publications), and a member of the board for ORBICOM, a network of UNESCO professorial chairs in Communication.